India's Evolving Economy

About the Author

Currently honorary fellow of the Centre for Development Studies (CDS), Thiruvanathapuram, A. Vaidyanathan's professional career spans academic and policy-centric research on diverse aspects of development. He worked in the National Council of Applied Economic Research (1956-1962); Planning Commission (1962-1972); as professor in CDS (1976-1984) and Madras Institute of Development Studies (1984-2004); as senior economist in FAO and the World Bank. During this long career, he has combined sustained empirical-analytical research on varied aspects of the country's socioeconomic development with active involvement in planning and policy formulation. Besides numerous articles in professional journals, he has written more than a dozen books some dealing with broader aspects of strategy and policy and others exploring issues relating to specific sectors notably agriculture, water and education. As member of the PM's Economic Advisory Council and the Planning Commission of Centre and Tamil Nadu, he has first-hand knowledge of the processes of policy making. He has served or chaired several official committees to review policies in specific areas (such as pricing of irrigation, revitalisation of rural cooperative credit structure and improvement of the current system of agricultural statistics). His areas of interest ranges from critical assessment of recent growth experience and strategies for poverty alleviation, the role of politics and institutions, importance of reliable data for informed policy making, the current state of available data and its utilisation for research.

India's Evolving Economy

Puzzles and Perspectives

A. VAIDYANATHAN

ACADEMIC FOUNDATION
NEW DELHI

www.academicfoundation.com

First published in 2013
by

ACADEMIC FOUNDATION
4772-73 / 23 Bharat Ram Road, (23 Ansari Road),
Darya Ganj, New Delhi - 110 002 (India).
Phones : 23245001 / 02 / 03 / 04.
Fax : +91-11-23245005.
E-mail : books@academicfoundation.com
www.academicfoundation.com

Cataloging in Publication Data--DK
Courtesy: D.K. Agencies (P) Ltd. <docinfo@dkagencies.com>

Vaidyanathan, A.
India's evolving economy : puzzles and perspectives / A. Vaidyanathan.
p. cm.
Includes bibliographical references.
ISBN 8171889921
ISBN 9788171889921

1. Economic development--India. 2. India--Economic policy--1991- I. Title.

DDC 338.954 23

Typeset by Italics India, New Delhi.
Printed and bound by The Book Mint, New Delhi.
www.thebookmint.in

Contents

List of Tables 11

Acknowledgements 15

Introduction
V.K. Natraj 17

I

Macro Perspective: The Economy

1. **India's Recent Growth Experience: Some Puzzles** 31
   The Agricultural Puzzle
   Tertiary Sector Growth
   Role of Foreign Financial Resources

II

Poverty, Inequality and Access

2. **Food Consumption and Nutrition Status: Indian Evidence Re-examined** 61
   Introduction
   Food Consumption Patterns and Trends
   National Level Comparisons
   Interstate Variations
   Relation between Consumption and Production at State Level

Food Intake and Nutritional Status
Body Size
Health Indicators
The Position of Poorer and Underprivileged Groups
Conclusions

3. Globalisation and the Quest for Food Security 91

Prospects for Global Food Security
Quest for National Food Security
Limits to Augmenting Domestic Supplies through Imports
Trade Liberalisation and Agricultural Growth
Aspects of the Food Security Problem
Assessing Nutritional Deficiency
Determinants of Food Consumption
Measures to Achieve Food Security
Faster Overall Growth
Poverty Alleviation
Public Distribution System
Alternative Strategies
Conclusion

4. Political Economy of Employment Guarantee Programmes 113

The Rationale for Wage Employment Programmes
Evolution of Wage Employment Programmes
The Need for Inclusive Growth
NREGP
Impact
Criticisms
Deeper Causes
Political Factors

5. Private Sector in Education: Supplement to or Substitute for the State 137

Trends
Current Position
Within the Private Sector
Private Expenditure on Education
What Encourages Privatisation?
Consequences and Impact
The Way Forward
We Need to Start at the Base: The Schools
The Issue of Equity
Summing Up

III

Finance and Banking

6. Commercial Banks: Has Growth Widened Coverage? 169

Expansion Facilities
Trends in Scheduled Bank Credit 1990-2008
Differences in Reach of SCBs to Different Users
Distribution of Loans across Sectors
Distribution by Institutional Categories
Credit Relative to Production
Caveats
Financing Credit Needs of the Unorganised Sector

7. Consumption of Gold in India: Trends and Determinants 189

Trends in Consumption: An Overview
Economic Impact of Gold Imports
Factors Determining Gold Imports
Estimation and Results
Conclusion

IV
Political and Institutional Dimensions

8. Irrigation Institutions: An Evolutionary Perspective 209

Introduction

Evolution of Irrigation in India

Framework for Study of Institutions

Small Scale Local Systems

Large Scale Systems

By Way of Summing Up

9. The Political Class and Development in India 227

Politics and Politicians

Politicians and the Constitution

Poverty Alleviation Programmes

Burgeoning Subsidies

Politics and Public Sector Inefficiency

Impact of New Economic Policy

The Way Ahead

10. Decentralisation and Community Action 241

Introduction

Chequered History

Corruption

Capacity of PRIs

Institutions

Strategy for Reform

The Experience of Cooperatives

Democracy and Equity

Conclusion

V
Data Base: Availability and Application

11. State of the Indian Statistical System 261

An Overview of the Statistical System

Censuses

Executive Agencies

Sample Surveys

Critique

Some Remedies

Postscript

12. Role and Relevance of Social Science Research 277

Role of Social Science Research

Quality and Reliability of Data

Need for Broader Perspectives

Inadequate Analysis

On Interdisciplinary Research

Some Illustrative Examples

Current State of Social Science Research

Revitalising Social Research

13. Econometric Analyses of Agricultural Growth: Reflections of a Non-Econometrician 293

Growth and Fluctuations

Sources of Growth

14. Socioeconomic Characteristics of Villages in North Arcot: An Exploratory Study 311

Villages of North Arcot: An Overall Profile

Variations by Village Size

Level of Economic Development

Female Literacy
Sex Ratio
Non-agricultural Employment
Caste-Class Differentiation
Conclusion

15. Crop-Weather Relationship: A Review 335

The All-India Crop Weather Scheme
Analytical Work on Crop-Weather Relations
Forecasting Crop Yields on the Basis of Weather Parameters
Conclusion

List of Tables

1.1 Expenditure Elasticities of Cereals, Non-cereal Food, Total Food and Non-food 33

1.2 Trends in Estimated Demand and Actual Consumption of Food and Cereals and their Prices Relative to that of Manufactures 35

1.3 Service Sector Growth, India 1950-2004 40

1.4 Composition of GDP from Services 2004-2006 at Constant Prices 41

1.5 Elasticity of Sectoral GDP Relative to Total GDP 42

1.6 Implicit Elasticities of Tertiary Sector GDP Relative to GDP in Different Periods, India 1950-2002 48

2.1 Estimated Mean Per Capita Intake of Calories and Proteins in India 64

2.2 NNMB Estimates of Mean Intake of Nutrients Per Consumption Unit in Rural Areas 67

2.3 Variability of Per Capita Nutrient Intake across States in Selected Years 68

2.4 Correlation between Per Capita Nutrient Intake between Rural and Urban Areas 68

2.5 Correlations between Nutrient Intakes at Different Points of Time 69

2.6 Interstate Variation in Calorie Intake and Foodgrain Production Per Capita 71

2.7 Nutrition Status of Preschool Children based on Weight for Age 75

2.8 Percentage of Undernourished Rural Children by Age Group in Selected States 75

2.9 Incidence of Chronic Energy Deficiency among Adults 77
2.10 Still Birth Rate, Perinatal and Child Mortality Rates.................. 79
2.11 Food Intake and Body Size of Different Socioeconomic Groups 1996-97.. 81
2.12 Access to Health Care Facilities for Social Groups 82
3.1 Agricultural Exports and Imports Relative to Agricultural GDP 2003 96
3.2 Trends in Mean Calorie Intake Overall and for the Poorest Quartile of Rural and Urban Populations India............. 101
4.1 Growth of Rural Wage Employment Programmes in India 1985-86 to 2009-10 125
5.1 Growth of Enrolment in Different Categories of Schools at Different Levels in India 139
5.2 Estimated Number of Students Attending Educational Institutions, and Proportions Attending Private Schools at Different Levels, India, 1995-96 and 2004-05 139
5.3 Students Attending Private Schools as Percentage of Total Attending Different Stages of Education in Rural and Urban India 1995-96 and 2004-05 140
5.4 Estimate of Private Expenditure on Education based on Official Enrolment Figures and Annual Fees per Student, 2003-04.. 143
5.5 Comparison of Official and NSS Estimates of Enrolments in Higher Education.. 144
5.6 Inequality in Access to and Private Expenditure on Education Rural and Urban India, 2004-05.............................. 152
6.1 Growth of the Commercial Banking System, 1982–2009 169
6.2 Growth of Banking Facilities in Rural and Urban Areas, 1980-2009... 170
6.3 Growth of Outstanding Deposits and Outstanding Loans, 1982-2009 172
6.4 Growth in the Number of Loans (in Millions) for Different Purposes 2000-2008 173
6.5 Distribution of Loans Outstanding by Sector 1995-96 to 2007-08 176

6.6 Distribution of Outstanding Loans by Institutional Categories 1991-2008 177
6.7 Trends in Credit-Deposit Ratios of Major Sectors 178
6.8 Share of Government and Private Companies in Loan Outstanding of SCBs 1991 and 2006 179
6.9 Output and SCB Loan Outstanding in Organised and Unorganised Sectors 2005-06 180
7.1 Net Import of Gold into India 189
7.2 Trends in Gold Consumption after Liberalisation 194
7.3 Gold Imports and Related Macroeconomic Variables, India: 1970-71 to 1997-98 195
7.4 Estimated Multiple Regressions to Explain Level of Gold Imports in India 198
7.5 Estimated and Actual Gold Imports, and the Contribution of Significant Explanatory Factors in Recent Decades, India 202
13.1 Characteristics of Best Filling Trend Lines to State Time Series of Area, Output and Yield, 1970-1990 296
13.2 Distribution of Districts by Average Annual Growth Rate of Crop Output 298
13.3 Distribution of Districts by Rainfall-Irrigation Zones and Percentage Change in Crop Yields during Different Periods 299
13.4 Distribution of Districts by Rainfall Zones and Trend in Yield Growth Rates during the Sixties, Seventies and Eighties 306
13.5 Linear Multiple Regression of Crop Output Per Hectare on Rainfall, Irrigation and Fertilisers for Different Rainfall-Irrigation Zones based on Pooled District Level Data for 1962-1965, 1970-1973 and 1980-1983 307
13.6 Linear Multiple Regression of Crop Output Per Hectare on Irrigation and Fertilisers by Major States, 1970-1990 308
14.1 Average Characteristics of Villages in Tamil Nadu and North Arcot District in 1981 313

14.2 Mean Values of Selected Characteristics and their Variability in North Arcot District, 1971 and 1981 314
14.3 Weighted Mean Value of Selected Characteristics of Villages Grouped according to Size of Population in 1981 315
14.4 Weighted Mean of Selected Characteristics of Villages of North Arcot Grouped according to Prosperity of Agricultural Classes and Extent of Non-agricultural Employment 318
14.5 Weighted Mean Value of Selected Characteristics of Villages Grouped According to Female Literacy Rate in 1981 North Arcot, 1971-1981 320
14.6 Results of Multiple Regression of Male and Female Literacy Rate on Selected Variables in 1981 (North Arcot, 1971-1981) 323
14.7 Weighted Mean Value of Selected Characteristics of Villages Grouped according to Sex Ratio 1981 (North Arcot, 1971-1981) 325
14.8 Results of Multiple Regression of Sex Ratio in 1981 and Changes in Sex Ratio during 1971-1981 on Selected Variables, North Arcot District 328
14.9 Mean Value of Selected Characteristics of Villages Grouped according to Ratio of Male Non-agricultural Workers to Male Agricultural Workers in 1981 North Arcot, 1971-1981 329
14.10 Results of Multiple Regression of Male Non-agricultural to Male Agricultural Employed on Selected Variables (North Arcot District, 1971 and 1981) 330
14.11 Weighted Mean Value of Selected Characteristics of Villages Grouped According to Degree of Caste-Class Differentiation (North Arcot, 1971-1981) 332

Acknowledgements

This collection of essays would not have come about without the encouragement and support of Prof V.K. Natraj. Besides helping in the selection of papers and grouping them to reflect different areas of my research, he readily agreed to my request to write an introduction to the collection. He went through all the essays carefully and with a critical eye, made extensive substantive comments on errors of fact and on clarity of arguments. The entire script has been meticulously edited by him with the assistance of Ms H.L. Sheela of Mysore with word processing and formatting and with academic and professional advice of Dr G.S. Ganesh Prasad, faculty of MIDS, Chennai. My sincere thanks to all of them and to Academic Foundation and especially Sri Sanu Kapila for expeditious publication of the collection.

Most of the essays in this volume were written during the last 10-15 years. Several are edited versions of invited lectures sponsored by the Indian Statistical Institute, Kolkata; Institute of Development Studies, Kolkata; Council for Social Development, Hyderabad; Centre for Socioeconomic and Environmental Studies, Cochin; Gujarat Institute of Development Studies, Ahmedabad; and the Indian Econometric Society. The essay on "Globalisation on the Quest for Food Security" was sponsored by the Centre for Trade and Development in 2009. My sincere thanks to all these organisations for giving an opportunity to reflect on diverse themes. Some of the essays (2, 7, 11, 13 and 14) are already published. They have been edited and updated for inclusion in this volume with permission from publishers: Dasgupta & Co, Kolkata; Economic and Political Weekly, Mumbai; Review of Development and Change, Chennai; Indian Journal of Agricultural Economics and Journal of the Indian Econometric Society.

Introduction

The papers in this volume may appear, at first blush, somewhat eclectic. This is in fact a reflection of the author's long and scholarly commitment to development both as a discipline and at the policy level. Although primarily a researcher of the first order and a social scientist of eminence, A.Vaidyanathan is also well known in his role as an advisor to and interlocutor for the state. Despite the appearance of eclecticism, and as these papers will bear out, this is no negative attribute; the sensitive reader, specialist and non-specialist alike, is sure to discern some common themes running through them. These common pursuits are more perceptible in some than in others but their flavour is present throughout. To capture these common themes is not easy but an attempt will be made even if in the process some violence is done to the collection and its author.

The papers are grouped into five sections: macro perspective; poverty, inequality and access; finance and banking; political and institutional dimensions; and data base: its availability and application.

Vaidyanathan being first and foremost an economist, it was thought appropriate that this collection should commence with an economic overview. But the first paper, rather than being a chronicle of economic achievements or a saga of missed opportunities, focuses on what the author calls 'puzzles' in India's recent growth. With his masterly expertise in handling data and his concern with macroeconomic policy issues he takes us through an exciting journey during which he helps locate the puzzles. The first relates to agriculture. Growth of production and availability of food for consumption have remained constant despite the increase in the overall rate of growth especially over the past two decades. In the very recent past there was concern that agricultural growth had fallen below even the trend rate of 2.5 per cent per annum. Going by received wisdom, with high income elasticities of demand for food there ought to have been strong pressure on food and cereal prices but this has not occurred (Events since this was written have made a difference but they do not alter the principal point of the paper). In view of this it is plausible that the 'old apprehensions' (as propounded long ago by Vakil and Brahmanand in their critique of the Mahalanobis model) about the supply of wage goods becoming a constraint on the overall growth of the economy may not be valid. In fact for a considerable period non-agricultural growth reached very high levels in spite of sluggish agricultural performance. But the author wisely points out the 'flip side', that if this sluggish performance were to continue it may dampen overall growth. What is witnessed today amply justifies the fears expressed in this paper that it would be a 'serious folly' for planners to ignore agriculture because it is not vital to sustaining overall growth of the economy. His recommendations are for more public investment in agriculture, quick completion of ongoing irrigation projects and limiting government's role to laying down the broad principles and institutional framework for resource development and management, for conflict resolution and for regulatory functions. "Direct management of land, water and common service facilities for agriculture should be taken out of government and entrusted to autonomous participatory organisations in the public space functioning within well specified rules with government playing a supporting role." He also wants changes with regard to pricing, both of outputs and inputs. He admits candidly that his suggestions are perhaps present in official pronouncements and pious policy statements but these are rarely implemented with seriousness.

There is also a study of the tertiary sector's growth and while he notes its quite impressive performance he makes a comparison with China and remarks that the "differences in the growth of commodity production especially in manufacturing are staggering. Between the early 80s and 2000-2002, manufacturing output has increased nearly 30 fold in China while in India it increased a little over 7 fold. Exports have been a major driving force in growth in the Chinese economy both overall and particularly in manufacturing industry. It is fashionable to attribute it all to liberalisation and surge of foreign direct investment. But this is a gross oversimplification." Commenting that India too has travelled along the liberalisation route, we are reminded that it has not generated the kind of growth momentum that is observed in China. Vaidyanathan points to the critical difference which lies in the nature and scale of foreign resource flows. In China the scale of these flows was not only large but came from overseas Chinese entrepreneurs with experience in a wide range of manufacturing. By contrast FDI (foreign direct investment) flows to India have been very much smaller and that too mostly from MNCs (multi-national corporations) seeking to expand their operations in growing markets and shift them to countries where labour costs are comparatively low. Overall foreign resource flows into India have also been not only much smaller but also mostly in the financial sector. This analysis should be of special interest to students of development who are sometimes prone to laud the LPG (liberalisation, privatisation, globalisation) model as the wonder *mantra* for India. Indeed, of late, there appears to be an obsessive attachment to FDI in governmental and of course business circles. At the moment of writing, FDI in the retail sector has become a live political issue.

In the next section are papers concerned with the issues of poverty, inequality and access which may be described as the pivots of development and to which Vaidyanathan has an abiding commitment and as a theme, these run through the volume in one form or another. A noticeable feature of virtually every paper in this collection is Vaidyanathan's attempt to locate the subject under inquiry within a larger frame of reference. For instance in his examination of the 'Political Economy of Employment Guarantee Programmes' he traces the historical evolution of this type of intervention with particular emphasis on the Maharashtra EGS (Employment Guarantee Scheme). What follows is an incisive discussion of two quite different variants in the approach to employment programmes as an income generator and a security net, one suggested by Dandekar and Rath and the other by Minhas. Far from being of historical interest alone, this brings to light what is of relevance even today. Among these may be mentioned the following: should employment generation focus essentially on rural works or on other forms of work? Further, should the programmes be entrusted to the local community Panchayati Raj Institutions (PRIs) or should they be administered from above? These questions remain important at this juncture decades after the divergent views of Dandekar-Rath and Minhas came into the public domain.

A paper in this part discusses in detail the question of access to food and the reliability of the presently utilised norms for assessing food and nutritional adequacy. Vaidyanathan argues with evidence that "per capita calorie and protein intake by itself is neither a reliable nor an adequate basis to assess nutrition and health status. Ultimately, balanced diet is not an end in itself but a means to ensure the many facets of healthy, active living." He goes on to urge that mean intake of calories should be combined with "data on indicators such as body size, mortality and morbidity, and nature and intensity of activity which reflect the net effect of quantity and quality of food intake." He invites us to remember that the very notion of ideal health and functioning in all dimensions as well as the possibility of attaining that optimum is open to question. This piece of analysis is another example of Vaidyanathan's desire to place specific questions, such as nutrition in this instance, within a holistic development frame of reference. In this context he raises another complex issue and this too contains policy implications. It is the puzzling fact that average calorie intake is declining or is constant (at low levels) and this is so both for the population as a whole and for the poorest segments. This should be juxtaposed with the diversification in consumption patterns both within food from cereal to non-cereal and from food to non-food items. Further, it should be remembered that this diversification is seen to be taking place in a country with low incomes. We should agree with the author's contention that this has implications for state policy and intervention with respect to food security. In his analysis of food security and nutrition we find the author once again aiming at a blend of the several dimensions that dot the development policy landscape as witness to the attempt to examine agricultural growth, food consumption and nutritional status against the backdrop of globalisation and its impact on the country's reform strategy.

In another paper also relating to food security Vaidyanathan explores the validity of the argument that further liberalisation of Indian agriculture in respect of foreign trade will accelerate growth in this sector. He posits the contrary view, also taken by other specialists, that "all available evidence suggests that aggregate supply response to changes in overall terms of trade per se is miniscule" and that non-price factors including climatic conditions, technology and the like are much more important.

His complaint is that there is hardly any visibly serious effort at addressing the issue of improving resource use in agriculture and he rightly cautions against unfounded or exaggerated optimism that agricultural exports will become buoyant due to diversification into floriculture, animal husbandry, etc. In the light of the recent trends in the country's economic profile, these warnings are obviously well taken. Continuing attempts to persuade India to agree to further liberalisation of her foreign trade in agriculture are based on the argument that it will stimulate faster growth in domestic production. This advice is to be treated with care. The nature and extent of shifts in the average level of producer prices and in the relative price structure cannot be assessed on the basis of past experience or current trends.

This brings us to another major area of interest for Vaidyanathan, namely, education and within this the expanding role of the private sector. It is unnecessary to speak of the potential which education has as a transformative agent over time. In passing we are tempted to add that the inadequacy of longitudinal studies relating to education and in particular the profile of beneficiaries of positive discrimination is a big lacuna. They would throw considerable light on the role of education in increasing access to employment and, in general, to a better quality of life. In a broader sense this paper goes to the vortex of the question of what the state should do to promote development through education and this is highly relevant in a context in which the role of the state is steadily getting diluted. The exponential expansion of the private sector's role in education, particularly higher education and more specifically in courses relating to medical and engineering, management and computer science and applications, is an established fact. Its implications and ramifications are very wide. Some states have made vast strides in this sphere and today there is active talk about the entry of foreign players into the education sector. In other words, the privatisation syndrome is enveloping higher education almost with a vengeance. At the school level also a number of factors contribute to the burgeoning of the private sector including the woeful state of government run schools and the rising demand for instruction in the English medium. There is evidence of parents spending impressive amounts on such school education which is interpreted often wrongly as 'willingness to pay' as Jandhyala Tilak has argued in his Adiseshiah Memorial Lecture (MIDS, 2003), while the fact is that several factors virtually compel parents to incur this expenditure.

In a long discussion of this scenario Vaidyanathan poses the all-important question whether private education is a supplement to the efforts of the state or is threatening to become a substitute for it. He warns quite rightly against mistaking quantitative expansion (necessary though it is) of facilities in higher education for achievement in the meaningful sense since the standard of teaching (and of teachers) is far from satisfactory. While this is a fair point, the problem is how to attract committed teachers and retain them and do it in such a way that equity and excellence are blended. And this applies to selection of students as well. Vaidyanathan focuses on this knotty issue and appears to be in agreement with the composite index of backwardness which was much discussed in the aftermath of the introduction of the 27 per cent reservation for the backward classes mooted by the then HRD minister, Arjun Singh in 2006. Since the paper is an examination of the whole of the education sector, one should not perhaps expect the author to answer every question relating to student and staff selection but it does appear that some of his strategies will provoke critical debate. The composite index formulated first by Satish Deshpande and Yogendra Yadav is not free from fault lines; at the very least it is open to debate. As a scholar specialising in analysis of data one need not be surprised at Vaidyanathan's displeasure at detailed data by caste not being available with respect to student applicants in entrance to technical/professional courses although I harbour a slight suspicion (based not only on his writings but very many instructive personal discussions) that he might be glossing over some of the complexities in the collection of such data. This paper should be read in conjunction with others in the collection which discuss, directly or otherwise, the role of the state under the 'reform regime'. In this our author is in the company of several equally distinguished contemporaries of his who, while disapproving of the stifling system of controls that had evolved over the decades and contributed to rent-seeking proclivities in the economy, nevertheless did not endorse the reforms and the LPG package ushered in the 1990s. His quest is for a State which will promote equity and justice along with growth. An issue of great consequence Vaidyanathan discusses is that a vast proportion of graduates from the engineering stream (including from prestigious colleges/institutes) opt for software or management with the result that only a relatively small percentage is engaged in actual engineering/manufacturing tasks.

Vaidyanathan has critiqued the contribution of commercial banks and their contribution to financial inclusion. He has noted that the progress is not as impressive as one would expect. He sees some merit in the model of the SHG (self-help group) and also notes that cooperatives can make a more substantial contribution to institutional credit than they do presently. His lament is that waiving of loans, frequently resorted to by the state, is not a remedy for the problems that bedevil rural credit. While the growth of commercial banks was expected to improve the reach to the most needy sections, reality is quite another and sad story. Around 60 per cent of loans go to the corporate sector, about 20 per cent are accounted for by personal loans and only the rest is available for those whose interests were supposed to be looked after by an expanding banking sector. He has also turned his attention to the consumption of gold, another unusual paper in this collection. He posits the view that the price of gold relative to share prices and international gold prices is an important determinant of gold imports. IOSP (index of share prices) is emerging as an increasingly important factor, even as the margin between domestic and foreign prices of gold has dwindled largely as a result of changes in the exchange rate and gold import policies. If gold imports are allowed to be determined by the market, IOSP seems likely to emerge as the crucial determinant of gold imports. However, the results need to be confirmed by incorporating the *hawala* premium in the estimating equation.

A principal concern for Vaidyanathan is governance. For him governance is not just the effects of policy decisions on society, rather it represents the sum total of what he often describes (in his writings as well as in discussions) as processes and outcomes. Naturally this makes him acutely sensitive to the manner in which processes work and the constellation of factors which affect outcomes. There are at least two examples of this genre of thinking in the collection. One is the paper on the 'Political Class and Development' and the other a somewhat unusually conceived article on 'Irrigation Institutions: An Evolutionary Perspective'. In the first of these he speaks of the need to "distinguish politics from politicians." And then goes on to perceive "politics in its broad sense as the mediation, balancing and resolution of competing interests of different segments of society—regions, religions, castes, and classes—and conflicts arising from them." Vaidyanathan's academic objectivity is seen clearly in that, unlike quite a few critics of the Indian system, he recognises the areas in which the political process works to a reasonable degree of satisfaction. At the same time he draws pointed attention to the several spheres in which action is called for and reminds us of the positive role that public awareness has played in bringing to light quite a few of the maladies bedevilling the system. He sees in the public and civil society, important instruments of ushering in change. This belief is almost an article of faith for him. It is tempting to speculate on what he would write as an afterthought to this in view of the Anna Hazare movement and its various ramifications. My own intuitive guess is that his welcome, if it were there, would be hedged with serious reservations and caveats!

The second paper was described earlier as somewhat unusual in conception. In this paper Vaidyanathan operates at two levels. In the first place he discusses the role of institutions. Later he attempts to illustrate this with respect to water and its uses. Starting from the premise that society needs to have "mechanisms for achieving a workable balance between the diverse and changing goals and interests of constituents and to resolve conflicts among them" he goes on to argue that "such mechanisms are built into the design of all social institutions but their functioning depends on those who design and control them" and further that the "manner and extent to which they cope with changes necessitated by internal and external factors depend both on their magnitude and the institutions' resilience to respond and adapt themselves to changing situations without unmanageable disruptions." He provides more than adequate reasoning for the necessity of regulations in relation to this resource by stating that since water is a fluid common pool resource, the market mechanism cannot perform these functions. In his words the "conditions necessary for an effective market mechanism to mediate allocations (and in particular clearly defined and enforceable private property rights) are nearly impossible to fulfil. Entitlement to access (geographical and by use) to a given source (which could be a tank, a reservoir, a river basin, or an aquifer) as well as the sharing of the available supplies from that source among diverse claimants is therefore, everywhere regulated through social institutions." His conclusion is worth recalling: "a proper understanding of the performance of public institutions therefore calls for studies in a wider evolutionary perspective sensitive to the complex and intricate ways in which they are shaped by material conditions, social and political configurations and the economic context."

A social scientist interested in governance and the processes attending on it would naturally be expected to probe into the nexus between the state, community and the voluntary sector/civil society. Vaidyanathan has had an abiding interest in these issues and especially in the realm of people's participation in democratic and development processes. He is a strong votary of decentralised governance and constantly advocates more powers for local bodies, that is, PRIs. And he is sharply critical of the hurdles placed in their way by power-hungry state-level politicians as also the bureaucracy. Almost predictably, he makes a strong plea for more powers to PRIs. One wishes though that he had found it possible to discuss some of the limitations that these institutions confront in relation to planning. For instance, at that spatial level, the temporal horizon of planners is bound to be short, while development requires a blend of the short and longer terms. Further, with respect to scale also, the emphasis is more likely than not to focus on the small while the necessity for the large scale cannot be ignored. Some of these are unexplored dimensions of decentralisation; indeed they do not figure with any prominence in the extant literature. They deserve to be labelled 'conundrums in decentralisation'. And it would be nice if Vaidyanathan were to direct his acute and perceptive focus on them. Another issue worthy of his attention is the difference in perception that appears to exist between politicians at the state level and those at the local level. The reference here is to politicians from the subaltern, principally Dalit category. From some, admittedly not extensive, field work carried out by me in Karnataka, the impression that surfaces is that the ones at the local level are more optimistic about the positive/emancipatory effects of local government on the Dalits than their counterparts at the higher levels. And it would be wrong to dismiss the 'state level' perspective as occasioned by a desire not to encourage competition from the local level or that it is due to lack of vibrant contact with grassroot reality. It would be a good exercise to examine whether this is not due to two basically different approaches to the problem of 'liberation' of the Dalits.

Practically an entire section is devoted to an examination of the state of data in India, a staunch favourite of the author's, a result of both his attachment to and remarkable expertise in data analysis. The paper on the state of India's statistical system should be a must read for anyone wishing to be acquainted with the numerous sources of data in India and their reliability. The paper has been updated to take account of the work of the Rangarajan Committee which reported after the paper was completed in its original form. As one may expect we find Vaidyanathan expressing unhappiness at the weak tradition of 'data based' policy analysis in India. There is an important contribution to the role of social science research wherein Vaidyanathan explodes the myth that academic research is mostly abstract in nature and can therefore contribute little to policy making. It is best to let him speak for himself. "In point of fact, ideas generated in 'academic' debates have a profound influence in shaping views on the appropriate strategies, programmes and policies for tackling current problems at different levels. Several important broader issues of development strategy and policy have been and continue to be under intense and lively debate among scholars. Academic debates and critiques have influenced several of the major changes in strategies relating to such diverse areas as employment and poverty alleviation, agricultural and rural development, fiscal policy, industrialisation, economic liberalisation, and decentralisation of governance and development. Perceptions and understanding on many of these aspects have changed in the light of studies of emerging experience." Space constraint prevents me from doing more than mention another major point he raises, which is with respect to the impact of 'sponsored/project' oriented work on the ethos of research in the social sciences. This latter point is especially significant in the present context where research centres and universities confront difficulties in recruiting and retaining truly good minds in research. It is to be hoped that this will be read, and read avidly, by policymakers but that, one fears, may not happen since the report prepared under the chairmanship of Vaidyanathan on social science research just a few years ago has resulted in no action.

Two papers in the last section deal with themes somewhat different from those of the others in this collection. One is a modestly titled piece on the reflections of a non-econometrician on econometric analysis of agricultural growth. A salutary warning in this is worth quoting and this relates to the much used approach of trend fitting. Vaidyanathan has this to offer as a critique of the method and he prefaces it by remarking that it may not enthuse those who are devoted to the econometric method and hopes that his "criticisms of mindless application of this method to evaluating trends, and estimating ill specified 'production functions' for agriculture" will attract serious attention. Further, "possibly there are econometrically tractable ways" of handling the complex interactions between inputs. Finding them would certainly be welcome. Meanwhile his appeal to econometricians is to "examine dispassionately the logic of my approach and assess its capacity to give us a better understanding of the technical factors underlying agricultural growth and the role of economic and institutional forces in determining how much and how prudently different inputs are used."

The second paper in this category is an analysis of the relation between the weather and crops. This is not an area generally visited by economists but even to a relatively unfamiliar academic in the area such as this writer, the analysis opens up interesting vistas of inquiry. After surveying some of the work done in this sphere Vaidyanathan has a few suggestions to offer based on his critical reflections. He remarks that his review is "obviously far from complete in its coverage of the work done at the India Meteorological Department (IMD) and other scientific bodies on crop-weather relations." But insofar as the papers covered form a fairly representative cross-section of the work, we could, at some risk, attempt to summarise the state of knowledge they reflect. It is evident that the AICWS (All India Coordinate Crop Weather Scheme) was a well-designed enquiry and that it did generate a mass of crop-weather information under controlled conditions for different parts of the country. Unfortunately, much of this data remains unpublished, and its quality and utility for analysis of weather-yield relations remain to be properly tested." This work suggests attractive possibilities for further work but they need to be tried out on many more stations and crops on the basis of much closer and conscious interaction with plant scientists to enable the formulation of meaningful hypotheses for testing. He believes that it would be useful to examine the "predictive power of these models in the case of other crops and regions" and the closeness of actual yields to the advance yield forecast reportedly made by the IMD every year for the use of the Ministry of Agriculture. The extent to which this plea has had an active response from the powers that be is not known but there can be no doubting the soundness of the advice.

One of the last papers is again on an area in which Vaidyanathan has had a long standing involvement, namely, village studies for which there is a deep tradition in certain academic circles. A most important point in this study is the manner in which Vaidyanathan summarises the value and the limitations of the data generated by different methods and from different sources at the village level. In his view, data generated from the village level has certain limitations. The population data is subject to post-enumeration checks which ensure that the degree of reliability is high but this is not equally true of other kinds of data. Yet he suggests that they can provide valuable insights and help develop typologies and assist in identifying backward villages. Above all they can prove useful in tracing the relative position of villages in terms of socioeconomic characteristics through time.

One conclusion that emerges from the papers on data application is that data collected at enormous cost is not fully utilised and in Vaidyanathan's view, both collectors and users ought to share the blame for this. His North Arcot paper illustrates this quite clearly.

A final word. What is presented in this collection is only a part of the rich contributions A.Vaidyanathan has offered academia, policymakers and the interested public in an active career stretching over several decades. Other writings of equal significance have appeared in the form of papers and books. Taken all in all, these represent the results of enormous and unceasing labour and a mind almost restless in its quest for more knowledge and always in search of ways to improve the state of our society. It is a pleasure and an honour to introduce this selection to prospective readers.

—V.K.Natraj

I

Macro Perspective: The Economy

1 India's Recent Growth Experience
Some Puzzles

The exceptionally rapid growth of the Indian economy during the past decade and a half has attracted much admiring attention and comment. That the economy has moved to a distinctly higher growth path following internal and external liberalisation is not in doubt. But the nature and extent of its contribution to growth and the socio-political consequences of the pattern of 'development' remain contentious issues. In particular there are serious concerns regarding widening socioeconomic disparities, the decline in the quality of basic education, health care and social protection to all citizens, and rapid privatisation of these functions, and resultant social tensions. The purpose here is not to address these larger issues directly but to draw attention to some features, and their implications, of the growth experience in agriculture and tertiary sectors and of trends in the balance of payments.

The Agricultural Puzzle

A distinguishing feature of India's agriculture is that the growth of production and availability of food for consumption have remained more or less constant even as the pace of overall growth, particularly in the last two decades, has increased over time (from around 3-3.5% pa between the early fifties and the early seventies to the current levels of 8-9% pa). Since the mid-sixties, the sectoral pattern of gross domestic product (GDP) growth to achieve the targeted overall growth rate has been estimated on the basis of models that set targets of production for various goods and services to match their projected demands for consumption, investment, trade and intermediate inputs. The target of agricultural GDP growth ranged between 3 and over 4 per cent; and that of gross agricultural output was higher. Actual trend rate of growth of agricultural GDP remained more or less constant at around 2.5 per cent per annum over most of the period 1950-2000, which was consistently short of the target. In fact, there is concern over signs that of late the growth has fallen even below this level as the current and projected growth of GDP (9% pa) is estimated to require agricultural GDP to grow at around 4-4.5% pa.

According to conventional wisdom, at the low levels of per capita income characteristic of India, the income elasticity of demand for food, which accounts for the bulk of agricultural production, is high. Based on data generated by consumption surveys of the National Sample Survey (NSS), the expenditure elasticity of food relative to per capita private consumption expenditure was estimated at around 0.85 in the early seventies and that of cereals around 0.6. On this basis and given the rate of growth and per capita total consumption expenditure from national income estimates, the expected rate of growth of food demand in different periods are as shown in the Table 1.1. In fact, there is widespread concern that, during the last decade, agricultural growth may have fallen below the long term trend. This would imply a large and growing excess demand for food and cereals which should have exerted a strong pressure on food and cereal prices relative to the general price level. But this has not happened: there is in fact no significant or sustained rise in the ratio of the indices of food prices and non-food prices over the last three or four decades.

Part of the reason could be changing patterns of consumer preferences. NSS consumer surveys (as well as surveys conducted by the National Nutrition Monitoring Bureau (NNMB)) show that: (i) on an average, consumer expenditures on food, food grains and non-cereal foods account for a smaller proportion of total household consumption expenditures in urban areas compared to rural areas; (ii) in both segments there is a progressive shift in the pattern of household consumption from food to non-food and from cereal to non-cereal food; (iii) the expenditure elasticity of demand of urban households for all food, cereals and non-cereal foods is also lower than those of rural households; (iv) the demand elasticity for these items has been declining in both rural and urban areas; (v) the decline is most pronounced in the case of cereals, less so in the case of non-cereal food and the least for total food; and (vi) in all three categories, the decline is more pronounced in urban areas (Table 1.1).

The general decline in demand elasticity and the growing proportion of population in urban areas as well as that of the incomes generated there would together have contributed to dampening the growth of demand for food and especially cereals. In order to allow for this trend, which is possible though only in a rough way, we have estimated the demand for all food and for cereals based on NSS estimates of demand elasticity with reference to per capita private consumption expenditure, and National Accounts Statistics (NAS) estimates of actual private consumption expenditure during different (roughly quinquennial) periods since 1970.

Table 1.1

Expenditure Elasticities of Cereals, Non-cereal Food, Total Food and Non-food

		Rural				*Urban*			
Round	*Year*	*Cereals*	*Non-cereal*	*Food*	*Non-food*	*Cereals*	*Non-cereal*	*Food*	*Non-food*
25	1970-71	0.5975	1.3027	0.8804	1.3285	0.5052	1.2037	0.8837	1.2679
27	1972-73	0.49	1.2018	0.7914	1.4119	0.337	1.1105	0.8129	1.3334
28	1973-74	0.5719	1.1723	0.8222	1.3994	0.513	1.1737	0.8971	1.2205
32	1977-78	0.7465	1.1011	0.9201	1.143	0.6053	1.0067	0.8693	1.1635
38	1983	0.4785	1.1525	0.8042	1.3526	0.451	1.0933	0.8407	1.2407
42	1986-87	0.6339	1.1008	0.8988	1.1749	0.3559	1.066	0.8045	1.3533
43	1987-88	0.3646	1.0604	0.7701	1.3585	0.215	0.9158	0.7217	1.3393
44	1988-89	0.3843	1.0781	0.7843	1.3588	0.2059	0.9158	0.7113	1.3838
45	1989-90	0.3308	1.1149	0.7954	1.3672	0.174	0.922	0.7138	1.3728
46	1990-91	0.4667	1.1374	0.8707	1.2411	0.2877	0.9488	0.7615	1.335
48	1992	0.5787	1.0731	0.8571	1.2634	0.3756	0.9821	0.7945	1.3023
50	1993-94	0.3231	1.0519	0.7643	1.3678	0.2207	0.9172	0.7229	1.3458
51	1994-95	0.3285	1.0102	0.7309	1.4066	0.2578	0.9342	0.7271	1.3626
52	1995-96	0.3345	1.053	0.7415	1.4005	0.2436	0.8715	0.6806	1.3971
53	1997	0.3789	1.103	0.7865	1.3473	0.3004	0.9359	0.7275	1.3429
55	1999-2000	0.3054	1.1415	0.8171	1.2569	0.2237	0.905	0.7171	1.2788
56	2000-01	0.304	1.1092	0.8076	1.2417	0.2199	0.8871	0.7012	1.2552
57	2001-02	0.2934	1.1022	0.7948	1.249	0.2447	0.8734	0.7028	1.2485
59	2003	0.3358	1.0664	0.8016	1.2335	0.2567	0.8722	0.7019	1.2511
61	2004-05	0.2867	0.9301	0.7096	1.3294	0.225	0.7832	0.6413	1.2966

Note: The elasticities are estimated using the cross-section consumption data from various rounds of NSS consumption data.

The estimates summarised in the table are derived as follows:

(i) The entire period is divided into sub-periods, each centering around the year when consumption surveys were done on the basis of a large sample.

(ii) Estimates of cross-section demand elasticity for these two groups are available for rural and urban areas, courtesy Prof C. Ravi; the elasticity for the entire population is assumed to lie between the values for rural and urban areas and closer to the rural values.

(iii) Year-wise estimates of total population and per capita private consumption at 1999-2000 prices are taken from NAS 2008.

(iv) Percentage change in per capita demand for food and cereals is estimated for each year by applying their respective elasticity (which changes from period to period) to the change in per capita total private consumption expenditure in that year.

(v) The base period demand is taken to be the actual consumption in 1970-71.

(vi) Estimated per capita demand is multiplied by the population of each year to get the total demand.

(vii) The total demand for each period is then compared with the actual consumption in that period.

(viii) It turns out that the demand for both total food and for cereals is in excess of the actual availability for consumption (which is reflected in the NAS estimates of consumption) throughout the period and that the difference shows a progressive increase.

(ix) We have also estimated the change in the price of food and cereals relative to that of manufactures in each period.

As stated above, even allowing for declining elasticity, the demand for both total food and for cereals exceeds the actual availability for consumption (which is reflected in the NAS estimates of consumption) throughout the period and the difference is growing both in absolute and relative terms. But this does not seem to have any consistent relation to the behaviour of the food and cereal prices relative to that of manufactures. This estimate of relative prices at an aggregated level is crude. Prices are not in all cases and always determined by the balancing of supply and demand through the market mechanism. Apart from macroeconomic factors that affect the general price level, government fiscal and monetary policies as well as direct intervention (through price and distribution controls) affect relative prices. Nevertheless, it is reasonable to expect that persistent and growing excess demand will be reflected in greater pressure on their prices relative to other commodities.

Table 1.2

Trends in Estimated Demand and Actual Consumption of Food and Cereals and their Prices Relative to that of Manufactures

Period	*Demand **		*Consumption**		*Consumption–Demand as % of Demand*		*Change in relative Prices during Period*	
	Food	*Cereals*	*Food*	*Cereals*	*Food*	*Cereals*	*Food*	*Cereals*
1970-1974	1200222	481512	1164350	453846	-3.1	-5.7	0.016	0.162
1975-1979	1403806	559148	1101386	509426	-27.5	-8.9	-0.160	-0.291
1980-1985	2082340	799334	1992231	704074	-4.5	-11.9	0.055	0.049
1986-1990	2109373	777502	1972832	695583	-6.9	-10.5	0.010	-0.105
1991-1996	3071029	1078518	2862381	945789	-7.3	-12.3	0.165	0.199
1997-2003	3222855	1047529	2798291	833311	-15.2	-25.7	0.136	0.087
2003-2006	3942840	1190825	3035043	879170	-29.9	-35.4	-1.418	-1.110

Note: * Estimates of demand and consumption in crore Rs.

1. Elasticities are weighted averages of elasticities for rural and urban areas based on NSS consumption surveys for various rounds.
2. These have been applied to aggregate private consumption expenditures from national income accounts published by CSO. Estimates of actual food and cereal consumption are also taken from national income accounts.

That this is not happening can be due to one or both of two factors. NSS data tend to overestimate demand elasticity; production is underestimated. That there are serious deficiencies in the system for compiling agricultural statistics is well known, but there is little basis to judge whether and to what extent they systematically underestimate outputs and supply. There are stronger reasons to believe that elasticity based on cross-section data on aggregate consumption and consumption of food may be over-estimated: richer households in the NSS sample are not only relatively small in absolute numbers, but they are also known to be less willing to respond and/ or tend to underestimate their consumption. The fact that total consumer expenditure derived from national income estimates are consistently and substantially higher than NSS lends credence to this belief. Underestimation of consumption of richer households would lead to under-estimation of the inequality in distribution of aggregate consumption and overestimation of the demand elasticity for essential consumer goods like food.

If the above reading of the evidence is correct, old apprehensions that the rate of agricultural growth and hence the supply of 'wage goods' set a severe constraint on the pace of non-agricultural and overall rate of growth without inflation are no longer valid. Despite continued low, and possibly declining, rates of agricultural growth during the last two decades, non-agricultural growth has been sustained at historically unprecedented levels. The flip side of this is that, if current trends continue, slow growth of demand for agricultural products may well turn out to be a dampening influence on agricultural growth. And policymakers and planners may be tempted to ignore or underplay the role of agriculture because it is not crucial to sustaining rapid overall growth of GDP. This would be a serious folly.

The burgeoning of the non-agricultural economy accompanied by increased concentration of incomes among the better off classes has no doubt created opportunities for non-agricultural employment and higher real wages in rural India. Despite this 'trickle down', the majority of the country's population and working population continue to depend on agriculture. A large segment of them are socially underprivileged depending on wage employment which is both inadequate and provides very low incomes. A substantial segment of cultivators also lives precariously close to subsistence. The bulk of the rural population does not have and cannot afford education of a level and quality that enables them to take advantage of growing and better paid non-agricultural job opportunities in urban areas. Widening disparities in income and opportunity, both real and perceived, between agriculture and non-agricultural sectors, and between rural and urban areas, are not only unacceptable but are also the root cause of growing social tensions.

The only way out of this is to increase the rate of expansion of incomes and employment generated within the rural sector. Achieving and sustaining faster growth of agriculture and related activities, which after all constitute the foundations of the rural economy, is therefore essential. This faces a twin challenge: besides addressing the constraints that impede agricultural growth, it is necessary to find ways to arrest and reverse the looming demand constraint. Improving the quality of land and water management, ensuring sustained progress in agricultural technology and restructuring institutions and public policy to facilitate and induce more efficient use of technology and inputs are essential to achieve faster agricultural growth. The positive impact this will have on rural demand for agricultural products needs to be reinforced by strategies and programmes to reduce the disparities in agricultural growth between regions and especially between irrigated and rainfed areas. It is however also necessary to address the trend towards increasing inequality in overall income distribution between rural and urban areas and within urban areas. These compulsions are barely recognised by the policymakers.

The slowing down of agricultural growth is widely attributed to slowing down of investment, especially public investment in agriculture. The Planning Commission seems to share this perception and sees increased investments in irrigation and watershed development as the means to achieve the projected step up in growth. Both in money terms and after due adjustment for rising prices, public as well as private investment has indeed slowed down especially in the nineties. But what is relevant is not the magnitude of investment but its contribution to increasing production capacity. For a variety of reasons peculiar to agriculture, production capacity has not increased in proportion to quantum of investment.

Thus surface irrigation, which accounts for the bulk of public investment in agriculture, is concentrated on projects that have taken an unconscionably long time to complete. Costs have risen and outlays have not resulted in any significant additions to irrigated area. The efficacy of public investments in soil and water conservation is in serious doubt. They (indeed much of outlays on rural development and poverty alleviation) are marked by huge waste and corruption; and there are hardly any mechanisms at the local level to maintain and manage the works and ensure that the potential for expansion is properly exploited. They have had hardly any impact in raising product potential or productivity of rainfed lands.

Private investment in agriculture has largely been concentrated on ground water exploitation and mechanisation. In recent years private investment in ground water has gone increasingly into deepening wells of all types and installing more and more powerful pumps to access water from a falling ground water table. In the context of falling water tables—which is a sure sign of overexploitation of ground water—these investments do not increase the volume of ground water available for irrigation and therefore production capacity. The impact of mechanisation, the other important component of private investment, is primarily to replace human and animal labour by tractors, harvesters and threshers. They reduce costs farmers have to incur for conduct of various agricultural operations; their contribution to increasing productive capacity is, if at all, of a very secondary importance.

It is therefore important to focus on deeper, and more basic, reasons for the slowdown of agricultural growth and the constraints that need to be overcome to reverse the trend and step up the pace. For this purpose it is useful to distinguish between three broad phases of agricultural growth in the post-Independence period. During the first phase, lasting roughly from the early fifties through the mid-sixties, the major part of growth came from expansion of area. Expansion of surface irrigation and fertiliser use brought about a modest pace of yield improvement. During the second phase, lasting from the mid-sixties through the eighties, the scope for extending area was more or less exhausted. But this was more than compensated by an unprecedented increase in the rate of yield improvement due to a combination of massive investment in public and private irrigation and the advent of the new seed-fertiliser technology. The pace of expansion in surface irrigation slowed down during the latter part of the period, despite continuing large scale investments. Simultaneously, falling ground water levels over more and more tracts signalled overexploitation of this resource. During the third phase (since the nineties), the flow of improvements in varieties, and agronomic practices from the research system was fitful and inadequate. Progress was particularly disappointing in respect of rainfed agriculture. The sharp reduction in growth of output reflects the combined effect of these factors. This was also a period marked by gross imprudence and waste in the use of land, water, fertilisers and other key inputs due to failures of governance, poor management of public systems catering to agriculture and pricing, and subsidy policies inimical to the prudent use of resources and effective exploitation of the potential of available technology. With the scope for expanding area being exhausted and the scope for further expansion of water for irrigation getting diminished, the institutional barrier—comprising governance, the quality of public systems and economic policies—has become the most serious impediment to agricultural growth.

Overcoming this barrier calls for major reorientation of strategy, priorities and policies along the following lines:

1. Strong shift in public investment priorities in favour of modernisation of surface irrigation works (to facilitate higher yield per unit of water used) and for watershed development.

2. Prioritisation of incomplete irrigation projects after stricter scrutiny of the technical quality, costs relative to benefits and close monitoring of their implementation.

3. Limit government's role to laying down the broad principles and institutional framework for resource development and management, for conflict resolution and for regulatory functions. Direct management of land, water and common service facilities for agriculture should be taken out of government and entrusted to autonomous participatory organisations in the public space functioning within well-specified rules with government playing a supporting role.

4. Vigilant and strict enforcement of preventive and punitive measures is critical to contain gross violations of rules governing access to and use of resources. This calls for much greater transparency and strictness of governance than is presently the case.

5. The public research system has not been generating a steady flow of technological improvements to reduce costs and increase the production potential of the limited land and water resources. There is need for a serious critical review of the measures—organisation, priorities and incentives—needed to make it more effective.

6. These need to be combined with changes in policies relating to pricing of outputs and inputs (especially canal water, fertilisers and electricity) to create strong incentives to reduce the huge and avoidably wasteful, inefficient and unsustainable use of agricultural resources.

These may be obvious to discerning observers and some elements of it even figure in official rhetoric. That they pose tough challenges is also obvious. But they have to be confronted and determined efforts made to overcome them in order to relax the institutional constraints and disincentives, which are now the critical bottlenecks to realising the potential for increasing production. Without it, the target of four per cent sustained growth in agriculture will remain a dream.

Tertiary Sector Growth

Even though growth of agriculture has been slow, and is possibly slowing down, the tertiary sector has been booming. Throughout the last five decades, the tertiary sector, consisting mostly of activities that provide services, has grown faster than the growth of GDP. Its share in GDP has increased progressively from around 30 per cent in the early fifties to nearly 53 per cent currently. It accounted for about 34 per cent of the increase in overall GDP in the fifties and rose to 62-63 per cent in the nineties. In both respects the role of the tertiary sector in India is exceptionally high compared to other economies at a comparable stage of development. (Table 1.3) The high rates of growth recorded by the Indian economy during the last two decades are largely driven by the rapid expansion of tertiary activities. It is important to examine whether and to what extent this perception is valid, what the underlying factors are and whether they will continue to drive future growth.

Table 1.3

Service Sector Growth, India 1950-2004

	% increase				
	1950-1960	*1960-1970*	*1970-1980*	*1980-1990*	*1990-2002*
Total GDP	47.1	40.6	41.1	65.6	99.4
Commodities	44.1	33.7	32.6	51.5	66.2
Total services	54.4	55.9	57.0	88.0	142.1
Elasticity (w.r.t.) GDP					
Commodities	0.93	0.83	0.79	0.79	0.67
Services	1.15	1.38	1.39	1.34	1.43
Increment in service	34.3	42.9	48.0	51.6	62.5
Sector GDP to increase in total GDP %					

Source: CSO, National Income Estimates at 1999-2000 prices.

According to conventional wisdom (dating back to Colin Clark), the share of tertiary sectors in GDP is expected to be relatively low in economies with low levels of per capita income, high dependence on agriculture and low levels of industrialisation, and is expected to increase with the level of per capita incomes. Comparisons based on UN estimates of GDP and its composition corroborate the Colin Clark hypothesis. A comparison across selected countries (Table 1.4) shows that in the US and Japan, which rank among countries with the highest per capita incomes, tertiary sectors currently account for 75 per cent and 65 per cent of their respective total GDP. Their share in the emerging economies of Asia, which have much lower per capita incomes, is around 55 per cent in India, 49 per cent in South East (SE) Asian countries and 21 per cent in China.

Table 1.4

Composition of GDP from Services 2004-2006 at Constant Prices

(bill $)

	Trade	*Transport/ Communication*	*Others*	*All*	*Services/ GDP*100*	*Total GDP*
US	1675	603	3875	6154		8462
	27	**10**	**63**	**100**	**73**	
Japan	523	282	1706	2511		3838
	21	**11**	**68**	**100**	**65**	
SE Asia	125	66	169	360		734
	35	**18**	**47**	**100**	**49**	
China	109	135	104	348		1669
	31	**39**	**30**	**100**	**21**	
India	115	77	197	389		711
	30	**20**	**51**	**100**	**55**	

Note: Figures in bold are percentages.
Source: United Nations *Statistical Year Books*.

There are also significant differences in the composition of the tertiary sector across countries. Trade (wholesale and retail), hotels and restaurants, and transport and communications account for a lower proportion of tertiary sector output in US and Japan than in S E Asia, India and China. Differences between these two groups in contribution of trade and restaurants to total GDP are not as pronounced as in transport and communications. The share of the latter is much higher in emerging economies of Asia, most strikingly so in the case of China.

'Other services' (comprising finance, insurance, real estate, business services, public administration, defence, community and personal services) contribute a much higher proportion of both tertiary sector output and total GDP in high income countries. These differences in composition of tertiary sector output reflect differences in the composition of demand for various services and the technology used by these, both of which vary across countries, activities and over time. However, the exceptionally high share of transport and low share of 'other' in China is not easy to explain.

Also striking are differences in trends in tertiary growth relative to that of GDP growth. (Table 1.5) Between early 1970s and 2002-2004, tertiary sector output has grown faster than overall GDP in all countries except China, but in varying degrees: by 19 per cent in SE Asia, around 25 per cent in USA and Japan, and most strikingly by as much as 70 per cent in India. In sharp contrast, tertiary sector in China has grown much slower than GDP. The share of tertiary sector output in total GDP has been rising in all countries albeit unevenly. But India and China stand out—the former recording an exceptionally high elasticity of total tertiary sector output relative to overall GDP and the latter—an exceptionally low elasticity. India also has recorded a much higher elasticity than China in the three components of tertiary activities. That the tertiary sector in China is growing at a slower rate than overall GDP is the surprising feature.

Table 1.5

Elasticity of Sectoral GDP Relative to Total GDP

	Trade	*Transport/Communication*	*Other*	*All*
US	1.86	1.91	1.33	1.24
Japan	1.17	1.25	1.29	1.26
SE Asia	1.00	2.14	1.14	1.19
China	1.09	1.50	0.39	0.78
India	1.63	2.82	1.50	1.70

Note: Estimated from *United Nations Statistical Year Book 2007*.

There are also significant differences across countries in the elasticity of different components of the sector. As would be expected, the elasticities of all three sub-sectors are relatively high in the high income countries of

US and Japan. But the wide divergences between the emerging economies of Asia—all of which have much lower per capita incomes—are surprising. In this respect India and China present striking contrasts. The elasticity of tertiary sector growth in India, both overall and in all three sub-sectors, relative to total GDP is higher than that of the rich countries. In China, which has a higher and faster growing per capita income, tertiary sector elasticity is much lower, both overall and in all three sub-sectors. In fact, according to these estimates, tertiary sector output is growing slower than total GDP largely because the growth rate of public administration, defence, community and personnel services is less than half of the overall growth rate!

The growth of the tertiary sectors has also been much slower relative to GDP over the period taken as a whole. Its share in GDP, which rose from 26 per cent in the early seventies to around 30 per cent in the early nineties fell to 21 per cent in 2004-2006.

The above comparisons are based on UN national income estimates in terms of US $ at constant prices. The Standard National Accounts (SNA) framework of the UN provides a uniform framework of concepts, classification and measurement as well as the format of presentation to be followed by national agencies. The UN statistical office has little control over generation of the basic data and estimation by countries. It uses estimates provided by national statistical agencies and converts different components of national income accounts into a common currency base at current and constant prices, and on the basis of purchasing power parity. While most countries have adopted the SNA format, the methods of collection of the required data and their coverage and reliability are decided by national agencies. SNA has given an impetus and direction to national efforts at improving the coverage and quality of database. But progress is very uneven.

In India, estimation of output based on systematic sample surveys and detailed accounts of enterprises covers agriculture, government, public sector undertakings and corporate entities in the private sector. Estimates for unincorporated enterprises also make extensive use of sample surveys of employment and output. But these surveys are not yet a regular feature. Data from sample surveys, or for that matter from actual accounts, are subject to several limitations arising in part from their design and conduct, but more importantly because of the difficulties of getting reliable information from sample respondents. The difficulty is much greater in the case of the unorganised sectors—comprising own account workers and small scale enterprises, which do not maintain any accounts and responses are based entirely on recall. This category of enterprises—collectively called the 'unorganised sectors' are important in several sectors including tertiary activities such as retail trade, hotels and restaurants, road transport, private sector educational and health care facilities, repair and personal services.

Apart from these limitations, sample surveys, which form the basis of estimates, are relatively new and evolving. At present, in some cases they are used only for base year estimates; others are done at periodic intervals (in some cases once in five years) requiring interpolation in the intervening years. Real output series are based on volume of output in some cases, but in most they are derived by deflating current price estimates with a price index. In the absence of sector/service specific price indices, the implicit GDP or sectoral deflators, or one or other consumer price index (CPI) is used to derive constant price estimates. Deflators are based on assumptions, indirect indicators, and interpolations. The Central Statistical Organisation (CSO) publication "National Accounts Statistics Sources and Methods 2007" spells out the assumptions, empirical basis and methods of dealing with these tasks and their limitations in some detail. The CSO also revises the series every time there is a change in basis and methods of estimation. However, it is difficult to see how earlier series based on different sources of data and assumptions can be brought in line with the latest changes in these respects. This raises questions about the reliability of past trends estimated from the revised series.

These problems are by no means unique to India. The manner in which they are handled is unlikely to be the same in all countries. This may be the main reason for the huge difference in the pattern of growth, and especially of the tertiary sectors between India and China. This underlines the importance of a closer scrutiny of the basis—in terms of database, assumptions and estimation procedures—on which national statistical agencies cope with lack of or inadequacies of data for estimating real output of various sectors. Unless they follow reasonably similar or comparable procedures in all these respects, international comparisons of structure and growth of GDP, and interpretations of their underlying factors would not be robust. These caveats and caution also apply to analysing growth trends when, as it happens in most countries including India, the database and estimation procedures have been changing from time to time.

The tertiary sector comprises diverse activities providing infrastructural services that support production and exchange; a variety of professional services to business enterprises; maintenance and repair services for machinery and durable goods for businesses as well as consumers; community services (like education and health care); and personal services. The demand for these services is a function of several factors: the level and composition of overall economic activity, per capita incomes, technology, consumer preferences and the degree of commercialisation of the economy. In the early stages of transformation from predominantly agrarian economies with low levels of income, technology and commercialisation, the demand for services generally and for services provided through the market in particular is likely to be low. As the economy grows and becomes increasingly commercialised and industrialised, the demand for services and the extent to which it is met through the market will also increase. As per capita income increases, the proportion of incomes that consumers spend on services also increases. Technological changes in production, consumption and in the service sectors, expansion of public administration as well as defence contribute both to the growth of demand for services and its composition. Growing international trade in services—air and ocean transport, software and other professional services and tourism are good examples—becomes an increasingly important determinant of both the pattern and perhaps also the level of service sector activity. The cumulative effect of all these factors would be to increase service sector activity to rise faster than GDP. However, their impact on different segments of the service sector will also vary across countries and over time.

Table 1.6 gives an idea of the elasticity of output of tertiary activities as a whole and of their major components with reference to GDP growth in India. For purposes of discussion we have divided the period into 3 segments:

1950-1980 - which was a period of relatively slow growth

1980-1990 - period of cautious liberalisation and faster growth than earlier

1990-2002 - when the liberalisation was carried much further and overall growth also increased.

The following features are noteworthy:

1. Overall elasticity has been consistently above unity throughout the last five decades.
2. It was highest during the first period at 1.45, declined in the eighties and has recovered since nineties to 1.43.
3. Elasticities and their time trends differ across sectors.
4. In the first period, it was greater than 1 in all except real estate and other services. The highest was in the communications, banking and finance sectors (over 3).
5. The second period witnessed a decline in elasticity in all sectors except real estate and other services, which recorded a substantial increase.
6. During the nineties, the elasticity declined in half of the sectors and increased in the rest. The decline is marked in railways, public administration/defence and most strikingly in banking and finance. Trade, hotels and restaurants, and communications sectors show a large increase in elasticity.

Some of the changes have plausible explanations. For instance, the growth of transport sector as a whole depends on the growth of freight and passenger traffic. Freight volumes are a function of commodity production, which is growing relatively slower than GDP. On the other hand, passenger traffic, which is a function of overall income, has grown much faster. The elasticity of the transport sector as a whole is greater than unity and has increased over the three periods which is in line with the quickening in the pace of GDP growth. The progressive increase in the share of road transport in both freight and passengers can account in part for the decline in the elasticity of railways.

Growth of trade is also more a function of growth in commodity production and the proportion which is traded, than of GDP. While its elasticity with reference to GDP growth is rather erratic, the elasticity relative to growth of GDP from the commodity sector is greater than unity. This suggests that traded volumes relative to commodity output are growing. Increasing commercialisation of the economy is one factor. But one would suppose that this process would have been much more important in the first period. The increases in subsequent periods suggest that the process is continuing.

Banking/finance and communications are among the fastest growing sectors. The coverage and scale of banks, cooperatives and other 'modern' financial institutions in the organised sector is driven by sustained growth of economic activity, progressive commercialisation and inflation. During the first period (1950-1980), they grew three times as fast as GDP but, for reasons that are not obvious, the elasticity dipped in the eighties. Financial sector liberalisation and reform led to a spurt in growth of this sector in the nineties and later.

Much of the same pattern is seen in the communications sector: growth in the first period largely reflects expansion of postal, telegraph and telephone networks. The subsequent spurt in growth, especially from the early nineties, is driven by the major technological advances which triggered the rapid spread of courier services, cable operators and cellular telephones.

Activity under hotels and restaurants, 'other services' (comprising community and personal services) and repair and business services (subsumed under real estate) have grown because of a combination of factors: rise in per capita incomes, urbanisation, more unequal distribution of incomes, changing consumer tastes and technological change. Whether the national income estimates capture these adequately is a question that needs closer examination.

These 'explanations' seem plausible but are obviously not adequate to corroborate the veracity of the growth elasticity of service sectors implied in the CSO estimates or explain the reasons for the differences between sectors at different points of time. Among other things, the rationale for and the sensitivity of, using macro price deflators—wholesale price index (WPI) and various CPIs—to convert nominal outputs into real terms in these sectors merit critical scrutiny.

Table 1.6

Implicit Elasticities of Tertiary Sector GDP Relative to GDP in Different Periods, India 1950-2002

	1950-1960	1960-1970	1970-1980	1950-1980	1980-1990	1990-2002
Trade	1.51	1.30	1.42	1.64	1.09	1.54
Hotels/restaurants	1.48	1.29	1.38	1.59	1.25	2.03
Railways	1.41	1.20	1.00	1.30	0.76	0.61
Other transport	1.85	1.77	2.44	2.84	1.34	1.50
Storage	0.59	0.76	3.61	1.64	0.50	0.26
Communications	1.95	2.35	2.14	3.15	1.31	7.38
Banking insurance	2.20	2.08	2.14	3.16	2.92	1.66
Real estate	0.55	0.79	1.05	0.72	1.83	1.19
Public administration/ defence	1.61	2.64	1.62	2.65	1.29	0.91
Others	0.76	1.09	0.82	0.84	1.09	1.21
All tertiary sectors	1.15	1.38	1.39	1.45	1.34	1.43

Source: CSOs National income estimates of aggregate GDP and GDP of specified sectors for different periods.

The increasing share of tertiary sectors in GDP has been widely interpreted to mean that the recent quickening of overall growth is driven by growth in services. This is wrong because, as would be evident from the foregoing discussion, most of the activity caters to domestic demand linked to the growth of commodity production and domestic incomes. There is room for scepticism over whether, at current levels of per capita income, the income elasticity of demand for services is as high and increasing as fast as the national income estimates imply. In any case there is no warrant for assuming that these trends will continue.

Activities that cater to foreign demand (which includes export of labour and outsourcing of information technology (IT), business process outsourcing (BPO), technological research and other professional services by developed countries) can make a difference to GDP growth. Though growing rapidly, they are still relatively small in relation to the country's GDP. Thus GDP from IT and related services, the largest and fastest growing segment, is estimated at Rs 17,000 crore in 1999-2000, which is barely two per cent of tertiary sector GDP and one per cent of total GDP. Even in 2006-07 the net receipts from trade in these items amounted to around four per cent of GDP. A sustained 20 per cent growth of these sectors would make a difference of 0.8 percentage points to the overall growth. Given the current and prospective economic trends in developed countries—the main export market for services—it would be unrealistic to expect that growth in these sectors can be sustained at the rates achieved during the last few years.

The importance of increasing the pace of growth of commodity producing sectors to sustain the rate of overall economic growth at high levels cannot be overemphasised. This is underscored by the contrast between the growth experiences of China and India. While there are reasons to be sceptical about the reliability of estimates of tertiary sector growth in both countries, the differences in the growth of commodity production especially in manufacturing are staggering. Between the early eighties and 2000-2002, manufacturing output has increased nearly 30 fold in China, while in India it increased a little over sevenfold. Exports have been a major driving force in growth in the Chinese economy, both overall and particularly in manufacturing industry. It is fashionable to attribute it all to liberalisation and surge of foreign direct investment (FDI). But this is a gross oversimplification. After all, India too has gone along the road of liberalisation and globalisation without generating the kind of growth momentum that is observed in China. A crucial difference lies in the nature and scale of foreign resource flows. In China the scale of these flows was not only large, but came from overseas Chinese entrepreneurs with experience in a wide range of manufacturing. By contrast, FDI flows to India have been very much smaller and that too mostly from multinational corporations (MNCs) seeking to expand their operations in growing markets and shift them to countries where labour costs are lower. Overall foreign resource flows into India have also been not only much smaller but also mostly in the financial sector.

Role of Foreign Financial Resources

The scale and role of foreign financial resources in economic development, and the attitudes to it have undergone a sea change—nearly a 180 degree turn—over the past 50 years. This was not much of an issue in shaping development strategy during the fifties, partly because of the substantial volume of sterling balances available at that time and also because of the relatively modest targets and gradualist path of growth envisaged.

But the issue began to assume importance from the late fifties as reserves declined, the current account deficit in the balance of payments increased rapidly and planners sought to achieve faster transformation of the economy. It came into prominence in the sixties when the country's own foreign exchange earnings were proving to be, and also expected to be, inadequate to meet its growing import requirements, and the domestic savings were inadequate to finance investment needed to sustain a quicker pace of growth. Economists developed the so called 'two-gap models' to assess magnitude of foreign resource requirements on the basis of the relative magnitude of the foreign exchange and savings gaps, which were binding constraints on the feasible growth rates. Planners and policy makers of course had to make an assessment of the magnitude and terms on which foreign resources could be tapped.

It was a time when historical memories of the exploitative role of foreign investment (FI) were fresh and there was widespread antipathy to allowing direct FI. Nor were commercial borrowings considered desirable or likely to be available to the public sector on any significant scale. However, developed countries were showing increasing interest in providing substantial development aid to third world countries, in the form of grants and low interest loans. They were interested in providing to India not entirely out of altruism but in their own political interests. The desirability of seeking aid, which was likely to be subject to conditions, which may not be in the recipient country's interest was a contentious and hotly debated issue in the political arena. In the event, recourse to such aid was deemed necessary to achieve faster growth and that it could be used to become self-reliant within a reasonable period of time.

The volume of foreign resource inflow during the sixties was nearly eight times the volume during the fifties, almost all of it from bilateral and multilateral aid. The seventies were a difficult period for the economy, which is reflected in low growth and high inflation. Balance of payments deficits continued, though at a lower level than in the sixties. Receipts from external assistance declined in absolute terms, but were still the dominant source of external flows. This period saw the emergence of commercial borrowing and non-resident Indian (NRI) deposits as sources of foreign exchange. There has been a dramatic change since then.

The overall magnitude of capital inflows increased at an unprecedented rate. There was a six fold increase from the seventies to eighties and roughly doubling in the subsequent decades. More dramatic is the change in the sources of these inflows. While the flow of external assistance continued to be high in absolute terms, its share in total flows declined sharply to 38 per cent in the eighties and further to less than one per cent post 2000. Recourse to borrowing of all types increased sharply in the eighties, both in absolute and relative terms, reflecting largely the government's reliance on commercial borrowing for development projects and rise in NRI deposits. Thereafter, commercial borrowings increased apace, especially during the reform period (when government allowed corporations to borrow abroad), while NRI deposits were much less and not sustained. But their share in total flows has declined sharply, yielding place to foreign investors.

The beginning of liberalisation of policy on FI is reflected in an increase in its magnitude in the eighties, but it still accounted for barely four per cent of total inflows. The liberalisation of policy in this regard during the reform period led to an explosive growth from $1.4 billion in the eighties to $33 billion (44% of total) in the nineties and to $98 billion (68% of total) since 2000-01. Of the $130 billion inflows under FI, roughly half is in the form of FDI and another half consists of investments by foreign institutional investors (FII).

The other striking feature of the overall picture is that, while the total net foreign inflows from the fifties through the eighties were sometimes lower than the current account deficit (leading to a drawing down of foreign exchange reserves) and sometimes higher (leading to an increase in these reserves), the inflows have far exceeded the current account deficit resulting in a huge increase in forex reserves.

These changes in both the level and composition of inflows have significant impact on the economy. Different components have different effects. Thus, external assistance has augmented the resources available to the public sector for implementing its development programmes. Aided projects are expected to have the benefit of accessing advanced technology and expertise as well as training of indigenous personnel. The combined effect is expected to contribute to improving the quality of projects—in terms of design, technology choice, supervision costs and time schedules—

compared to those designed and implemented indigenously. Whether and to what extent this expectation is borne out by experience has not been assessed. On the other hand, agreements on aided projects—especially sectoral and programme aid—often contain conditions regarding policies relating to specific sectors as well as at a broader level. These conditions have tended to change from time to time and reflect changing views of donors on appropriate policy without much concern to check whether the conditions and prescriptions are in fact adopted and whether they had the intended impact on performance. In fact, there is ample evidence that in many cases donors have chosen to ignore failure to implement reasonable and sensible changes in policy as conditions of loans and continued to approve of fresh loans (water and electricity rates and policy on subsidies are cases in point).

The public sector's recourse to commercial borrowing during the eighties was meant to accelerate investment in key infrastructure sectors to facilitate more rapid overall growth. While the growth rate did increase during this period, poor macro management of the fisc and the balance of payments led to a huge rise in current account deficit, and a rapid drawing down of foreign exchange reserves to a point that culminated in the crisis at the end of the decade. Restrictions imposed on all commercial borrowing substantially reduced the levels through the mid-nineties. The restrictions seem to have been relaxed for a few years thereafter before being reimposed in a stricter form leading to a substantial retirement of short-term debt obligations in early years of the current decade.

But the policy on commercial borrowings by the private sector (mostly large corporations) has since been greatly liberalised leading to a huge increase in the last two to three years. This increase seems to have been driven by the huge differential between interest rates on domestic borrowing and the rates prevailing in other developed countries. Reduction in interest costs could be one of the factors in increasing corporate profits and stimulating and financing larger investments.

Of all the categories of inflows, FDI is expected to and can make a significant direct impact on growth by expanding productive capacity and improving efficiency by bringing in new technology. Between 1990 and 2008, the cumulative flow of FDI is estimated at $97 billion, comprising $75 billion in equity and $20 billion by way of retained profits. Nearly half the equity investments have come during the last two years. And about two-fifths has come via Mauritius.

Of the $58 billion of FDI in the form of equity that came in since 2000-01, about 45 per cent was invested in service industries (financial, non-financial, software and hardware services, business services); about a third was invested in a wide range of manufacturing industries. Construction and real estate, energy and transport are other sectors receiving sizeable FDI.

The scale of FDI flows into India is much less than expected and formal approval from government is required. That they are far less compared to other emerging economies of Asia, and especially China, is common knowledge. Since the reform of the early eighties, China has received 700 $ billion of FDI compared to 111 $ billion in India. The annual rate of FDI in China (currently 124 $ billion) continues to be much higher than in India (currently around 32 $ billion).

There are also significant differences in the sources of FDI in the two countries. This has been pointed out earlier. In China, the bulk of the investment is in an estimated half a million or more manufacturing enterprises set up by overseas Chinese mostly from Taiwan and Hong Kong, who have already established modern manufacturing enterprises in a wide range of industries with the capability to compete in international markets. By contrast, a large part of FDI flows into India are from MNC investments in the financial sector, computer hardware, software and telecom services. They have also invested in several industries but on a much smaller scale.

The Indian diaspora comprises mostly professionals, who have migrated and settled in the developed countries and much larger numbers of unskilled and semi-skilled labour working in the Middle East. Except for software, successful industrial entrepreneurs are relatively few compared to overseas Chinese. Judging from the available data on sectoral distribution of FDI, non-MNC investments (including NRIs) cover a wide range of industries and services. But little is known about the true provenance of these investments and about the contribution and role of NRIs.

FDI's contribution to increasing productive capacity and productivity depends on how much of it is in production sectors and supporting infrastructure facilities; how much goes to establishing new projects (green field) as against mergers and acquisitions of existing enterprises; the extent to which investment in acquisition of existing enterprises, joint ventures and technical collaborations for outsourcing of production leads to expansion of capacity and upgrading of technology. Recent trends point to a significant shift in FDI and foreign inflows generally into housing and commercial real estate in metropolitan cities and special economic zone (SEZs) in anticipation of huge profits. Whether they add to productive capacity is a moot question. So is the impact of the entry of foreign enterprise in some areas (food processing and retailing are good examples) on employment and output in indigenous enterprises in these sectors. Available information is inadequate to assess the relative importance of these categories and the extent to which they have contributed to capacity expansion and technological improvement.

As part of the liberalisation of the financial sector, the door was opened for entry of FIIs into India. Their investments have grown rapidly. Besides emerging as important players in share markets, their contribution to net capital inflows into the country has increased both in absolute and relative terms. Their primary business is to invest in shares and other financial assets. The sustained strong performance of the economy in terms of overall growth, profits of the corporate sector and the sustained rise in share prices leads to expectations of high returns by investing in domestic financial assets. This is the main attraction for FIIs to seek outlets for their funds in India. The large and increasing investments in Indian shares and bonds is known to be a major factor in driving share prices to dizzying heights. The market value of FII investments is currently about twice their cumulative investments. While it is true that these gains cannot be realised by disposing of their holdings in a short time, the magnitude of net inflows and the turnover of their portfolios is not determined only by the performance of the domestic economy and its corporate sector, but is strongly influenced by the opportunities of arbitrage arising from changing differential interest rates, exchange rates, general price levels, and movements in financial markets of other countries. Shifting in the composition and destination of portfolios involves a considerable amount of speculation in assessing the behaviour of the relevant variables and government policies in various countries. Given the size of FII investments and the freedom they have to shift funds into and out of India, the scale of net inflows and outflows of their funds have a significant influence on their expectations and behaviour of domestic share markets. Recent evidence shows the rapidity and extent to which disturbances and fluctuations in international financial markets are transmitted to Indian share markets and increase their volatility.

There are several well-founded reasons for the demand for restricting and even reducing FII operations. Effective regulation is also proving to be difficult because of the complexity of instruments they have devised, and lack of information on the sources of funds, identity of investors and their relation to the FIIs. There are apprehensions about the use of FIIs to gain control over domestic corporations. FII operations not only contribute nothing to increasing domestic production and incomes, but complicate the task of macroeconomic policy and sustaining high rates of growth without exacerbating inflationary pressures and social tensions.

Inflows in this form no doubt add to the supply of foreign exchange, which could provide an extra cushion to manage current account deficits and also be used to increase investments in the economy beyond the levels permitted by domestic savings and FDI flows. But it so happens that the flows are rising at a time when foreign inflows are increasingly in excess of the current account deficit and there are severe fiscal and institutional constraints on using them for increasing domestic investment.

An obvious consequence is appreciation of the rupee. It has made the task of evolving and implementing coherent and mutually consistent fiscal, monetary and exchange rate polices necessary to maintain the present tempo of growth with price stability. Supporters of appreciation (mostly those depending to a significant extent on imports for production and those using import-intensive products and services for consumption and investments) argue that it could serve as an effective instrument to control inflation. This is both wrong and socially unacceptable for the simple reason that imports and import-intensive products constitute only a fraction of the demand of even the middle classes and the rich; they constitute a miniscule part of the consumption of the vast majority of Indians. On the other hand, appreciation of the rupee hits exporters hard even as it puts producers for the domestic market at a disadvantage by making imports cheaper. The recent widening of the current account deficit, despite the continued increase in software exports and remittances, is a consequence of this trend. Its continuation can have serious adverse impact on long-term growth.

Of course exchange rates are not the only factor that determine the competitiveness of Indian products and services in export markets and against imports in the domestic market. They depend as much on the efficiency of domestic production, which is a function of technology, innovative capacity and the quality of management. But it is worth noting that the extraordinary growth of post-war Japan and of China since 1980 combined their strength in these real factors with a successful policy of maintaining an undervalued currency. India has not shown a capacity for absorption and improvement of technology, organisation and management comparable to those of East Asian countries. In this context a policy of continued appreciation of the rupee does not augur well for even maintaining the current rates of growth, much less for increasing it and achieving a more balanced sectoral mix.

The current trend towards greater globalisation not only of the financial sector but also of significant segments of organised industry and services has larger consequences, which give cause for concern. Perhaps, the most important of these is its asymmetric impact on different segments of the domestic labour market. The market for professionals is getting increasingly globalised. This is reflected in the high rates of migration of both students and trained professionals to seek careers in the developed world and the increasing alignment of salaries for executives and professionals in domestic corporations with international salaries. This is obvious in the phenomenal increase in salaries of corporate executives in finance, industry, IT and service sectors. This probably has some cascading effect on salaries of other segments in the organised private sector. It has certainly generated pressures for substantial increase in salaries from public sector employees at all levels. But these trends have little effect on conditions and terms of employment in the unorganised sectors, especially for unskilled and semi-skilled labour, which accounts for the bulk of employment in the country. As a result, disparities in income between blue and white collar workers with different levels of education in different segments of the economy have greatly widened.

Increasing economic disparities have collateral effects in widening the already serious social divide between rural and urban areas and between India and Bharat. Other collateral effects include—intensified competition for higher education, aggravation of difficulties for disadvantaged segments in accessing increasingly privatised and high cost higher education, the rising trend of elite youth to seek education and careers abroad, the strong preference for managerial jobs and jobs in the IT and financial services sector, its impact on the supply of personnel trained in specialised subjects for other sectors, and the alarming reduction in the number and quality of people available for higher level research and teaching.

II

Poverty, Inequality and Access

2 Food Consumption and Nutrition Status

Indian Evidence Re-examined

Introduction

The availability of food in terms of both quantity and quality is an important indicator of well being of the mass of the people. In the Indian context, the official 'poverty line' based on norms of calorie and protein intake needed for healthy, active life, has come to be widely used as the basis for assessing nutritional status of the population. The 'poverty line', used to assess 'income poverty', is also anchored on certain assumptions regarding the commodity composition of the food basket to achieve the nutritional norms with an allowance (rather arbitrary) for non-food consumption.

Much research effort has gone into documenting the near stagnation of mean per capita intake of food grains and calories, the progressive diversification in the pattern of food consumption from cereals to non-cereal products, the persistent inadequacy of actual intake relative to norms especially among the poor, and the necessity for policies and programmes aimed directly at increasing employment and income-earning opportunities to the poor and ensuring (through a subsidised public distribution system) that they have access to food at reasonable prices. The relative merits of different policy interventions to ensure food security, and the experience in their working have also been under active debate.[1]

There are however important issues relating to the measurement of levels and patterns of food consumption and current understanding of their implications for the nutritional status of the population. These issues are the focus of the present paper. Specially, it seeks to do the following: (a)

1. For a sampling of recent writings on these issues and for references to earlier contributions see Krishnaji and Krishnan (ed.) (2000).

present the main features, as revealed by National Sample Survey (NSS), of levels and patterns of food consumption and variations across regions and over time; (b) compare estimates from these different sources and assess the confidence with which we can speak of levels and composition of food intake from different sources and trends therein; (c) focus on the limitations of food intake as a measure of nutritional status and the need to look at 'outcome' indicators such as size of people, mortality and morbidity; and (d) present available data on some of these indicators, point out how they might modify inference about nutritional status based only on food intake, and suggest directions for further work to refine these indices.

Food Consumption Patterns and Trends

Data Sources

Household consumption surveys conducted by the NSS, more or less continuously since the early 1950s, are by far the most comprehensive and detailed source of data on food consumption. Published tabulations usually give data on value of consumption by major food and non-food items, and quantity estimates for different food grains. Detailed estimates of quantity and value of different food items are available for a few years. State-wise estimates for rural and urban areas and by per capita consumption expenditure levels are available for practically all years when the consumption surveys were conducted. With nutritional norms coming into prominence for defining poverty line and assessing poverty incidence, NSS has published estimates of calorie, protein and fat intake by state—rural and urban areas and socioeconomic class. These estimates, first published for 1971-72, are now available for 1972-73, 1997-98, 1983, 1993-94 and 1999-2000.[2]

Apart from the NSS, there are at least two other sources of data on food consumption: One is the Food Balance Sheet (FBS) based on official estimates of production, adjusted for seed, feed, wastage and stock changes, to get at private consumption of various food items. FBS for the country as a whole is estimated and published by the Food and Agriculture Organisation (FAO) (accessible on their website); no further disaggregated estimates are

2. NSS, report nos. 238 and 239 and *Sarvekshana* October-December 1989 and October-December 1997.

available. The other source is the National Nutrition Monitoring Bureau (NNMB), which has been conducting sample surveys of food consumption and nutrition status of rural population in selected states from the early 1970s. About 10 states have been covered at various points of time, 6-7 of them (4 in South India, Maharashtra and Gujarat in the West, and Orissa and Madhya Pradesh) more or less continuously. Summary tabulations of nutrient intake, body size and incidence of nutrition deficiency are published more or less regularly in periodic reports.[3] Estimates of food intake obtained from these sources differ significantly from each other.

National Level Comparisons

Estimated national average per capita intake of calories and protein for selected years based on FBS and NSS are presented in Table 2.1. Both show that intake levels are lower than the norms recommended by nutrition experts, and that there is no noticeable trend over time. But the differences between the two are striking.

While the level of calorie intake differs but marginally from that of FBS, the level of protein intake and the proportion of the two nutrients derived from cereals and their time profiles from these sources differ substantially. It is apparent from the table that:

1. The FBS estimates of calories pcpd is less than that of NSS in three out of four years but exceeds it in 1993-94.
2. FBS estimates of protein are consistently lower.
3. The two sources point to very different time profiles of change in nutrient intake: the FBS shows a progressive increase in both calories and proteins pcpd between successive points of time. The NSS shows

---

3. These reports, available in mimeographed form, include a series of annual reports giving processed tables for surveys for individual years and some special technical reports giving consolidated results for several years. They give estimated per capita intake of calories, protein and other nutrients based on household level measurements for a sub-sample and mean per capita intakes for different age and gender groups based on 24 hour recall by the individuals for another sub-sample; mean values and standard deviations of height, weight and other anthropometric measurements by gender and age group for all individuals in the entire sample; and incidence of under-nourishment, by age groups and gender based on energy deficiency and clinical assessment. Some reports give a limited amount of data by occupation and social groups.

Table 2.1

Estimated Mean Per Capita Intake of Calories and Proteins in India

	1971-72	*1977-78*	*1983*	*1993-94*
Calories (Kcal)				
FBS	2072	2085	2144	2330
NSS	2170	2370	2190	2132
Proteins (gms)				
FBS	50.4	51.3	54.1	56
NSS	61.4	70.7	59.9	59.4
% contribution of cereals and cereal substitutes to				
Calories				
FBS	66.3	64.6	64.4	61.4
NSS	80	72.3	72.4	70.5
Proteins				
FBS	62.4	63.3	58.9	60
NSS	NA	NA	NA	69.4

Note: NSS report numbers 238 and 329 and Sarvekshana O-D 1989; and O-D 1997. Figures are weighted averages of estimates for rural and urban areas, the weights being their population shares in the selected years.

Data from more recent surveys (summarised in NSS Report 513) show that the per capita intake of both calories and proteins has declined progressively over successive rounds of NSS from 1993-94 to 2004-05. While the major portion of both nutrients was derived from cereals, their contribution has declined progressively over the period from 71 per cent to 68 per cent for calories, and 69 per cent to 64 per cent for proteins.

Source: Food Balance Sheet (FBS) for India prepared by FAO, available in FAO website.

a sharp rise between 1971-72 and 1977-78 and a decline thereafter. Further, according to FBS, mean intake in 1993-94 was higher than in 1971-72. The NSS estimate points to the opposite.

4. The dominance of cereals in diets and its declining importance is corroborated by both sources. However, its extent is considerably higher in the NSS estimate compared to FBS. FBS, in other words, suggests a more diversified diet.

5. Between 1971-72 and 1977-78, the NSS shows a larger increase in diversification than FBS, but thereafter the FBS points to a faster diversification.

These differences are in part due to differences in scope, sources and methods underlying the two estimates. Thus NSS data relate to household consumption while FBS is broader in scope covering households, non-household institutions in the private sector and the public sector. The NSS estimate is based on information regarding the consumption of various foodstuffs obtained directly from sampled households. FBS is built on the basis of estimates of aggregate production of various food crops net of usage for seed, animal feed, waste in storage and transport, and changes in inventories. The food content of some major crops, namely rice, sugar and oilseeds, is estimated on the basis of some standard conversion factors. Losses in processing and cooking of raw foodstuffs before they are consumed are not taken into account. The NSS, on the other hand, gathers information on the quantities of a large number of items used by the sample household during 30 days prior to the interview. It distinguishes between unprocessed food (for example cereals and pulses), semi-processed food (such as flour) and processed foods obtained from outside (like bread, biscuits, snacks and even prepared meals). Losses in processing (but not in cooking) are likely to be better reflected in NSS estimates.

Other things being the same, one would therefore expect estimates based on household surveys to be less than those derived from production estimates. But this is not the case in 3 out of 4 years for which we have estimates; NSS estimate is in fact higher by 2 to 10 per cent than FBS in these years. Only in one is the FBS higher by about 10 per cent. The data also point to very different pictures of change even in respect of direction—not to speak of its rate. Given differences in scope, sources and method, the fact that they have changed in some respects, and that both sources are subject to errors (sampling errors, recall lapses, inadequate/ineffective field supervision, wrong and even biased reporting) of unknown magnitude, it seems impossible to judge which of the two estimates is closer to reality.[4]

Interstate Variations

Unlike the FBS, which provides estimates only at the national level and for the population as a whole, NSS gives disaggregated estimates of food consumption by state, rural and urban areas and economic classes at different points of time. Despite some changes in design, the scope, concepts

4. NSS estimates of consumption expenditure of food as a whole and its major components are substantially higher than those made by the CSO based on commodity flow approach. The underlying reasons have been explored in GoI, Planning Commission (1993), Minhas and Kansal (1989) and more recently by a committee of the CSO in 2008. Because of differences in concepts, coverage and underlying assumptions of the two estimates, their differences remain largely un-reconciled.

and methods, the NSS consumption surveys in the selected years are largely comparable. While one cannot vouch for the veracity of the estimates of absolute levels or rates of change, the data can be, and have been, used for studying spatial and temporal variations.[5]

The NSS gives estimates of per capita intake of calories and proteins, at different points of time, for rural and urban areas separately. These are presented in Annexure Table A-2.2. They show that in rural areas, per capita calorie intake is below the national mean in a majority of states in 3 of the 4 years. The southern states of Andhra Pradesh (AP), Kerala and Tamil Nadu (TN); Gujarat and Maharashtra in the West; and Bihar, Orissa, Assam and West Bengal (WB) figure in this group. In urban areas, the range of variation is much lower compared to rural areas and (except for 1977-78) the number of states with below the national mean is smaller. Four southern states, Maharashtra, Uttar Pradesh (UP) and WB figure in this group in all four years. In several states—generally the majority—intake levels in rural areas are higher than in urban areas. However, in a number of them—notably Assam, Bihar, Kerala, Orissa, TN and WB—urban intake levels are higher.

The only other source for state level estimates of calorie and protein intake is the NNMB. These estimates, based on weighing food actually consumed by sample households, relate to the nutrient content of food (after processing and cooking) available on plate to members of the sampled families.[6] This nets out losses in cooking and, perhaps, cooked food that is wasted. Since the quantities are measured, details of food taken outside the home are also ascertained, they give more accurate picture of food intake than information based on recall. On the other hand, the estimates are based on single day observations which, being more variable than average intakes over longer periods, may not give a reliable estimate of 'sustained' intake. Moreover, NNMB estimates are limited to rural areas in selected states and are not available for the same years as the NSS. For all these reasons, NNMB

5. See for example Radhakrishna and Ravi, 1992; Meenakshi, 2000; Suryanarayana, 1996 and 2000; and Meenakshi and Viswanathan, 2001.
6. Note that besides weighing food cooked and eaten in the sample households, meals, snacks and beverage taken from outside are also counted. Data on food intake of individuals during the previous 24 hours obtained based on their recall, from a separate sub-sample of households are also tabulated but only by age and gender groups. Weighted average of intakes for the sampled population as a whole are not published. A rough computation for one year suggests that the weighted average of individual intakes is less than that obtained from intake based on household level measurements.

and NSS estimates are not strictly comparable. Despite these limitations, the NNMB estimates (Table 2.2) point to some interesting features.

Table 2.2

NNMB Estimates of Mean Intake of Nutrients Per Consumption Unit in Rural Areas

State	*Calories*					*Proteins*				
	1975-1979	*1988-1990*	*1990-1991*	*1994-1995*	*1996-1997*	*1975-1979*	*1988-1990*	*1990-1991*	*1994-1995*	*1996-1997*
Kerala	1978	2140	2055	2188	2106	46.4	52.9	52.9	55.6	56.4
Tamil Nadu	2275	1871	1950	1845	1896	54.8	45.6	46.2	44.5	46.4
Karnataka	2932	2431	2293	2228	2108	79.3	65.4	59.7	56.2	53.3
Andhra Pradesh	2447	2340	2247	2446	2161	59.8	55.7	53.1	57.6	51.6
Maharashtra	2300	2211	2011	2100	2089	64.5	61.7	58.9	62.3	56.1
Gujarat	2162	2375	2079	2316	2105	64.2	69.3	60.5	63.4	61.5
Madhya Pradesh	2283	2614	2253	2245	na	71.5	82.5	56.1	59.1	na
Orissa	na	2285	2450	2157	2177	na	52.4	58.4	51.5	49.2

Note: Estimates for 1975-1979, 1988-1990 and 1996-67 relate to a common set of sample villages. In other years different sets of the sample villages were chosen.

Source: NNMB (1995, 1999, 2001).

First, NNMB estimates of calorie intake are considerably lower than that of NSS (Annexure Table A-2.2) in all the states and that of protein in six of them. This is to be expected in as much as they, unlike NSS, are net of losses in the process of converting raw foodstuffs into food on the plate. Second, comparison of calorie intake as per NNMB in 1994-95 with that of NSS in 1993-94, one finds no significant correspondence between the two sources in terms of levels of intake among the selected areas. Third, unlike with the NSS, the correlation between the NNMB estimates of intake of each nutrient and between the two nutrients, at different points of time is neither strong nor stable. This is consistent with the fact that daily intake levels are apt to be much more variable than mean intakes over longer periods. Finally, the two sources show directionally similar changes over time in six states but the time points to which the two estimates relate are not identical.

Reverting to NSS, Table 2.3 gives an overview of the pattern of spatial variation in rural and urban food consumption in selected years. In three out of four years, interstate variability (judged by the coefficient of variation) in calories as well as proteins in rural areas is higher than in urban areas. (1977-78 is the sole exception). A striking feature is that while interstate variation in per capita calorie intake has declined progressively in rural areas, no such trend is noticeable in urban areas.[7]

Table 2.3

Variability of Per Capita Nutrient Intake across States in Selected Years

Years	*Rural*				*Urban*			
	Calories		*Proteins*		*Calories*		*Proteins*	
	Mean	*CV*	*Mean*	*CV*	*Mean*	*CV*	*Mean*	*CV*
1971-72	2247	17.2	68.2	25.1	2129	9.3	61.5	13.5
1977-78	2429	11.4	70.9	16.5	2466	18.2	74.0	40.1
1983	2258	11.3	63.2	18.0	2131	5.3	58.2	11.9
1993-94	2182	9.4	61.3	18.1	2119	6.5	58.6	11.0

Note: Mean – Unweighted average CV – Coefficient of variation in per cent.

Calorie intakes in rural and urban areas are positively correlated, but the coefficients are variable and sometimes insignificant. The correlation between rural and urban protein intakes is much higher, and consistently so, than with calories. In rural as well as urban segments, calorie and protein intakes are also closely and positively correlated, the correlation being higher and more consistently so in rural areas (Table 2.4).

Table 2.4

Correlation between Per Capita Nutrient Intake between Rural and Urban Areas

Years	*Correlation Coefficients between*			
	Calories and Protein		*Rural and Urban*	
	Rural	*Urban*	*Calories*	*Protein*
1971-72	0.63	0.89	0.63	0.81
1977-78	0.95	0.93	0.32	0.32
1983	0.95	0.65	0.57	0.91
1993-94	0.93	0.84	0.69	0.89

Also significant is the fact that calorie (and protein) intakes at different points of time are highly and positively correlated in rural areas suggesting a relative stability in the relative position of different states over time.

7. This has been noted by other writers, Meenakshi, 2000 being one of the most recent examples.

In urban areas the correlations, though positive, are smaller and show substantial changes over time. Further, it is noteworthy that while inter-year correlations in successive period have weakened, even if slightly, in rural areas, they show a remarkable increase in urban areas (Table 2.5).

Table 2.5

Correlations between Nutrient Intakes at Different Points of Time

Years	*Correlation Coefficients for*			
	Calories		*Protein*	
	Rural	*Urban*	*Rural*	*Urban*
1971-72 and 1977-78	0.91	0.27	0.73	0.25
1971-72 and 1983	0.88	0.54	0.86	0.90
1971-72 and 1993-94	0.81	0.70	0.80	0.80

In all states, and in all years, food grains are by far the largest source of calories.[8] Their contribution to calorie intake of the rural population is everywhere larger compared to that of urban population. By this index, rural diets are most diversified in Punjab and Kerala and the least so in Bihar, Orissa and WB. In urban areas, Gujarat, Himachal Pradesh (HP), Kerala, Maharashtra and Punjab report the most diversified diet; the least diversified diets are in Orissa and Bihar.

There is also considerable variation in the time profiles of change. In rural areas, changes in both calories and proteins follow similar patterns: in a majority of them (10 out of 17) there was an increase between 1971-72 and 1977-78 followed by a reduction. In three years (Kerala, Madhya Pradesh (MP) and WB), 1993-94 levels were lower than in 1971-72. Gujarat, Haryana, Jammu and Kashmir (J&K) and Punjab show a progressive reduction over the four years. Urban areas experienced a pattern of change broadly similar to rural areas but with some significant exceptions—AP, J&K, MP and Rajasthan.

In most states (13 out of 17 in rural and 11 out of 17 in urban areas), there is progressive reduction in the share of calories contributed by food grains. The pace of diversification however differs widely, being most

8. Radhakrishna and Ravi, 1992 and Meenakshi, 2000 focus on diversification of consumption in terms of different kinds of foodstuffs. Our focus, like that of Meenakshi and Viswanathan, 2000 is on the share of cereals in total calorie and protein intake.

pronounced in Gujarat, Haryana, HP and Punjab and the least in Assam, Bihar, MP, Orissa and WB.

Relation between Consumption and Production at State Level[9]

Estimates of overall mean (for the total population) per capita calorie and protein intake in major states based on NSS in selected years are presented in Annexure Table A-2.1. The calorie intake pcpd in all four southern states, the eastern states, MP, Maharashtra and Gujarat have been consistently below the national average. That there is much variation in nutrient intake and composition across states in both rural and urban areas is not surprising. The degree of interstate variation in mean intake for the two segments taken together has however progressively declined between the selected years.

Moreover, in the early sixties, across states, the level of food intake was strongly and positively correlated with per capita food grain production. This correlation has however progressively declined and was non-significant in 1993-94. The growing disjunction between local food grain production and calorie intake is highlighted by the fact that interstate differences in calorie intake have narrowed substantially, even as the interstate variation in food grain production per capita—still by far the largest source of calories—has increased. The correlation between the two in 1971-72 was already substantially less than in the early sixties, but had since declined progressively and become non-significant in 1993-94 (Table 2.6). This trend is attributable to several factors: (a) increase in the proportion of food production sold and of consumption purchased, through the market; (b) increase in interstate flows in food grains; and (c) declining importance of

9. The motivation for this is the wide spread interest in this relationship. A Centre for Development Studies (CDS) study in the early seventies found, on the basis of data relating to 1961-62, a strong positive correlation between per capita food grain output derived from official production estimates and NSS estimates of per capita grain intake in rural areas. Meenakshi, 2000 also confirm this finding using more recent data. Our own findings suggests that while the correlations between food grain production and mean calorie intake pcpd for the entire population continues to be positive, they are becoming progressively weaker. However the interpretation of this association as evidence that cheaper sources of calories for more expensive ones (e.g., cereals as against non-cereal foods, and sorghum and millets as against rice and wheat) remain elusive.

food grains as a source of calories, reflecting the widespread diversification of diets.

Table 2.6

*Interstate Variation in Calorie Intake and Foodgrain Production Per Capita**

Years	*Calorie Intake*			*Food Grain Output***			*Correlation @ Coefficient*
	Mean	*SD*	*CV*	*Mean*	*SD*	*CV*	
1971-72	2221	338	15	215.4	121.8	57	0.74
1977-78	2435	266	11	219.8	133.1	60	0.634
1983	2230	214	9.6	245.9	180	73	0.649
1993-94	2164	178	8	243.0	220.2	86	0.481

Note: SD – Standard deviation CV – Coefficient of variation per cent.
* kcal pcpd weighted average of NSS estimates for rural and urban areas.
** kg pcpa based on official production estimates.
@ between calorie intake and production per capita.

Food Intake and Nutritional Status[10]

Nutrition experts have worked out norms of calorie, protein and other nutrients needed for healthy active life for males and females of different ages with specified characteristics in terms of height, weight and activity. These gender-age-size-activity-specific norms are weighted by the share of these different categories in a reference population to arrive at overall norm of desirable nutrient intake per capita. In India, the size parameters are specified normatively and the observed composition of the national population is used for specifying a uniform national norm. The current norm is 2,400 kcal per capita per day (pcpd) for rural population and 2,100 kcal per capita in urban areas. Comparison of actual intake with these norms, and, more specifically, the proportion of population who consume less than this norm, is widely used as an indicator of nutritional deficiency in the population.[11] This is questionable on several grounds.

Energy expenditure of a person depends on climate, body size and nature of activity. All these vary across regions and differ between age, gender and occupation groups. These variations are not taken into account

10. For a recent discussion of the issues involved see Osmani (2003).
11. This is evident in the importance given to per capita calorie requirements for a healthy active life recommended by nutritionists in defining the poverty line.

when per capita mean intake is compared with the national norm for a 'reference' population of specified composition. Spatial and temporal variations in age–gender composition can be taken care of by focussing on food intake per consumption unit. These estimates are available both from the NSS and NNMB. But differences in body size and climate are more difficult to allow for. NNMB measures various aspects of body size for all individuals in the sample households and of food intake for a sample of them. The joint distribution of body mass and calorie intake for individuals would provide a better bias to assess differences in nutritional status. The relevant data can be compiled from the unit record data of the NNMB surveys but the problem remains that intake measurements on a single day are not reliable indicators of sustained intake.

A more serious problem arises from the complexity of the relation between food intake on the one hand and health and activity on the other. An essential condition for healthy, active functioning is that intake of energy should be equal to the energy expended in maintaining basic body metabolism and for carrying out various (work and non-work related) activities. However, there are various adjustment mechanisms by which an individual can maintain healthy, active functioning over a range of intakes. The short run mechanisms include automatic adjustments in the metabolism; use of energy stores in the body; and more efficient use of energy from intake (lower waste through evacuation and/or increased conversion efficiencies). Over the longer run, adaptation of mechanisms operating via changes in size and nature of activity are important. It has been argued that lower intakes among adults, while reducing size (weight and BMI), may yet result in equilibrium consistent with healthy and active functioning over a certain range.[12] Within this range, smaller size does not result in functional impairment. And there is no reason why a certain size assumed in deciding norms should be considered 'optimal' or inherently desirable.

Another reason why a simple comparison of actual intake with nutritional norms is a misleading basis to assess nutritional capacity because it ignores interaction between food intake, incidence and treatment of infections and its impact on size and activity. Frequent or chronic

12. See essays of Sukhatme and Seckler in Osmani (2003).

infections are known to involve additional energy expenditure to fight them; they often reduce appetite and therefore food intake and result in greater waste (through excretion) and/or lowered efficiency of conversion on the body of intake into usable energy. Intake may remain constant at levels below the norm, but if improvements in water supply, environmental hygiene and public health services reduce infections and/or if infections are better controlled by medication (antibiotics), the conversion efficacy of a given level of intake and hence the state of health and functioning, could well improve. Also to be considered are possible adverse effects of low or unbalanced intake on, for example, the nature, intensity and efficiency of activity, of nutritional inadequacy in childhood on mental growth, cognitive ability, and intelligence, and of malnourishment of pregnant women on birth weights of their children.[13]

For all these reasons per capita calorie and protein intake by itself is neither reliable nor adequate basis to assess nutrition and health status. Ultimately, balanced diet is not an end itself but a means to ensure the many facets of healthy, active living. It is not appropriate to rely on mean intake of calories (or even mean—2 standard deviation) as the sole, or even the main, basis for judging nutritional status. It should be combined with data on indicators such as body size, mortality and morbidity, and nature and intensity of activity, which reflect the net effect of quantity and quality of food intake, environmental conditions and efficiency with which intake is utilised by the body on nutritional and health status. We should also note that the notion of ideal health and functioning in all dimensions as well as the possibility of attaining that optimum, is under question.

Available data do not permit mapping of all these indicators across all states and population categories. Estimates of body size by broad age and sex groups can be gleaned from NNMB publications only for rural areas of 7-8 states at different points of time. Estimates for different socioeconomic groups is available for one or two years. Time series estimates of mortality rates by age and gender are available from published reports of Sample Registration Surveys. Some data on maternal mortality rates are available from the National Family Health Surveys (NFHS). NSS employment surveys give disaggregated data on the nature and duration of employment

13. See Sukhatme's Essay in Osmani (1992).

for various categories of workers. There is hardly any information on the intensity of activity. Morbidity estimates for two years (1986-87 and 1993-94) are available from NSS surveys. But being based on respondents' perceptions of illness, comparisons across regions and over time are somewhat problematic. The subsequent discussion is largely confined to variations in size and mortality.

Body Size

The NNMB gives estimates of malnourishment for: (1) preschool children (2) children in the age group 6-17 years and (3) adults. In the case of children, nutrition status is assessed on the basis of weight for age. Those whose weight is 75 per cent or lower than the National Centre for Health Statistics (NCHS) standard is categorised as 'moderately' undernourished, and weights less than 60 per cent of the standard as 'severely' undernourished. The nutrition status of adults is assessed on the basis of BMI (defined as weight in kilogram divided by the square of their height in metres). Those with BMI between 18.5 and 25 are considered 'normal' and those above 25 as obese. People with BMI below 18.5 are rated as chronically energy deficient (CED). This class is divided into three groups: CEDI (17-18.5), CEDII (16-17) and CEDIII (<16). (Note that current levels of nutrient intake are likely to make much more of a difference to weight rather than height; that weight for age is more appropriate in the case of children in the phase of rapid growth; and that among adults, BMI reflects the combined effect of height and weight.)

The estimated incidence of under-nutrition among preschool children in the sampled rural population of seven states is presented in Table 2.7. The proportion of undernourished children in the 1-5 age group ranged, in 1975-1979, from 59 per cent (TN) to 71 per cent (Maharashtra). Overall incidence of undernourishment at the end of nineties is lower than in the mid-seventies and late eighties in all seven states—Kerala, TN and Karnataka show a progressive and significant decline; AP, Gujarat and Maharashtra also show an overall decline; and Orissa but a marginal change. However, the pace and consistency of the trend being variable, there are substantial changes in relative rankings of some states over the years.

Table 2.7

Nutrition Status of Preschool Children based on Weight for Age

State	Nutritional Grades							
	1975-1979		1988-1990		1996-97		2000-01	
	Moderate	Severe	Moderate	Severe	Moderate	Severe	Moderate	Severe
Kerala	46.5	10.3	32.9	2.0	25.1	2.0	26.9	1.9
Tamil Nadu	47.0	12.6	45.8	4.2	33.5	2.9	35.3	3.7
Karnataka	50.0	14.3	48.8	8.3	45.4	6.2	45.2	2.4
Andhra Pradesh	45.1	15.4	44.3	7.5	47.6	7.1	35.8	4.1
Maharashtra	49.5	21.9	47.5	7.8	49.5	7.7	45.0	7.2
Gujarat	54.3	13.8	45.8	13.0	47.0	16.7	40.0	8.9
Orissa	41.7	14.9	46.6	10.7	50.4	4.1	47.2	7.2

Source: NNMB: 1999, 2001.

State level estimates of the distribution of population by weight for age are not available for older children (6-17 years). Pooled data for the seven states suggest that both moderate and severe undernourishment is higher in this group than for pre-school children, the difference in the incidence of severe undernourishment being especially marked among adolescents. Further, it is noteworthy that among children of all age groups, the reported per capita calorie (and protein) intake in 2000-01 was lower compared to 1996-97 and yet incidence of severe and moderate undernourishment also declined over this period.

Table 2.8

Percentage of Undernourished Rural Children by Age Group in Selected States

Age Group	Proportion under Nourished					
	1996-97			2000-01		
	Moderate	Severe	Overall	Moderate	Severe	Overall
1-5 years	44.3	6.2	50.3	41.3	6.4	57.7
6-9 years	54.7	8.4	63.1	54.0	8.6	62.6
10-13 years	52.0	28.7	80.7	47.8	30.1	77.9
14-17 years	52.6	18.9	71.5	47.1	18.9	66.0

Source: NNMB: 1999, 2001.

For adults, published reports give height and weight of the sample population by age, separately for males and females, for several years. BMI calculated from these data for the years 1975-1979, 1988-1990 and 1996-1997—which relate to a common set of villages—are presented in Annexure Table A-2.3. (These data are also available for more years but we have not been able to access all of them.) In most states and in all age groups, BMI of adult males and females in 1996-97 was lower than in 1975-1979. But this is neither sustained nor uniform in all cases. On both counts, Kerala, showing the largest and most sustained increase in both sexes, stands out from the rest. Maharashtra also shows a sustained rise but of a modest magnitude. In Karnataka and TN, only males record a sustained increase in BMI over this period. In others, there is much variation in the time profiles of changes between males and females and across age groups. There are some striking differences between states in the age-BMI gradients and their changes. But no clear or consistent patterns are noticeable in gender relative movements of BMI between males and females.

The distribution of adults according to BMI gives a more meaningful basis for assessing the relative undernutrition across regions, gender and time. Estimates of this distribution are published for the nineties but not for earlier years. These are set out in Table 2.9.

In 1990-91 the proportion of males with BMI less than 18.5 (rated as CED) ranged from around 37 per cent (Kerala) to 56.7 per cent (Gujarat). Those with BMI below 16 (belong to the severely energy deficient group) constituted between 4 per cent of the population (Kerala) and close to 7 per cent (MP and Maharashtra). BMI values above 25 are classified as 'obese': the proportion falling in this category ranges from 2-3 per cent (Orissa and MP) to 14 per cent (Kerala).

The proportion of females with BMI below 18.5 ranged between 27.4 per cent in Kerala to 64 per cent in Maharashtra. In a majority of states the incidence of CED among females is higher than for males. The incidence of CED among females in Kerala and Gujarat is substantially lower than among males in all years, and in one year in TN and Orissa.

Table 2.9

Incidence of Chronic Energy Deficiency among Adults

State	Males								Females							
	1990-91		1994-95		1996-97		2000-01		1990-91		1994-95		1996-97		2000-01	
	1	2	1	2	1	2	1	2	1	2	1	2	1	2	1	2
Kerala	36.9	5.3	38.0	6.2	31.2	9.8	22.4	13.9	27.4	12.1	30.4	13.6	24.6	15.8	18.8	23.6
Tamil Nadu	42.1	5.0	38.0	7.9	42.4	6.3	35.5	7.0	45.0	6.2	41.6	8.6	40.4	8.6	38.2	8.9
Karnataka	52.1	2.8	52.0	3.2	49.9	4.2	36.2	7.1	53.1	4.0	54.6	5.6	57.0	3.4	41.7	7.9
Andhra Pradesh	41.3	6.1	45.2	3.7	52.4	3.0	37.4	7.2	47.3	5.6	50.0	5.1	56.9	3.6	42.0	7.8
Maharashtra	55.4	1.2	45.2	2.7	42.6	3.4	41.2	5.2	63.9	3.8	54.8	5.2	50.2	3.2	45.1	5.6
Gujarat	56.7	5.1	56.6	4.3	65.9	2.0	37.1	6.8	48.7	3.3	44.6	7.8	55.9	4.0	33.3	7.8
Orissa	50.4	2.1	51.5	1.1	43.0	1.1	38.6	2.3	48.2	1.3	57.5	1.8	53.2	1.6	46.0	0.3

Note: 1 – BMI<18.5; 2 – BMI>25.

Source: NNMB (1999, 2001).

Incidence of severe energy deficiency (CEDIII) among females is much higher than among males in 6 out of 7 states, so is the incidence of obesity the proportion ranging from a little over 3 per cent in Orissa to nearly 24 per cent in Kerala. Interstate variation in CED is higher among females in all years. Incidence of energy deficiency among males shows a strong positive correlation with that of females (coefficient of correlation >0.8) in two years but weak in the other two.

Incidence of energy deficiency at the end of the nineties is mostly lower than at the beginning of the decade, but the extent and time profile of the decline is quite varied: being marginal in a few cases and substantial in some, and more or less sustained in some and erratic in others. Gender disparity in incidence of CED at the end of the decade is narrower than at its beginning in four states. In two of them (Kerala and Gujarat) CED continues to be less among females, but in the other two (AP and Maharashtra) energy deficiency among females continues to be greater; the position at the end of the decade is somewhat worse than at the beginning. In the remaining three, where CED incidence among females was about the same (Orissa) or higher to begin with, their position relative to males at the end of the decade had worsened.

The striking feature is that, across the seven states, incidence of CED or even CED III among adults is not positively correlated with overall mean calorie intake per consumer unit per day. On the contrary, and surprisingly, there seems to be a positive, though non-significant, correlation between CED and overall mean calorie intake. If anything available data suggest that states with higher intake seem to have higher incidence of energy deficient population. Also striking is the decline in CED even as mean intakes have remained stagnant (or even declined).

One has to be cautious, however, in interpreting these associations. Firmer inferences require CED among adults to be related to mean intake of adults, and better still CED status of individuals with their intakes. Moreover, CED does not give the full picture of nutritional status. One must also take account of associated variations in the nature and intensity of activities performed. There is little information on this aspect. Nevertheless, the weak relation between calorie intake and body size underlines the role of other factors, and in particular health conditions, in determining nutritional outcomes. There are good reasons to believe that improvements in the overall health status of the population may have contributed to a reduction in incidence of CED despite stagnation, if not decline, in nutrient intake.

Health Indicators

The health status of a population is reflected in the incidence of illness and mortality rate. Some recent sample surveys (mainly the NSS) give estimates of incidence of illness overall and by nature of disease at a fairly disaggregated level. State-wise time-series estimates of mortality by gender and age group, in rural and urban areas are published by the Registrar General. Morbidity surveys show considerable variations in incidence of illness across regions and groups as well as over time. These variations do not seem to bear any relation to food intake. But this inference cannot be asserted with confidence because, apart from differences in perceptions of illness, reporting of illness is often incomplete, subjective and open to varying degrees of bias. Mortality estimates, which do not suffer from these limitations, provide a better basis to judge health status.

For the purpose of the present discussion, we need to focus on mortality rates of different age and gender groups. For infants and pre-school children, perinatal mortality rates (PNMR) and child mortality rates (CMR) are significant indicators. That these rates vary across states, both in terms of levels at a particular point of time and of the rate, or even direction, of change over time is evident from Table 2.10. So do still birth rates (SBR)—a significant indicator of the health of pregnant women. While CMR has declined in all the selected states, PNMR has risen in two and declined but marginally in two others. That five out of these seven states show a substantial rise in SBR, despite expansion of facilities for antenatal care and institutional deliveries, points to deterioration in women's health status during pregnancy.

Table 2.10

Still Birth Rate, Perinatal and Child Mortality Rates

States	*SBR*		*PNMR*		*CMR*	
	1981	*1991*	*1981*	*1991*	*1981*	*1991*
Kerala	11.3	10.3	28.6	20	12.8	4.7
Tamil Nadu	8.6	11.1	42.1	10.5	42.1	20.5
Karnataka	11.7	18	43.2	57.6	27.8	24.4
Andhra Pradesh	13.8	13.2	53.4	52.3	33.6	22.1
Maharashtra	8.3	13.8	45.2	44.7	33.3	18.4
Gujarat	4.4	6.5	54.5	42.8	43.7	29.8
Orissa	9.8	20.9	50.2	73.1	43.9	37.4

Note: SBR – Still birth rate PNMR – Perinatal mortality rate
CMR – Child mortality rate

Source: Registrar General of India.

Across states, in rural areas, mortality rates among children in the age group 5-14 is generally the lowest and increases progressively with age to reach maximum in the 60+ group. Mortality rates have declined everywhere and in practically all age groups, the rate being relatively more in the young age groups, declining progressively in higher age groups and reaching a minimum in the 60+ age group. There are, not surprisingly, substantial differences between states in both the level and the rate of decline in mortality in comparable age groups. Again, there is no relation between levels of overall mortality and level of food intake. The near universal decline in mortality has occurred in the context of stagnant or declining food intake and is largely attributable to government programmes for improving water supply and sanitation, for control of communicable diseases and creation of an extensive network of curative care facilities.

While serious deficiencies in the coverage and quality of the public health care system have rightly attracted much criticism, there can be no denying that public health care facilities have become far more extensive and accessible. Achievements in controlling and, in some cases, eradicating mass communicable diseases have unquestionably contributed to reducing mortality. The spread of curative services in the private sector and the use of antibiotics have also contributed to checking fatalities due to disease. That much is wrong with the health care system, and its capacity to contain and treat illness, should not detract from its contribution to reducing mortality.

Differences in mortality rates and their decline reflect differences in incidence and nature of disease, the environmental conditions that cause them and the effectiveness of preventive and curative health services in tackling them. These issues deserve more intensive scrutiny than they have received. The point to be emphasised here is that improvements that have taken place, limited as they are in relation to needs, can probably explain the apparent anomaly of reduction in indices of undernourishment in the face of constant or even declining nutrient intake. In particular, the rapid spread of antibiotics, its ready accessibility even in rural areas, and the fact that a great deal of it is dispensed by retail outlets for medical drugs has perhaps been a significant contributory factor. For one of the effects of containing infections is to reduce the energy expended by the body in fighting them and increase the efficiency with which a given intake is converted into energy available for work and for building body tissues.

The Position of Poorer and Underprivileged Groups

The foregoing discussion, based as it is on the levels of, and changes in, average food intake, body size and health indicators, relates to the population as a whole. It does not tell us anything about the position of different socioeconomic groups in these respects. The available published data do not permit a sufficiently detailed exploration of this aspect. NSS estimates for 1983 suggest that the calorie intake of the poorest quintile of the population averaged less than 1,500 calories in several states and was as low as 1,000 in several states; that though their intake has increased moderately, the level in most cases is still around 1,500-1,600; their diets are much more dependent on cereals than the top quintile and remain so despite increasing share of non-cereal food in recent times.

There is evidence of a progressive shift from kind to cash payments for wages and of increasing casualisation of wage labour. This would imply greater freedom to decide what to consume as well as growing dependence on market purchases. There are also indications of significant structural shifts in overall patterns of consumption even in these groups, reflected in the shift from food to non-food, from cereals to non-cereal food and among cereals from the so-called 'coarse' cereals to rice and wheat. A significant feature of this shift, which is difficult to explain in terms of conventional notions of economic rationality, is the switch from relatively cheaper sources of nutrients to more expensive ones (namely coarse as against fine cereals against non-cereal foods).[14]

NNMB surveys show that the incidence of both moderate and, more strikingly, severe undernourishment is markedly higher among the low-income groups than among the better off and among socially underprivileged groups (especially Schedules Castes and Tribes) than upper castes. In 1996-1997, more than 60 per cent of SC children were undernourished compared to 46 per cent among 'others', mostly upper castes; the corresponding figures for severe undernourishment being 10.4 per cent and 5.3 per cent. Among adults, those with BMI less than 18.5 constituted 53 per cent in SC compared to 41 per cent in 'others'. There is some indication that undernourishment by these indices may have declined in all categories, but the data are too patchy to permit a clear assessment (Table 2.11).

Table 2.11

Food Intake and Body Size of Different Socioeconomic Groups 1996-97

	Calories pcpd	*Proteins pcpd*	*% Undernourished Children*		*BMI Adults*		
			Moderate	*Severe*	*<16.5*	*<18.5*	*>25*
LLAL	1989	51.7	46.6	8.3	12.4	53.6	2.8
Other lab	2042	47.9	50.7	7.0	11.0	51.6	1.8
Culti	2205	55.2	44.6	6.0	11.3	50.2	4.0
Others	2187	54.4	na	na	8.8	35.3	9.4
Overall	2108	61.8	45.3	6.9	10.6	47.0	5.2
SC	2125	55.1	50.9	10.4	12.3	53.1	2.5
ST	2036	49.8	47.7	7.3	12.6	56.9	1.3
BC	2094	53.5	44.7	6.5	9.6	43.4	6.8
Other	2169	56.2	41.0	5.3	9.7	41.1	7.3

Note: LLAL – Landless agricultural labourers; Other lab: Other labourers; Cult: cultivators
SC: Scheduled Castes; ST: Scheduled Tribes; BC: Backward Castes.

14. This is clearly brought out by NSS consumption surveys.

The coverage of and access to health care facilities has improved for all classes in rural India. But the poorer groups and underprivileged social segments continue to be a disadvantage as it shown in the following table relating to maternal health care facilities. (Table 2.12) Unfortunately, available data on health outcome indicators for different socioeconomic groups is scanty.

Table 2.12

Access to Health Care Facilities for Social Groups

		1988-1992	*1995-1998*
Per cent of Deliveries in Health Facility/Institution			
All India		25.5	33.6
of which	SC	16	26.8
	ST	9.1	17.1
	Others	29.2	40
Attended by Doctor, Nurse and			
All India		34.2	42.3
of which	SC	25.1	36.8
	ST	17.5	23
	Others	37.9	48.9
	Rural areas	25	33.5

Source: National Family Health Survey 1992-93, and 1998-99.

Clearly a fuller, more meaningful assessment of nutrition and health calls for information disaggregated by income, caste-community and occupation groups. A good deal seems possible by appropriation retabulations of primary data from existing surveys and by analysis of unit record data. In some cases, particularly morbidity and mortality, better designed, more elaborate surveys will be necessary to generate the requisite data both for description and for analysis of these aspects, and the factors and processes underlying them.

Conclusions

To sum up: we have a great deal of data on food consumption patterns and trends. And despite their limitations and differences in estimates obtained from different sources, it is possible to discern some general patterns of spatial and temporal variation.

On the average, per capita and per consumption unit intake of calorie and protein seem to have generally remained stagnant and in some cases have declined; consumption surveys point to a moderate rise in intake levels in the poorest quintile population. Everywhere and in all classes the pattern of diet has diversified.

It is important to recognise that nutritional poverty and income poverty are not equivalent: even if people have enough income, they may choose not to consume a nutritive and balanced diet at the least cost. Factors, such as monetisation of rural economy, changes in wage payment systems, commercialisation of food economy, education and exposure to mass media—underlying diet diversification even among those with calorie intakes of 1,500 kcal or less—merit closer investigation.

In any case, assessment of nutritional poverty based on crude comparisons of mean intake with nutritional norms is misleading. For a variety of reasons, discussed in the paper, it is essential to also focus directly on outcome indicators such as body size, mortality and morbidity, nature and intensity of activity.

Available data, largely limited to body size and mortality, generally point to improvement in most age-gender groups and regions but in varying degrees and at different rates. The puzzle of course is the lack of correlation between food intake and these two outcome indicators. These indicators are the highest in states with the lowest intakes; they have improved even in the face of constant or declining mean intakes; and substantial improvements are seen even among the less privileged social and economic groups, whose intake levels are abysmally low. The only plausible explanation we can suggest is that improvements in health environment and adaptive mechanisms have increased the efficiency of utilisation of intake. The possibility that changes in nature and intensity of activity may have reduced energy requirements for work cannot be verified with the available information.

There is clearly need for improving the information base to cover more of the relevant indicators. And given that nutrition and health status indicators differ significantly across socioeconomic, age and gender categories, it is also necessary to go beyond mapping their average values for the population. It is important to have a disaggregated picture of these indicators and examine the factors accounting for intergroup differences. In particular we need to focus on the conditions of the poorest 20-30 per cent of the population and socially disadvantaged segments.

Annexure Table A-2.1

Per Capita Calorie Intake and Per Capita Food Grain Production in Major States, Selected Years

State	1971-72		1977-78		1983		1993-94	
	kcal/cap	fgp/cap	kcal/cap	fgp/cap	kcal/cap	fgp/cap	kcal/cap	fgp/cap
Andhra Pradesh	2112	159.0	2401	164.5	2157	207.2	2036	170.4
Assam	2134	133.6	2269	140.2	2054	139.2	1997	152.9
Bihar	2185	137.1	2342	153.7	2182	126.5	2125	128.2
Gujarat	2137	160.8	2226	120.5	2077	155.5	2005	98.3
Haryana	2763	461.7	3024	430.9	2483	499.3	2399	576.8
Himachal Pradesh	2489	220.0	2578	221.2	2620	273.4	2332	266.9
Jammu & Kashmir	2696	198.7	2749	193.8	2492	178.5	2479	171.1
Karnataka	2171	212.4	2390	209.7	2220	182.2	2058	181.8
Kerala	1618	64.0	2100	55.2	1886	47.7	1965	36.4
Madhya Pradesh	1900	256.1	2325	239.1	2284	272.7	2144	249.9
Maharashtra	2036	94.0	2169	183.6	2102	193.7	1959	151.3
Orissa	2034	209.0	2178	214.2	2117	248.2	2208	220.7
Punjab	2792	548.0	2728	645	2515	831.2	2316	976
Rajasthan	2553	267.0	2790	219	2395	295.5	2403	191.3
Tamil Nadu	1875	168.1	2121	170	1954	137	1898	137.4
Uttar Pradesh	2364	204.4	2533	203	2333	244.5	2268	251.1
West Bengal	1899	167.5	2479	173.8	2033	147.4	2188	173.6
Average	2221.1	215.4	2435.4	219.8	2229.6	245.9	2163.5	243.2
SD	338.9	121.8	266.0	133.1	213.8	180.0	178.8	220.2
CV	15.3	56.5	10.9	60.5	9.6	73.2	8.3	90.6

Note: Fgp/cap: food grains production per capita in kg pr annum.

Source: National Sample Survey for calories and proteins, and official estimates for food grain per capita.

Annexure Table A-2.2

State-wise Estimates of Mean Per Capita Calorie and Protein Intake according to NSS

States	1971-72				1977-78				1983				1993-94			
	Rural		Urban		Rural		Urban		Rural		Urban		Rural		Urban	
	Calories	Proteins	Calories	Proteins	Calories	Proteins	Calories	Proteins	Calories	Proteins	Calories	Proteins	Calories	Proteins	Calories	Proteins
Andhra Pradesh	2118	58	2087	54.2	2377	68.5	2487	78.2	2204	56	2009	50	2052	50.8	1992	49.6
Assam	2132	55.2	2163	58.7	2244	67.5	2509	79.0	2056	52	2043	52	1983	49.5	2108	53.5
Bihar	2178	66.2	2249	67.6	2330	70.0	2431	77.9	2189	65	2131	61	2115	60.2	2188	61.4
Gujarat	2142	62.2	2123	61.5	2231	63.0	2212	62.8	2113	50	2000	55	1994	55.6	2027	54.9
Haryana	2874	90.5	2250	71.8	2781	82.4	3979	175.7	2554	78	2242	67	2491	78.4	2140	63.6
Himachal Pradesh	2499	76.8	2364	68.7	2593	77.9	2388	68.7	2636	80	2429	70	2324	70.5	2416	70.0
Jammu & Kashmir	2793	80	2267	62.1	2776	86.6	2652	80.6	2569	71	2234	60	2507	75.4	2392	69.1
Karnataka	2254	61.1	1912	54	2437	63.9	2261	59.1	2260	60	2124	55	2073	55.1	2026	53.1
Kerala	1610	39.8	1658	44.2	2112	50.9	2052	51.0	1844	47	2049	51	1965	50.8	1966	52.4
Madhya Pradesh	1824	104.1	2289	67.5	2308	68.3	2357	305	2323	68	2137	62	2164	63	2082	59.8
Maharashtra	2033	61.8	2041	62.8	2189	65.6	2130	59.0	2144	62	2028	56	1939	54.8	1989	55.5
Orissa	2017	52.6	2213	59	2142	54.6	2478	73.2	2103	51	2219	56	2199	52.7	2261	57.2
Punjab	2954	88.4	2270	68.8	2881	85.8	2301	65.9	2677	79	2100	63	2418	74.7	2089	61.8
Rajasthan	2586	82.1	2393	73.2	2921	92.6	2257	67.6	2433	75	2255	69	2470	79.4	2184	66.5
Tamil Nadu	1910	52.7	1797	46.6	2076	57.8	2216	70.2	1861	47	2140	45	1884	46.8	1922	48.7
Uttar Pradesh	2407	76.8	2100	67.4	2597	78.9	2208	66.3	2399	73	2043	62	2307	70.4	2114	63.2
West Bengal	1860	50.7	2015	58	2291	70.0	3012	99.3	2027	52	2048	55	2211	54.8	2131	56.6
Average	2246.5	68.2	2128.9	61.5	2428.6	70.9	2466.5	74.4	2258.4	63.2	2131.2	58.2	2182.1	61.3	2119.2	58.6
SD	386.3	17.1	198.3	8.3	277.3	11.7	449.6	29.9	255.7	11.4	113.9	6.9	206.2	11.1	138.6	6.5
CV	17.2	25.1	9.3	13.6	11.4	16.5	18.2	40.1	11.3	18.0	5.3	11.9	9.4	18.1	6.5	11.0

Source: National Sample Survey for calories and proteins, and official estimates for food grain per capita.

Annexure Table A-2.3

Body Mass Index of Adults by Age Groups: Selected states

1975-1979	1988-1990	1996-1997	1975-1979	1988-1990	1996-1997
	Females			*Males*	
		Kerala			
18.3	19.2	19.6	16.8	17.7	18.5
18.9	19.0	19.6	17.4	17.8	18.9
18.8	19.3	20.3	18.1	18.6	19.7
19.0	19.9	20.9	18.6	19.6	20.5
19.0	19.7	21.6	18.9	19.5	20.9
18.8	20.1	22.0	18.4	19.7	20.9
18.6	20.2	22.5	18.6	20.3	21.1
18.3	19.7	22.2	18.2	19.7	21.5
18.6	20.5	22.4	18.6	19.9	20.8
18.1	20.0	22.2	18.6	18.9	20.4
18.1	19.0	20.8	17.8	18.9	19.8
		Tamil Nadu			
18.8	18.9	19.0	16.9	17.4	17.7
18.8	19.1	18.7	17.7	17.9	18.3
18.8	18.8	19.1	18.0	18.4	18.7
18.7	19.0	19.5	18.9	18.9	19.5
19.1	19.0	20.5	19.0	19.1	19.9
19.4	19.2	20.5	18.8	19.0	19.9
18.9	20.0	20.4	19.4	19.5	20.7
19.5	19.8	21.0	19.1	19.2	19.9
18.9	20.3	20.7	19.5	19.3	20.6
18.9	18.5	19.4	19.3	19.3	20.2
18.2	18.8	19.7	18.5	18.7	18.8
		Karnataka			
18.2	18.1	18.6	17.4	17.4	17.8
174.8	19.4	18.3	18.0	17.7	17.8
18.3	18.7	18.5	18.0	18.2	18.4
18.5	18.5	18.4	18.3	18.7	19.0
18.5	18.6	18.6	18.3	18.8	19.5
18.0	19.3	18.8	18.6	18.9	19.6
18.3	18.9	18.7	18.2	18.8	19.7
18.2	19.0	19.0	18.4	18.6	19.5
18.2	20.0	18.6	18.3	19.4	18.7
18.1	18.8	18.7	17.5	19.4	19.5
17.5	18.4	18.3	17.6	18.7	18.3

		Maharashtra			
18.6	18.6	18.7	17.6	17.8	18.0
19.0	18.1	18.2	17.6	17.9	18.1
18.3	18.4	18.7	18.1	18.5	19.0
18.3	18.5	18.7	18.7	15.4	19.3
17.8	18.2	18.8	18.6	18.9	19.5
18.3	18.6	19.0	18.9	18.7	19.2
17.8	18.6	19.1	18.3	19.0	19.7
17.7	18.4	19.8	18.1	19.6	20.2
17.9	18.6	19.7	18.1	19.0	19.4
18.5	18.7	20.0	19.2	18.3	19.8
17.6	18.4	19.1	18.3	18.5	19.1
		Gujarat			
18.2	17.8	19.1	16.8	17.4	17.5
18.3	18.7	18.9	18.1	18.3	17.0
18.7	18.5	18.3	17.5	18.0	17.6
18.1	18.4	18.4	18.1	18.3	18.3
18.8	18.7	18.7	17.6	18.4	18.6
18.5	18.5	19.0	18.2	18.1	18.6
18.5	18.6	18.9	17.7	18.2	19.3
18.2	18.2	19.3	17.5	18.1	18.1
19.7	18.9	18.6	18.2	17.8	18.3
18.3	19.3	19.1	17.9	17.3	18.5
17.6	17.9	18.9	17.4	18.3	18.1
		Orissa			
19.4	19.3	18.7	17.9	18.3	18.2
19.0	19.7	19.1	18.1	17.9	18.4
19.5	19.0	18.7	18.7	18.5	18.7
18.9	18.9	18.6	18.9	19.0	19.1
19.2	18.7	18.5	19.1	19.1	19.1
18.8	18.8	18.5	19.5	19.1	19.1
18.6	18.7	18.6	18.7	18.9	19.1
19.1	18.4	19.0	18.9	19.0	18.9
19.2	18.7	18.3	19.5	19.1	18.5
17.9	18.6	18.1	18.8	18.9	18.6
18.1	17.1	17.8	18.8	18.8	18.2

References

Gopalan, C. (1992). "Under Nutrition: Measurement and Implications", in Osmani (1992).

International Institute of Population Studies (1995). *National Family Health Survey, India 1992-93: Main and Summary Report*. Mumbai.

———. (2000). *National Family Health Survey, India 1998-99*. Mumbai.

Krishnaji, N. and T.N. Krishnan (eds.) (2000). *Public Support for Food Security: The Public Distribution System in India*. Sage: New Delhi.

Kumar, B.G. and A. Vaidyanathan (1988). "Morbidity in India: Some Problems of Measurement Interpretation and Analysis". Paper presented at annual conference of Indian Society of Medical Statistics (*mimeo*).

Kumar, B.G. (1990). "Quality of Life and Morbidity: A Reconsideration of Some Paradoxes for Kerala, India", Trivandrum: Centre for Development Studies. (*mimeo*).

Meenakshi, J.V. (2000). "Food Consumption Trends in India: A Regional Analysis", in Krishnaji and Krishnan (eds.) (2000).

Meenakshi, J.V. and Brinda Viswanathan (2000). "Nutrient Intake Patterns in Rural India: 1983-1999/2000: Evidence from Unit Record Data". Paper presented at *the Indian Econometric Society Conference,* Chennai. (*mimeo*).

National Nutrition Monitoring Bureau (1995). *Report for the Year 1994-95*. Hyderabad: National Institution of Nutrition.

———. (1999). *Report of the Second Repeat Survey: Rural Technical Report 18*. Hyderabad: National Institute of Nutrition.

———. (2001). *Diet and Nutrition Status of Rural Population, Technical Report 21*. Hyderabad: National Institute of Nutrition.

Osmani, S.R. (eds.) (1992). *Nutrition and Poverty*. Oxford: Clarendon.

———. (1992). "On Some Controversies in the Measurement of Under Nutrition", in Osmani (ed.) 1992.

Payne, P. (1992). "Assessing Under Nutrition: The Need for a Reconceptualisation", in Osmani (ed.) (1992).

Panikar, P.G.K. and C.R. Soman (1982). *Health Status of Kerala*. Trivandrum: Centre for Development Studies.

Radhakrishna, R. and C. Ravi (1992). "Food Demand in India: Some Emerging Trends and Perspectives", *Economic and Political Weekly 27*.

Rudra, Ashok (1978). *Basic Needs Concept and its Implementation in Water Development Planning*. Bangkok: ILO, ARTED.

Suryanarayana, M.H. (1996). "Food Security and Calorie Adequacy Across States: Implications for Reform", *Journal of the Indian School of Political Economy* 8(2). Reprinted in Krishnaji and Krishnan (ed.) 2000.

Srinivasan, T.N. (1992). "Under Nutrition Concepts, Measurements and Policy Implications", in Osmani (1992).

Seckler, D. (1982). "Small but Healthy: A Basic Hypothesis in the Theory, Measurement and Policy of Malnutrition", in Sukhatme (1982).

Sukhatme, P.V. (1982). *Never Concepts in Nutrition and their Implications for Policy.* Pune, Maharashtra: Association for the Cultivation of Science.

Sen, A.K. (1990). *Objectivity and Position: Tolerance of Health and Well Being.* Centre for Population and Development Studies and Harvard University.

Vaidyanathan, A. (1985). "Food Consumption and Size of People", *Economic and Political Weekly*, June.

———. (1986). "On Validity of NSS Consumption Data", *Economic and Political Weekly.*

Acknowledgements: I am grateful to R. Rajagopalan for getting me the annual reports of the NNMB, Brinda Viswanathan for discussions on the analysis of the data and for comments on the draft of the paper, and Dharumaperumal for help in computer processing and computations. The usual disclaimers apply.

3 Globalisation and the Quest for Food Security

The past three to four decades have been a period of unprecedented economic growth in the world and more so in developing countries as a whole. The proportion of people living in poverty—measured in terms of income (necessary to afford a rather conservatively defined minimum living standard)—has declined. But in absolute terms the number of people deemed to be poor by the income criterion (estimated to be around two billion) remains unconscionably high. Massive investments in irrigation, research and other support facilities for agriculture, and the spread of yield-augmenting biochemical technology has led to growth of food production in developing countries. But increases in per capita output have been modest, uneven and rather volatile. Food and Agriculture Organisation (FAO) estimates that four decades back nearly one billion people in the world had less than 2,000 kcal per capita per day (pcpd) considered to be essential for adequate nourishment. The current level of people below this threshold remains more or less unchanged. The bulk of them are in Asia, Africa and Latin America and comprise nearly a fifth of their total population.

Prospects for Global Food Security

FAO has long been highlighting the adverse impact of low and poor quality of food intake on the health and well being of large sections of the population in developing countries. Besides emphasising the need for national governments to focus their domestic policies to address the problem of hunger and malnutrition, it has played an important role in mobilising the support of developed countries for programmes to provide emergency food aid to people affected by natural and man-made disasters. More recently, by drawing attention to the fact that the incidence of hunger and malnutrition has not diminished in scale or spread, FAO has been instrumental in bringing the problem to the centre stage of international concern.

In 1996 it organised the World Food Summit in which heads of governments of practically all countries of the world participated. They found it intolerable and unacceptable that "... more than 800 million people throughout the world, and particularly in developing countries, do not have enough food to meet their basic nutritional needs." In a historic Declaration, they affirmed "...the right of everyone to have access to safe and nutritious food...and the fundamental right of everyone to be free from hunger," and committed themselves to "... implement policies aimed at eradicating poverty and inequality and improving physical and economic access by all, at all times, to sufficient, nutritionally adequate and safe food and its effective utilisation."

The Declaration recognised that the primary responsibility for devising and implementing appropriate policies for expansion of agricultural production, poverty alleviation and equitable distribution of food rests with the national governments. At the same time it emphasised the key role of the international community in helping to achieve the objectives by '...supporting the adoption of appropriate national policies and, where necessary and appropriate, in providing technical and financial assistance to assist developing countries and countries with economies in transition in fostering food security'. It also reiterated their collective commitment to provide the technical support and financial aid to developing countries to 'prevent and be prepared for natural disasters and man-made emergencies and to meet transitory and emergency food requirements in ways that encourage recovery, rehabilitation, development and a capacity to satisfy future needs' and 'ensure that food, agricultural trade and overall trade policies are conducive to fostering food security for all through a fair and market-oriented world trade system'. But these were not backed by any concrete and firm commitments on the part of developed countries. They were left to be decided through bilateral and ongoing multilateral negotiations in various international forums.

In the event, there has hardly been any progress in any of these respects. On the contrary the dire agricultural situation in Africa showed no signs of improvement. In many developing countries there were signs that the pace of agricultural growth was slowing and that the momentum of the 'green revolution' was weakening. International negotiations on agricultural trade remained in stalemate because of the refusal of developed countries to reduce their agricultural subsidies. The scale of international aid for agricultural development in developing countries declined. So did the contributions to international food aid programmes to deal with emergencies. According to FAO the incidence of undernourishment had increased to nearly a billion. In the meantime potential impact of climate change and worldwide financial and economic crisis on agriculture and food security had emerged as a major area of concern.

The growing concern over the seriousness of these trends led the recent (July 2009) summit meeting of heads of governments of the G8 countries, select members of G20 group and international organisations to focus specifically on the need for urgent action to achieve sustainable global food security. Besides emphasising the need for inclusive and sustainable growth both overall and in agriculture, the joint statement on Global Food Security adopted at the meet recognises the importance of social safety nets and social protection to ensure for the most vulnerable groups access to food. It further stresses the need to use a variety of mechanisms for this purpose supported by 'sufficient, more predictable and flexible resources'. The statement exhorts nations to fulfil their commitments to increase overseas development assistance, and welcomes participants' offer to contribute $ 20 billion over the next three years as international aid for agricultural development and food security. The idea of building a stock to deal with 'humanitarian food emergencies and limit price volatility' is mentioned, but leaves its scope and feasibility to be examined by experts. On trade the statement does not break any new ground to give hope of if, when and to what extent outstanding differences are likely to be resolved.

The Aquila declaration marks a welcome appreciation of the seriousness of the food problem, especially in the context of climate change. It rightly recognises that the responsibility to formulate and implement strategies for increasing domestic food supplies and providing more and better food to the underfed and malnourished in developing countries will have to be borne by their national governments. International support by way of developmental and food aid and improvements in international trading arrangements generally, and for agricultural products in particular, can make a difference. The commitments made at Aquila to increase the quantum and terms of international aid for expanding agricultural production and food security programmes and to bring about changes in the environment of international trade are inadequate. In key respects the implementation of these commitments depends on developed countries, whose willingness and ability to deliver is in serious doubt. The ability of developing countries to expand domestic agricultural production, increase food supplies through international trade and manage large-scale food security programmes will continue to be constrained by uncertainties in developed countries' policies relating to trade, flow of technology and the scale and terms of aid. International action is therefore unlikely to make a significant contribution to ensuring food security and to improvement of nutrition of vulnerable people in developing countries. Progress on this front depends, and will continue to depend, almost entirely on their national governments.

Quest for National Food Security

An influential body of opinion holds that restrictions on domestic and international trade in agricultural commodities are a major reason for slow growth of production. They are alleged to dampen incentives for productivity, augmenting investments by depressing prices that farmers get for their produce and for raising output through more efficient allocation of resources. This argument is contestable on several grounds, at any rate, in the case of India.

Over time, there has been a progressive expansion of transport and communications network in the country. Restrictions on internal movements of produce across states have been substantially reduced, though not eliminated. Both have contributed to promote greater integration of produce markets across regions. Guaranteed minimum support prices (MSP) and procurement of several important food and fibre crops at prices higher than MSP work to the advantage of farmers. The remaining restrictions and the uneven effectiveness of MSP could well have affected the levels and structure of relative prices across regions and crops. But there are hardly any credible studies quantifying the magnitude of these effects.

Limits to Augmenting Domestic Supplies through Imports

The argument against foreign trade restrictions used to be that domestic farm prices are out of line with prices in the world market because of trade restrictions and that trade liberalisation would correct the anti-agricultural bias in fiscal policy and bring about a substantial improvement in the agricultural sector's terms of trade. Besides shifting income distribution in favour of agriculture and aligning domestic prices with world prices, it would give a strong impetus to growth by inducing production augmenting investments, faster diffusion of improved technology and more efficient allocation of resources. Thanks to the progressive depreciation of the rupee, reduction of tariffs and relaxation of trade restrictions, the disparities between domestic and world market prices have narrowed substantially. Even so, the above argument resonates in ongoing world trade negotiations to press developing countries to allow free trade in agricultural products.

India (along with other developing countries) has been unwilling to do so for several reasons. Traded volumes comprise a small proportion of world production. The bulk of agricultural products that enter international trade originate from and flow to developed countries. World market prices are much more volatile than domestic prices. The two often do not move in the same direction. Prices at which trade takes place are strongly influenced by heavy direct and indirect subsidies provided by developed country governments to their producers. Moreover, trade in commodities (food grains, oil seeds, oils and other basic food stuff) of greatest interest to developing countries are cartelised. Taken together with discriminatory tariff and non-tariff barriers to import of products from developing countries, these put third world farmers at a great disadvantage.

Foreign trade relative to GDP in the agricultural sector averages around 42 per cent in the world as a whole. The value of exports as well as imports of developed countries is much higher, both in absolute terms and relative to their agricultural GDP, compared to developing countries. Much of the developed country trade is among countries within that group. It is noteworthy that their trade in agricultural products is well developed despite all of them subsidising their farm sector heavily. The situation of developing countries is very different for a variety of reasons: relatively small export surpluses, less diversified domestic demand, desire to limit dependence on imports to meet domestic needs of staple foods, limited capacity to produce and process crops for which there is a market in high income countries, and impediments for their products to access developed country markets.

Table 3.1

Agricultural Exports and Imports Relative to Agricultural GDP 2003

Billion US $

	GDP	*Exports*	*% of GDP*	*Imports*	*% of GDP*
World	1237	522	42	518	41.9
Developed countries	501	369	70.2	395	73.6
Developing countries	735	153	21	154	21
South Asia	159	9	5.6	10	6.3
East and South East Asia	308	56	18.2	64	20.8
Africa	162	22	13.5	48	29.6
Latin America& Caribbean	106	63	59.4	32	30

Source: FAO, *State of Agricultural Commodity Markets 2004.*

In these respects the situation among developing countries is heterogeneous. Thus South Asia has followed policies that enabled production of basic food and fibre to increase in tandem with demand and, at the same time, restricted both imports and exports. Food self-sufficiency was an important guiding principle of policy. Much the same is true of other parts of Asia, but several of the constituent countries being both relatively small and more prosperous, have larger and more diversified demand, which could not be met from domestic production. Africa's exports are constrained by the adverse effects of prolonged drought on overall production, and the fact that the market for some of its main exports is not growing. Production of basic food has been severely affected and shortages have led to high dependence on imports. With limited export growth, their ability to import food depends heavily on foreign aid. Latin American agriculture is very different: it is far more foreign trade-intensive, both in absolute terms and relative to GDP. It has the resources and the capacity to produce and export a variety of crop and animal products. They are the only region among developing countries that have significant net exports.

The importance attached by developing countries to food self-sufficiency arises from concerns about the impact of large scale food imports on their balance of payments, uncertainties in the availability and costs of imports, and attendant risks to domestic food security. Balance of payments concerns are directly related to the performance of exports, and import needs of non-agricultural sectors. They are not a constraint on food and agricultural imports in several emerging economies of East and South East Asia, which have comfortable balance of payments based on exceptionally rapid expansion of exports of manufactured products and large inflows of foreign capital. But this is not the case in India, whose balance of payments has been and continues to face persistent current account deficits and dependence on volatile inflows of foreign funds to maintain reasonable reserves. While growing domestic demand for food has been met mostly from rising domestic production, there are several occasions on which reductions in output due to adverse weather conditions have necessitated sizeable imports when the balance of payments were under severe strain and recourse to foreign food aid became inevitable. Experience has shown that such aid does not come without strings: aid was in fact used by donors as instruments of political pressure on the government in its foreign and domestic policies.

The situation has eased considerably in the recent past and the country has been able to meet marginal shortages through direct purchases in the world market. Though a minor player in world markets, India's intermittent entry—sometimes as exporter and more often as importer - of significant quantities of different commodities—has had a significant influence on their world market prices. The recent rapidly rising trend in world prices of key food crops reflects the emergence of new sources of demand for grains and vegetable oils even as unusual speculative activity has greatly increased the volatility of prices. That this is happening at a time when there are signs of slackening in the pace of growth in domestic food production and relatively rapid growth in overall GDP, gives cause for worry. Even allowing for ongoing changes in consumption patterns indicating shifts from food to non-food products, and diversification of food consumption towards non-cereal foods, the current trends in food, and especially food grain production have to be arrested and reversed to achieve a faster rate of growth.

Trade Liberalisation and Agricultural Growth

Continuing attempts to persuade India to agree to further liberalisation of her foreign trade in agriculture are based on the argument that it will stimulate faster growth in domestic production. The nature and extent of shifts in the average level of producer prices and in the relative price structure cannot be assessed on the basis of past experience or current trends. All available evidence suggests that aggregate supply response to changes in overall terms of trade per se is miniscule and that non-price factors (climatic conditions, irrigation and technology changes that increase productivity per unit of land and of inputs affecting yields) are far and away more important. Expectations of significant changes in crop patterns underestimate the constraints imposed by agro-climatic factors (soil, climate, water availability) and the political resistance on account of the uneven impact (regionally, across crops and classes of farmers) of major shifts in relative prices, and the capacity to adapt production patterns to them. The pace of yield improvement of a wide range of staple crops continues to be limited by the diminishing scope for expansion of irrigation, serious deterioration in the quality of soil and water management and the inability of the research system to generate improved crop and animal production technology adapted to varied local conditions. These are largely due to institutional deficiencies and perverse pricing policies.

Correcting these deficiencies is critically important to improve resource-use efficiency and realise the full potential of biochemical technology. But there are hardly any signs of a serious attempt to address them. It is difficult to be optimistic about the prospects of stepping up the growth of domestic food grains production in the coming years. Without it, the country will have to depend on rising imports to provide basic food without raising prices. In theory this is possible without balance of payments problems, provided exports of goods and services grow at a much faster and sustained rate than in recent years. The prospects of this happening on a large enough scale do not seem bright.

In particular, the current optimism about the role of diversification into animal husbandry, horticulture, floriculture and other high value crops as a means to raise the overall rate of agricultural growth and generate large export surpluses is misplaced. Growth of these segments also faces technological and institutional constraints. It is far from clear that even if they produce more than domestic demand—which is also growing and rather faster than food grains—the surpluses will be large enough to make a significant difference to export growth. Also in question is whether they can be produced and processed efficiently enough to be able to compete in world markets in the face of large-scale producer subsidies and various tariff and non-tariff barriers.

Aspects of the Food Security Problem

Ensuring adequate supplies of food to meet demand in the aggregate is one aspect of the quest for food security. The other, and in many ways, more important and difficult task, in the words of the FAO summit declaration, is to improve '...physical and economic access by all, at all times, to sufficient, nutritionally adequate and safe food.' The task has several components: (1) determining the level and composition of 'sufficient and nutritionally adequate food'; (2) identifying groups and persons whose food consumption does not meet this standard; (3) determining the scope and nature of interventions needed to correct the deficiency; (4) devising effective mechanisms for implementing the interventions.

Assessing Nutritional Deficiency

In order to assess adequacy of actual food intake from the nutritional viewpoint, we need to have an objective standard of requirements for healthy, active functioning. The common practice, both nationally and internationally, is to measure the incidence of undernourishment by comparing average intake with a uniform norm of requirement for healthy, active functioning. The norm used in India is 2,400 kcal pcpd for rural areas and 2,100 for urban areas. Relative to these norms, the incidence of nutritional inadequacy would be much higher at 80 per cent of the rural and 60 of the urban population compared to the FAO estimate of about 40 per cent with less than 2,000 kcal pcpd.

Assessing undernourishment or hunger in this way poses several problems: (1) these norms relate to requirements for a reference population of specified composition in terms of age, gender, body weight and the kind of activity—all of which are highly variable across and within countries, occupations, between rural and urban areas and also between individuals. This raises questions about the validity of using a uniform norm for diverse populations and comparing it with mean intakes for different groups; (2) calorie intakes derived from consumption surveys are based on gross quantities of numerous foodstuffs in unprocessed, semi-processed and processed (in varying degrees) forms, whose levels and composition vary between class, space and time. The appropriate measure would be the calorie content of processed food on the plate; (3) healthy, active functioning does not depend only on the quantum of calorie intake but the extent to which it is used to fight and contain infections; the higher the incidence and severity of infections, the smaller the proportion of energy intake that is available for maintaining and building body mass and for other activity. (4) there is credible basis for the argument that there are biological mechanisms that enable individuals to maintain health and activity levels even when intake varies over a considerable range.

These limitations can be mitigated to a considerable extent by focussing on more direct measures of nutritional and health status namely morbidity and mortality rates, body mass index (MBI) for adults, weight-for-age for children, and incidence of anaemia for females. BMI less than 18.5 is considered to indicate chronic energy deficiency (CED) among adults. Available data in 8-9 Indian states show that currently (2004-05) about a third of adult males and 36 per cent of adult females fall in this category. Based on the weight-for-age criterion, between 41 and 48 per cent of children in different age groups are considered undernourished. For adult females the incidence of anaemia—an important indicator of nutritional and health status—is around 50 per cent.

In all these respects there has been progressive improvement overall: CED among adult males in 1987-88 was 56 per cent (about 70% higher compared to current levels); among males it was 52 per cent (45% higher than current levels). Other indicators also show significant improvement over the period. A significant and rather puzzling feature of these trends is that there has been a sustained improvement in nutrition status in all these dimensions over the last three decades despite declining average per capita calorie intake in the country.

There is reason to believe that this is due in significant measure to control of major communicable diseases and to expansion and improvement in basic health care and education. This reinforces the caution against judging the magnitude of nutritional deficiency in the population by comparing mean per capita calorie intake relative to a uniform national norm. This is not to deny the importance of undernourishment as a problem which even by outcome indicators is cause enough for concern. That more than a third of adults are in the CED category and nearly half the children have weight-for-height below desirable levels shows an unsatisfactory, indeed worrisome, sign of nutritional deficiency in our population. The merit of outcome indicators is that they permit a more meaningful and disaggregated assessment of the situation by region and by class, which is essential for designing measures to alleviate the conditions of the more vulnerable sections of the population.

But this overall improvement may conceal significant differences between different sections of the population. For, calorie intake of the majority of the population is less than the average. In rural areas, the poorest quartile of the population gets less than 80 per cent of the average. Consumption of the poorest quartile of urban population is about 60 per cent of the average. The mean intake of this segment has been declining in both rural and urban areas. It is important to know the incidence of, and trends in, CED and other indicators of nutritional status in these segments. This aspect can be, and needs to be, examined based on disaggregated analysis of the data from the National Nutrition Monitoring Bureau (NNMB) surveys.

Table 3.2

Trends in Mean Calorie Intake Overall and for the Poorest Quartile of Rural and Urban Populations India

		1983	*1987-88*	*1993-94*	*1999-2000*	*2004-05*
Rural	All	2240	2233	2153	2148	2047
	Poorest quartile	1580	1683	1659	1658	1624
urban	All	2070	2093	2073	2155	2021
	Poorest quartile	1309	1354	1316	1289	1259

Source: Deaton and Dreze (2008), Estimates based on National Sample Survey data.

Determinants of Food Consumption

Besides recognising the limitations of the minimum calorie intake norm to assess the incidence of nutritional deficiency and hunger, it is also important to understand the factors that account for actual food consumption patterns and their nutritive content. Sample surveys of food consumption give estimates at the household level, which show large variations reflecting differences across and within regions and classes of population in terms of size, sex and age composition of households, their incomes as well as food habits and preferences. In general, poorer households tend to be larger and have, on the average, a larger proportion of children compared to those higher up in the per capita income scale. It is also likely that there are systematic differences in age composition of adults across per capita income groups. These differences can be taken care of by focussing on consumption per adult units.

That there is a strong positive relation between per capita calorie intake and per capita incomes/consumption expenditure is well known. In 2004-2005, in rural areas, per capita calorie intake of the bottom decile (in terms of per capita expenditure (pce)) of the population was less than 1,500 kcal pcpd compared to more than 3,000 in the top decile. Average intake, overall and in all deciles of the urban population, was lower; so is the differential between the bottom and top deciles. Compared to urban areas, rural areas have lower per capita incomes, spend a larger proportion of their income on food and their food basket is far less diversified. On the average, 70 per cent of calorie intake in rural India is contributed by food grains compared to 55 per cent in urban areas. The importance of income as a determinant of the level and pattern of food consumption is also seen in the positive correlation between mean calorie intake and per capita incomes and in the fact that the relative contribution of cereals declines as incomes increase.

As already noted, mean calorie intake in both urban and rural areas is barely 2,000 kcal pcpd, about the same as the norm used in international discussions and well below the official Indian norm. Average intakes have declined progressively over the last two decades in both segments, the decline being more pronounced in rural areas. The average intake of the poorest decile of rural population—which one would expect to be prone to the greatest nutritional deprivation—has improved slightly relative to the average in both rural and urban areas. But the level of intake of this group—barely 1,500 kcal pcpd in rural and 1,200 in urban areas—is by any reckoning abysmally low. That despite this there is no indication of deterioration in outcome indicators is noteworthy.

Also puzzling is the fact that average calorie intake, both for the population as a whole and for those in the poorest segments, is declining or constant at relatively low levels and that consumption patterns are getting diversified to a degree that is quite unexpected when incomes are as low as in India. Significant changes in consumer tastes and preferences—reflected in the shift from food to non-food goods and to services, from cereal to non-cereal foods and from cheaper cereals (sorghum and millets) to more expensive rice and wheat—are evidently taking place. All this has important implications, both for identifying undernourished and more so for the design of effective policies for ensuring food security.

Measures to Achieve Food Security

The main issues relate to: (1) the basis for determining what constitutes 'food security'; (2) whether it is to be assessed in the aggregate, or by groups and regions, or with reference to individuals and households suffering from or prone to high risk of hunger and malnourishment; (3) the criteria and procedures for assessing and identifying segments and households who are vulnerable to nutritional deficiency; (4) alternative means of augmenting effective food consumption of target groups; and (5) implementation problems.

All these issues are subject to contention in the current debate on strategies to ensure food security. At one extreme are those who believe that the best way is to increase incomes of the poor to enable them to acquire adequate and nutritious food. And that for this purpose the focus should be on achieving and sustaining rapid overall growth. But there are few takers for this view. Experience shows that the impact of overall GDP growth is highly uneven. Overall economic growth does lead to increased incomes for the poorer segments but not a proportionate increase in incomes of all classes and regions.

Faster Overall Growth

During the fifties and sixties, the country's GDP was growing at barely 3.5 per cent per annum overall and average per capita incomes at less than 1.5 per cent per annum. There were apprehensions of worsening inequalities and increasing incidence of poverty. At the same time, the difficulties of implementing any drastic measures to reduce inequality of income and wealth were also recognised. The emphasis therefore shifted to accelerated overall growth as the critical instrument for eliminating poverty in the sense of ensuring that everyone could afford a minimum standard of living consisting of nutritive food and other basic needs, including education and health care. This was the thrust of a provisional outline of a long term plan prepared by the Perspective Planning Division of the Planning Commission: it suggested that the targets of minimum living standards could be achieved over a 15 year period if the rate of growth could be stepped up to and sustained at seven per cent per annum. It also articulated changes in the structure of production, the level and pattern of needed investments and how they could be financed. Significantly, it emphasised that with no change in income distribution, publicly funded programmes for education, health and basic social amenities combined with a redistributive fiscal policy would be essential to realise the minimum income objectives. In the event this strategy failed to take off, thanks to severe droughts, military conflicts during the sixties and their impact on government fisc and balance of payments. Overall growth continued to hobble around four per cent or less per annum through the seventies. While the advent of 'green revolution' in agriculture eased the food situation, it was widely perceived to be aggravating rural inequalities. Poverty incidence remained high and showed no signs of sustained decline.

Poverty Alleviation

This led to a growing emphasis on special programmes to increase employment opportunities and incomes of the poor segments especially in rural areas, programmes for subsidised supply of basic food through the public distribution system (PDS), and subsidised supply of key farm inputs (water, electricity, fertilisers and credit) ostensibly to help small and marginal farmers to reduce costs and increase production. Most of these programmes originated in the seventies and have proliferated under various guises and grown vastly in scale. The process has continued and gained in strength even after the eighties when the economy shifted to a much higher growth trajectory. The growth was lopsided with agricultural growth showing little or no improvement even as urban, non-agricultural sectors were booming. Despite significant diversification of employment into non-agricultural activities, rising real wage rates and reduction in poverty incidence, and economic and social disparities, both between and within rural and urban areas have increased at an alarming rate.

Particularly worrying is the fact that after six decades of development, the incidence of poverty (measured both in conventional ways and by levels of consumption of food and access to basic social services) is still unconscionably high. Nearly 30 per cent of the population is still below a rather modest poverty line; average calorie intake has been declining with more than a third reporting intakes of less than 1,500 kcal pcpd; a little over 30 per cent of the adult population suffers from CED; more than half of adult females and nearly three-fourths of children are anaemic; and the country ranks low in most human development indicators. Increasing awareness of these deficiencies and greater assertiveness of the underclass in voicing their discontent has forced the government to pay much greater attention to addressing them.

The National Rural Employment Guarantee scheme (NREGA) has emerged as the flagship programme for poverty alleviation. It aims at providing 100 days of assured employment in a financial year to any rural household whose adult members are willing to do unskilled manual work on local labour-intensive development projects at prescribed minimum wage rates. The current year's budget provides for an outlay of over Rs 300 billion for this programme. Even as it has caught public imagination, the scope, content, organisation and implementation of the programme are also the subject of intense and ongoing public debate.

Concurrent audits of performance have highlighted several deficiencies in the operation of the programme. Notable among these are: poorly designed and fragmented projects; widespread leakages and corruption; failure to meet the commitments on the scale of employment provided and payment of minimum wages; the nature and quality of works undertaken; and the lack of transparency and accountability to check these deficiencies. In effect they have created a situation in which the additional employment and incomes accruing to target groups fall much short of expectations and a large part of the resources get diverted to the benefit of the relatively well-to-do and powerful local elite. Concerted measures to address these deficiencies are imperative. But it would be wrong and short-sighted, as an influential section of opinion suggests that creation of employment and incomes for the poor can be a permanent solution to their problems. It is important to recognise that NREGA cannot provide an enduring solution to poverty of landless and land-poor, who depend on wage employment for their livelihood. Nor can the exchequer afford to fund it (alongside numerous other subsidies being justified in the name of benefitting the poor) on the present scale indefinitely.

Public Distribution System

Despite all this, it is widely recognised that the programme has generated employment opportunities for the poor, increased rural wage rates and therefore incomes of this segment. But increased incomes have not led to increased calorie intake among the poorer segments. The average calorie intake of the poorest quartile of the population is less than 1,700 kcal pcpd compared to the 2,400 that nutritionists recommend. This shortfall is widely viewed as a measure of chronic food deficiency and insecurity. In order to address this problem, the government has decided to enact a national law guaranteeing the supply of 25 kg of food grains per month at a price of Rs 3 per kg to all families below the poverty line (BPL) in all parts of the country. If actual consumption increases by an equivalent amount, BPL families will have about 600 more kcal pcpd, which will raise their total intake to nearly 2,300 kcal pcpd. Some 18 million tonnes of grains will be needed to supply 59-60 million households. The subsidy will cost the exchequer about Rs 21,000 crore a year. The assumptions underlying this programme in terms of nutritional improvement and its logistic, organisational and fiscal implications are currently under debate.

The programme presumes that nutritional deficiency is limited to the BPL households, that its nature and extent is uniform across households in this class and providing 25 kg per household per month to each of them would result in an equivalent increase in their actual calorie intake, and that this by itself would raise their nutritional status to the desired level. All these presumptions are open to question.

While it is certainly true that nutritional deficiencies are likely to be much higher in the BPL segment, not all those in this group suffer from malnutrition nor are all malnourished individuals poor. Calorie intake of nearly three-fourths of the population is below the reference norm. Given the difficulties involved in defining a uniform norm of intake for healthy active functioning and the fact that the size, composition and activity as well as level of intake vary widely within the category of BPL households, the average per capita intake is not an adequate basis to assess the nutritional status of individual households in this class. This also means that the extent of deficiency and its underlying factors are too varied to be effectively tackled by a uniform increase in the quantum of availability. Interventions must be capable of addressing this aspect.

The proposed programme assumes that low intakes are essentially due to inadequate supply and high prices of food grains. This flies in the face of the fact that food grain (and overall calorie) intake is well below the reference norm for nearly three-fourths of the population and that both have declined across poor as well non-poor groups despite significant increases in income. Available evidence on actual consumption patterns at all levels of income shows clear reduction in the overall elasticity of food intake relative to income, along with a marked shift from high calorie food grains to low calorie foods.

Even if the programme succeeds in reaching 25 kg of grain to all BPL families at far below market prices, actual food consumption may not increase. Our long experience with operating the PDS system shows that not all beneficiaries are able to purchase the full entitlements; on the other hand, subsidies create incentives to trade in these entitlements, illegal diversion of supplies to the market and attendant corruption. Those who trade their entitlements will of course have an income gain, but they may not use all or part of it for eating more and increasing their calorie intake.

There are also serious doubts about the ability of government to ensure that the targeted quantity in fact reaches all BPL families. The existence of a nationwide network of PDS outlets, which are assured of adequate and timely flow of supplies and which are easily accessible to the target groups throughout the country, is a critical precondition. The existing network is patchy and is weakest in regions with high concentrations of the poor. The system depends almost entirely on the grains procured and distributed by the Central government, which also meets the bulk of the subsidies. Identification of BPL families, operating PDS based on a system of centralised procurement in two or three states, ensuring smooth and predictable supplies to the network and checking leakages and misuse

—all these present horrendous problems. With a few exceptions, state governments have not shown much interest in building and maintaining the network or to procure grains locally to feed the system. If there were no subsidies and states were required to contribute a part of the supplies and share part of the costs, there would be little interest in PDS.

Alternative Strategies

Given these problems, it is appropriate to consider alternative strategies to achieve food security. Several possibilities have been suggested and are under active debate. These include: (1) getting the state governments and/or *panchayats* to create and maintain local grain banks; (2) make access to PDS open to all households; (3) a system of food vouchers to BPL families exchangeable with traders for a specified quantity of grains at subsidised rates and traders being reimbursed the subsidy in cash; and (4) programmes focussed on groups that suffer from serious nutritional deficiency for lack of adequate food of satisfactory quality.

Of these, the first alternative has no takers in the centre or state governments. It seems highly unrealistic to expect that local *Panchayats* as presently constituted will, or can, take this responsibility. PDS with universal coverage will avoid the problems of identifying BPL families. But what it will do to achieve food security in the sense of ensuring adequate and assured food to all is far from clear. PDS was designed basically to ensure that poor people get a minimum quantity of food grains and other essentials at 'affordable' prices. It also served as a useful medium for distribution of food in times of acute scarcity and natural disasters.

Subsidised supplies are necessary and justified when food prices are rising and incomes of poor segments are too low and/or stagnant to access adequate food from the market. But over the years, governments have found it expedient to commit themselves to maintaining and even reducing PDS prices, while market prices were rising. The resulting phenomenal growth in food subsidies was sought to be justified as a poverty alleviation measure. In the event, the efficacy of this strategy, both in terms of coverage and the extent to which the benefits reached the ostensible target groups, has been extremely limited. An extension of this approach to a universal PDS may seem to avoid the messy problems of identifying eligible poor. But providing assured supply of a specified quantity at subsidised prices to everyone is simply not feasible in terms of procuring the needed quantities, ensuring that they reach all sections in towns and villages, and of the ability of the exchequer to meet the costs.

The idea of food vouchers has the merit of avoiding the difficult problems involved in procurement and distribution of supplies through a widespread network of PDS outlets, and limiting the role of government to the responsibility of maintaining and managing buffer stocks for ensuring reasonable stability in market prices. There are also apprehensions about the potential for corruption and misuse of the system, though it is difficult to see why they should be any greater than in PDS. But the problems of defining criteria for eligibility to these vouchers and identifying specific households who meet the criteria remain.

Given the serious difficulties in design and effective operation of the PDS strategy in any form, the suggestion to focus on groups and individuals with clearly identifiable nutritional deficiencies and devise interventions appropriate to correct different types of deficiencies deserves serious consideration. These groups and the nature of their deficiencies can be identified on the basis of BMI for adults, weight-for-age/stunting for children, incidence of anaemia and other recognised outcome indicators of nutritional status, which can be measured directly or through objective clinical tests. This approach is already the basis of existing Integrated Child Development Services (ICDS), school feeding and other special nutrition improvement programmes. The merit of these programmes is that they combine measures to improve nutritional status with appropriate health interventions. Expanding the coverage of these programmes to cover all infants, preschool and school going children, and women requiring ante/postnatal care, combined with adequate funding and supplies, would enable identification and treatment of all those in these groups that need special treatment.

That leaves children not attending school, adults suffering from CED and people (such as widows, disabled, old and chronically sick) with meagre incomes of their own and without any family support. In the case of children, the aim should be to make attendance compulsory for all with access to school, feeding being used as an incentive. In other cases, families of adults, all those identified through universal screening to be in CED category, and those who are near destitute would be enabled to increase their food intake through PDS, food vouchers or cash transfers through various pension schemes. The process of identification of eligible groups could be done using dominant characteristics of households (size, age composition, assets and consumption levels) with low per capita incomes derived from an analysis of National Sample Survey (NSS) and National Family Health Survey (NFHS), cross-checked with first hand information available within each community.

Such a differentiated approach would reduce problems of identifying those that need to be helped and enabled to get and eat more food and adapt interventions to their diverse requirements. The chances of leakages and misuse as well as the costs to be borne by the exchequer will also be substantially less than in any of the variants of PDS being currently debated. Being very different from the PDS-centric proposals of the Food Security Bill, the implications of this strategy in terms of modalities, procedures, institutional arrangements and costs need to be examined in depth. One aspect is obvious: such a programme cannot work if the design and implementation of its components are left to bureaucracies of different line departments without effective involvement and participation of local communities, better coordination of personnel engaged in related activities, and credible arrangements for ensuring accountability.

Conclusion

In sum, there is a welcome recognition, globally and nationally, that the persistence of malnourishment on an unacceptably large scale in developing countries demands that more determined efforts be made to address the problem. That international contribution, and more especially of developed countries, to solving this problem is likely to be quite limited is evident from the G20 summit declaration. It sees the solution primarily in developing countries' efforts to achieve faster and more equitable growth both overall and especially in their domestic food production and through poverty alleviation programmes to ensure that the poor have incomes to acquire adequate and nutritious food. The international commitment is limited to providing technical and financial aid to support these efforts; to exhortations to provide emergency food aid (of unspecified magnitude);

to meet acute shortages and distress caused by natural and man-made disasters; and work towards a freer and fairer international trade regime.

The prospects of freer, fairer international trade making a significant contribution to securing adequate access on reasonable terms to meet even temporary, let alone chronic, domestic shortages are quite limited. The claim that trade liberalisation is in the interests of developing countries because it would increase efficiency and give a powerful stimulus to growth of domestic agricultural/food production is untenable. Programmes and policies to promote faster and more diffused growth and those specifically meant to increase employment and incomes of the poor and give social protection to the disadvantaged are important. But they will not solve the problems of unequal income distribution. Moreover, as the recent Indian experience shows, increases in incomes do not necessarily lead to increased food consumption.

In this context the paper has highlighted the limitations of using uniform average calorie intake norms as the basis for assessing the extent of hunger and malnourishment. The determinants of requirements for healthy, active functioning vary greatly across and within regions. The nutritional status of individuals is not determined only by the volume and composition of food intake. Despite calorie intake levels being well below the reference norms and declining in most groups, size and health status indicators show a progressive, if modest improvement. Conditions of water supply, sanitation and health also have a significant impact. This is not to suggest that malnourishment is not a problem. Its incidence judged by outcome indicators is unacceptably high and calls for special measures to tackle it.

Expanding programmes for increased employment and incomes for the poor, social protection schemes for the disadvantaged and programmes to improve health and nutrition of children and women are important for improving conditions of the poor. Their effectiveness is however less than expected because of unevenness of coverage and numerous deficiencies in their implementation. Even as the scale of outlays on these programmes is increased, measures to correct these deficiencies are imperative. The strategy of subsidised supply of food grains through PDS has not worked well. The extraordinary complexity of organising and managing procurement and distribution to reach all parts of the country and the inherent difficulties of identifying the poor have been highlighted. These difficulties, it is argued, cannot be avoided in any variant of the subsidised supply of grains to the poor. It is suggested that a better way would be to identify the malnourished individuals and groups on the basis of objectively measurable indicators of malnourishment, recognise that the nature and extent of deficiencies vary, and focus on ways to directly increase food intake along with measures to improve their intake more efficiently. There is much to commend a serious and detailed study to design an intervention programme using this approach.

4 Political Economy of Employment Guarantee Programmes

Generating adequate employment opportunities at rising levels of income for a rapidly growing population has been and remains a central concern of India's development strategy. That this calls for rapid growth and diversification of economic activity through investments in physical and human capital and progressive technological improvement is beyond controversy. However, from early on, there have been divergent views about how to implement it in the Indian context. Thus, during the fifties, advocates of the big push strategy argued that the prevalence of unemployment in countries like India is not due to lack of effective demand but to the limited size of market and low elasticity of production both of which called for simultaneous expansion of demand and supply by '... a synchronised application of capital to a wide range of industries' and in 'public overhead facilities' (Rodan, 1943). Others saw the mobilisation of surplus labour in poor agrarian economies (manifest in open and, more importantly, disguised unemployment) as the means to increase investment for augmenting productive capacity.

The economic, organisational and political factors that limited the scope for either strategy were elaborately and persuasively argued by Raj (Raj, 1957). For one, unemployed and underemployed workers are mostly unskilled. Using them for work outside the household on large scale raises major tasks of organisation and management of works. Second, for effective capital formation that will augment productive capacity they need to be combined with substantial equipment, materials and technical skills, all of which are scarce. Third, increased capital formation requires larger savings. Average incomes of most of the population are far too low to leave any margin for savings. There is also the problem of meeting the consumption needs of workers employed in capital construction. These workers are contributing, even if in a limited way, to family income by participating in household production activities and/or working as hired labour. Their consumption needs (consisting mostly of food) are met out of the pooled family income. The extent to which this is possible is limited by the scope for increasing overall production of food and/or reducing the consumption of producer households through taxation or compulsory procurement, and then distributing the physical food 'surplus' so mobilised for meeting these needs.

These problems were managed with apparent success in the early post-revolutionary phase of China. But it evidently involved using coercive methods of mobilising food supplies and labour which were unthinkable in India given its complex and diverse social structure and its commitment to democracy. Therefore, the solution to the employment problem depended basically on the rate at which capital formation and thereby the pace of growth and diversification in overall production could be increased. Given the socio-political constraints, the long term strategy outlined in India's First Five Year Plan argued for adopting a gradualist path of transformation from the initial state of low saving, low capital formation and low growth to a progressive and mutually reinforcing increase in these dimensions with public investment playing the role of a driving force.

By the time the Second Plan was formulated, the mood of caution changed as a result of the better-than-expected performance during the early fifties. The Second Plan opted for the 'big push' strategy (suggested by Mahalanobis) for accelerated increase in the rate of capital formation by massive public investments in heavy industry and simultaneously ensuring employment opportunities by using labour-intensive techniques in the rest of the economy. This approach was carried further in a draft outline of a 15 year plan presented to the Planning Commission in the early sixties (PPD, 1962). It argued that GDP growth at a much faster rate than envisaged earlier was feasible and that a sustained growth at the rate of seven per cent path over a period of 15 years would generate adequate additional employment to absorb the increase in labour force and also ensure a reasonable minimum level of living to all.[1]

In the event, this vision suffered a severe setback in the wake of the military conflicts with China and Pakistan, and the unprecedented droughts of the mid-sixties. Planning was suspended for a while. Growth targets were scaled down even as concerns about unemployment, poverty and inequalities came under close scrutiny. The advent of the green revolution in the latter half of the sixties signalled a revival of agricultural growth prospects. But this revival was concentrated in a few regions and among those who had access to irrigation, and there were apprehensions about the magnitude of their impact on labour use, especially of wage labour. These concerns were heightened, among other things, by the proliferation of small and marginal holdings and attendant rapid increase in dependence on wage labour as a source of livelihood in rural areas, indications of widespread stagnation (and, in many areas, a decline) in real wage rates for rural labour, and the slow pace of employment diversification.

There was a general consensus on the crucial role of rapid growth and diversification of economic activity for sustained increase in employment and poverty eradication. At the same time, development economists were veering to the view that the success of development strategy should not be judged only by the increases in mean per capita real incomes but by the extent to which it enables everyone to afford basic minimum needs. The view that a high rate of overall growth was neither a sufficient nor a necessary condition for poverty eradication gained ground. The need for special programmes focused directly on increasing incomes and access to basic education and health of the poor came to be widely accepted as an

1. Subject to two caveats: 1. The projected employment growth was based on the assumption that productivity growth in construction and services, which accounted for most of the increase, would be much slower than in other sectors. (2) Given that a large proportion of the population lives in remote areas, isolated from the mainstream of the economy; that much of rural economic activity is loosely integrated with the rest of the economy; and that the vast reserve of underemployed labour in rural areas is unskilled and has limited mobility, 'the condition of a considerable proportion of the people (which it estimated at one-fifth) will remain stagnant or, at any rate, improve much less than the average unless specific steps are taken to deal with their problems'. Measures needed to provide additional incomes for these segments were not spelt out (PPD, 1962).

essential component of development plans. The concept of a minimum standard of living as a measure of absolute poverty, and the pace of its reduction as a basis for assessing the efficacy of development plans found widespread resonance among scholars and policy makers.

The moral and political rationale for special poverty alleviation programmes arises from the fact that the benefits of growth do not reach all classes and regions in equal proportion. Hence, the need for special programmes to enable areas and classes of people who do not benefit at all from overall growth, or do so only to a very limited extent, to reach an acceptable minimum level of living. Since the factors underlying uneven distribution of benefits of growth vary across regions and between different socioeconomic groups, it was considered appropriate to adopt a differentiated strategy designed to address the constraints and opportunities facing different laggard regions and groups.

Thus small and marginal farmers and artisans, who had very small endowments of productive assets needed assistance to augment their productive asset base and increase its productivity; regions (hill areas, tribal areas, drought prone and desert regions) with stagnant or low productivity of agriculture called for special programmes for developing their resource potential; raising incomes of the unemployed and underemployed required special schemes to provide them additional wage employment opportunities and to equip them with skills and resources; and distribution of subsidised food and essential consumption goods for the poor, as well as material and financial inputs for agriculture. The rural employment programmes were one of several elements, and a rather small element at that, of the poverty alleviation strategy. The special rural works programmes included in the Third and Fourth Plans were very modest in scale and impact.

This strategy, which was evolving during the fifties and sixties, found sharper articulation in Indira Gandhi's 20 point programme for '*garibi hatao*'. Its huge success in mobilising electoral support of the poor led to a wider recognition among the political parties of the importance of these groups on account of their sheer size. Thereafter, election manifestos of all political parties declared their commitment to take up special measures to address their problems. Besides giving it a prominent place in their election manifestos, parties that gained power at the centre and the states competed with each other in extending and expanding these programmes and devising their own schemes to attract support from particular groups of the poor. Wage employment schemes were one of their several components. The number and variety of targeted poverty alleviation schemes and magnitude of public spending on these schemes have grown manifold. While some of the new schemes were more in name, there have also been significant changes in substantive aspects of their scope and content and organisation.

The Rationale for Wage Employment Programmes

The Maharashtra Employment Guarantee scheme marks a radical departure from this approach in two important respects: a massive rural works programme was seen as crucial to mitigating poverty of the rural unemployed, and it gave legal sanction to the concept of Right to Work. Started as an experimental project as early as 1965, it was expanded in scale to provide relief to large parts of the state affected by an unprecedented drought, and subsequently institutionalised under a law that guaranteed employment to anyone who seeks work and is willing to do unskilled jobs in public works. Rightly hailed as a creative and imaginative initiative, several evaluation studies done during the seventies showed that they made a significant impact both in terms of the magnitude of additional employment created and wage rates, thereby increasing the incomes of rural wage labour and their bargaining power in the rural labour market.

The case for adopting a similar approach at the national level was strongly advocated by Dandekar and Rath (D-R, 1971). They highlighted the fact that the large majority of the poor are from rural households with very little or no land, who depend exclusively or mostly on wage labour. Their poverty is due to lack of adequate employment opportunities and low wages. Neither of which is likely to be addressed adequately or soon as a result of overall growth and diversification of the economy. Therefore, it was argued, effective and speedy reduction of poverty would be possible only through a massive programme of rural public works on a scale that would meet the gap between their current incomes and the minimum desired level.

They argued that such a programme would be the most effective way of addressing both unemployment and poverty. By providing additional wage employment to all or most of the unemployed and underemployed at prevailing wage rates, it could provide them additional incomes to cover the gap between the current income of the rural poor and the income required to bring their per capita incomes to the desired minimum. Such a scheme would be much larger than envisaged by the Planning Commission at that time but quite feasible. There was no dearth of worthwhile schemes. The extra costs, justified from the larger social viewpoint, could be met by a special cess on the rich.

They went into considerable detail about problems of operationalising it. They were not in favour of some features of the Maharashtra scheme including the condition that works should be within the village or its vicinity, and that the village *panchayat* should be made responsible for implementation. They were also against entrusting the welfare of the poor to local communities on the ground that "because of their long acquaintance with poverty at close quarters, they have developed a certain amount of callousness or hardened conscience towards poverty" (D-R, 1971). Given the nature and geographical scope of works they envisaged, the responsibility for planning and implementation of the programme should, in their view, be vested with the state bureaucracy. This point of view continues to be voiced by influential segments of politicians, bureaucrats and civil society to this day.

Minhas (1972), while not supporting the idea of an employment guarantee, also emphasised the potential of large scale rural works programmes to solve the employment problem in a manner that would also help to raise agricultural production. He was critical of the belief current at the time, that radical redistribution of land (even if it were feasible), or through ill-planned works programmes of the make-work variety could solve the problem. He argued that a speedy progress towards this goal required effective measures to provide all sections free basic education, vocational training, basic health facilities, water supply and sanitation to remove disabilities from which the poorer segments of the community suffer, along with an integrated programme designed to address structural constraints to rural economic growth, and at the same time utilise idle labour in such a way that "...employment and income opportunities for the poor and the productive capabilities of economically weak producers can be significantly increased" (Srinivasan and Bardhan, 1974: 402).

Emphasising excessive fragmentation of land holdings as a critical constraint on agricultural growth, he advocated a programme for compulsory consolidation of holdings, followed by a complementary programme of public works for land leveling, soil conservation in dry lands, and development of local potential for irrigation with appropriate distribution and drainage networks for the entire land in the village. This process would offer ample opportunities for utilising the unemployed and underemployed and in the process increase the production potential of agriculture. After development, the land was to be parcelled and redistributed in compact blocks to the original owners taking into account the area they owned before consolidation with adjustments for improvements in land quality as a result of development works, thereby providing the basis for sustained employment at higher levels.

The programme was radical both in concept and in the legal and institutional arrangements needed to implement it. Unlike D-R, Minhas envisaged entrusting the task of the consolidation and land improvement phase to teams of technical specialists. The fact that the scheme would make a significant and demonstrable improvement in the overall production potential would, he argued, facilitate getting stakeholders' agreement. The institutional problems of the process would be manageable with transparent and rule-based procedures for allocation of developed land, and open consultation with communities. But the modalities of the consultation process were not spelt out. And the definition and enforcement of criteria were left to extra community agencies.

It is noteworthy that both proposals viewed the role of works programmes not merely as a means of creating additional wage employment in the short run but as part of a larger, more integrated programme of overall development that would increase the production potential of rural economy and sustain higher levels of employment over the longer run. They also envisaged that these programmes would give special attention to regions with high levels of unemployment and poverty. But they had very different views on the appropriate institutional arrangements for implementing the programme.

Evolution of Wage Employment Programmes

In the event, the response of policy makers and the political class was slow and hesitant. The Minhas approach that emphasised land consolidation as a prelude to integrated programme of land and water development for increasing production and employment potential was never given serious consideration. Nor did the concept of employment guarantee through large scale public works even after the Maharashtra Employment Guarantee Scheme (EGS) demonstrated its feasibility and significant positive impact. Except Gujarat, no other state showed much interest in adopting that approach. Nor did the national plans of the sixties and seventies. Special rural employment schemes figured in the rhetoric of the plans but actual outlays were quite small and the focus was on particular but variable target groups/regions. This reflected the widespread belief at that time that rapid overall growth and diversification of economic activity was the most effective means to reduce poverty and unemployment. Poverty alleviation programmes targeted on selected disadvantaged sections of the population and economically backward and laggard regions seemed a better, and also politically more attractive, alternative to employment. Resource constraints also were a limiting factor.

Attitudes changed in the face of failure to realise targeted acceleration of growth in incomes and employment, continued high dependence on agriculture for livelihood, the rapid rise in the proportion of landless and land poor, and growing public concerns over persistence of high levels of rural poverty and unemployment. Interest in rural wage employment programmes grew in response to increasing political pressures to address these concerns. This process was rather slow and hesitant through the seventies but gained in intensity thereafter. The eighties witnessed the launch of several new and larger wage employment programmes with wider reach but still selective in coverage and content. The nineties saw a major effort at combining and rationalising different ongoing programmes of this genre.

The scale, scope, content and priorities of wage employment programmes have thus undergone many changes over the last four-five decades. The main features of the programmes, in terms of their objectives, target groups and kinds of works taken up, from the sixties to the current National Rural Employment Guarantee Programme (NREGP) are highlighted below.

Scheme	*History*	*Scope*	*Objective*	*Target group priorities*	*Nature of works*	*Funding*
Rural works programme/ food for work	Included in draft Third Plan with allocation of Rs 100 crore but scaled down because of economic crisis. Replaced by food for work programme in Fourth Plan	National	Providing wage employment in unskilled and semi-skilled works in slack season	Densely populated areas	Schemes under block and village plans	Central government
Employment guarantee	Started in 1972 and continuing	Maharashtra	Legally guaranteed 100 days of unskilled and semi-skilled employment to all able bodied unemployed persons at wage rates somewhat below lean season village rates	All able bodied unemployed persons	Durable, community assets, village industry	State government
Employment Assurance Scheme (EAS)	1975 merged with Jawahar Rozgar Yojana (JRY)	National	100 days of employment in lean season at statutory minimum wage	All persons above the age of 18 and below 60 years who need and seek employment on economically productive and labour intensive social and community works.	Watershed development, agro-horticulture, felt needs for village community buildings, and master plans in drought prone and desert development blocks	No data
National Rural Employment Programme (NREP)	1984-1988 merged with JRY in 1989	National	Wage employment in slack season	Groups not likely to be benefited by other sectoral programme	Rural roads, social forestry, housing, community buildings	50% Central and 50% states

contd...

...contd...

Scheme	*History*	*Scope*	*Objective*	*Target group priorities*	*Nature of works*	*Funding*
Rural Landless Employment Guarantee Programme (RLEGP)	1983-1989 merged into JRY 1989	National	Guaranteed employment of 100 days for one member of eligible families	Limited only to the landless	Earmarked allocations for social forestry, houses for SC/ST, Indira Awas Yojana (IAY) and Million Wells scheme (MWS).	Wholly funded by centre
JRY	1989-2006	National	Generation of additional gainful employment for unemployed and under-employed persons, both men and women, in the rural areas through the creation of rural economic infrastructure, community and social assets with the aim of improving the quality of life of the rural poor	All people BPL but preference to SC/ST and low productivity areas at statutory minimum wage	Works contributing to creation of rural economic infrastructure, community and social assets for sustained benefit to the poor	80% Central, 20% states
NREGP	2005 continuing	National	Provide guaranteed employment of 100 days of wage employment in unskilled manual work for all rural households who seek it.	Universal	Projects to be taken up decided in consultation with elected representatives and local communities,	90% Central; 10% states

With the exception of Maharashtra's EGS and Gujarat's Right to Work scheme, others have been conceived and funded by the Central government but implemented by states. States are expected to share the costs, but the proportion to be met by them has come down from 50 per cent in some components during the eighties to 10 per cent currently. Central funds are transferred to states on the basis of specified but changing criteria. The scope and content of the programme, funding patterns as well as guidelines on prioritisation of target groups and regions, the nature of projects that can be undertaken are laid down by the centre. In all these respects there have been substantial changes in successive plans. The changes are not based on systematic learning from experience nor do they have any coherent and consistent rationale. Guidelines are meant to be followed uniformly throughout the country leaving little flexibility for adaptation to local conditions.

The geographical scope of the programme is specified variously at different times covering 'areas with high pressure of population and considerable unemployment' (Third Plan), 'areas affected by scarcity', 'drought prone, desert and tribal areas' (in the earlier version of EAS) and low productivity areas (JRY). These criteria were meant to focus on programmes on areas that needed those most. But they were loosely defined and tended to change over time. Moreover they were used as the basis for allocating the programme funds to states. While in earlier programmes the release of funds was based on predetermined allocation criteria, under NREGA actual releases to states, and by states to districts and lower levels, are based on the number of persons who register for employment and the progress of actual expenditure on the schemes.

Eligibility for employment under the scheme is left undefined in some; limited in others (e.g., 'those not likely to benefit from other sectoral programmes', 'landless' and 'unemployed men and women in BPL families'); and more inclusively ('those who seek work', all adults aged between 18 and 60 who seek work') in more recent times. In several programmes, central guidelines require priority to be given to works that benefit specified groups such as landless, SC/ST, and agricultural labourers. In general, the schemes aim at providing work in unskilled or semi-skilled jobs in construction of local works during the slack season at statutory minimum wages. Beneficiaries under pre-NREGA programmes were claimed to be self-selecting on the argument that statutory minimum wages in most states were higher than market rates. Some schemes (NREP and the early version of JRY) did not specify any target employment per person, while others (RLEGP, EAS) set the goal as 100 days of work per household or registered applicant per year. Eligibility under NREGA is in principle unrestricted: individuals are free to decide whether they want to seek work under the programme.

The schemes that can be taken up under wage employment programmes are also indicated in the guidelines relating to each of them. A general condition is that they must be of a type that requires mostly unskilled and semi-skilled labour and uses local materials. Some programmes specify that the wage component should be at least 60 per cent of the total cost. The kinds of works to be taken up vary in scope and detail: some are of broad scope (e.g., 'productive works and community assets', 'productive works of sustained benefit to the poor', 'contributing to creation of rural infrastructure'), while others are more specific (e.g., watershed development, rural roads, social forestry, houses, community buildings). In some cases funds are required to be earmarked for particular schemes such as social forestry and those that benefit SC and ST. The choice is to be decided by state government officials on the basis of integrated development plans at different levels and felt needs ascertained in consultation with village communities. Interpretation of the guidelines and decisions on what projects are taken, when and by which agency at the sub-state level have been largely left to the state bureaucracy.

Scattered evaluations by official agencies and studies by scholars and activists highlight several deficiencies: programme funds not reaching district and local levels; their unauthorised diversion to other programmes; widespread use of private contractors (often influential local party functionaries and their associates) for construction; failure to maintain proper accounts and records of work taken up; and lax monitoring of the nature and quality of works and their impact. Like other poverty alleviation programmes, wage employment schemes are widely seen to be affected by organised and extensive corruption. There was widespread criticism of the continued emphasis on selectivity in prioritising target groups/regions and nature of works to be taken up. At the same time, the social impact of the new economic policy has given rise to widespread concern.

The Need for Inclusive Growth

While overall growth rate had increased to unprecedented levels, it was largely concentrated in organised urban sectors. Growth of employment in the organised sectors of the economy, which propelled the rapid growth in the rest of the economy was very little compared to that of the total labour force. Inequalities between rural and urban areas and between classes increased. Agricultural growth remained slow (and was possibly slowing down) without any significant decline in the proportion of labour, especially wage labour, dependent on the sector. Growing dissatisfaction of the poor and underprivileged that were not benefitting from the growth process reflected itself in the wider and stronger articulation of a demand from these classes, civil society groups and sections of the political class for corrective action to address these problems and promote 'inclusive growth'.

Civil society groups actively campaigned for a strategy that would radically expand and redesign wage employment programmes to cover all those who need additional employment, making Right to Work a justiciable right, and ensuring greater transparency and public accountability by empowering elected local bodies to plan and implement the programmes. The political initiative for implementing NEGP was taken by the United Progressive Alliance (UPA) government and supported by the Left parties. It formed a key part of the alliance's 2004 election manifesto and was implemented soon after it came to power. The requisite legislation was approved by Parliament in 2005. It has since become the most important, and the largest ever poverty alleviation programme of the country. The total outlay on this programme is currently (2009-10) around Rs 390 billion (about 8% of the total public sector plan outlay), which is 10 times the outlay (2.4% of total public sector plan) in 2000-01 and more than 3 times the level recorded the year before it was launched (Table 4.1).

Table 4.1

Growth of Rural Wage Employment Programmes in India 1985-86 to 2009-10

		1985-86	*1990-2001*	*1995-2006*	*2000-01*	*2003-04*	*2009-10*
1. Total public sector plan outlay	Rs crore	33060	58370	107380	185740	224800	447900
2. Outlay on wage employment programmes	Rs crore	1000	2600	6170	3790	12100	39000
3. (2) as % of (1)	Per cent	3.0	4.5	5.7	2.4	5.4	8.7
4. Additional employment created	Million Days	764	874	1240	406	1570	1829

Source: Various plan documents.

Details of actual outlays on wage employment and estimates of employment generated are not available for years prior to 1985.

These estimates are based on reporting by the state governments. There are no systematic and independent surveys.

NREGP

The objectives of NREGP and institutional arrangements for its implementation are governed by a special law enacted by Parliament. Under this law, the government is obligated to provide guaranteed employment of 100 days of wage employment in unskilled manual work for all rural households who seek it, irrespective of region, caste, occupation or poverty. Applicants can indicate their preference regarding time and location of work in the vicinity of their village and are entitled to compensation if they are not given work according to their preference. The programme now covers all the districts in the country.

The law also envisages significant changes in funding the programme and institutional arrangements for its implementation. The Central government finances 90 per cent of the cost of the programme. An important innovation is that the allocation of Central assistance to states is no longer predetermined on the basis of poverty, unemployment and social backwardness but on the basis of the actual demand for employment reflected in the applications for work under the programme. Funds are transferred directly to the districts into separate bank accounts for NREGA. Permitting unspent balances in this account to be carried over and used in subsequent years is a special feature of the programme.

Like earlier programmes, NREGP is also to be implemented through the state governments and its agencies. The types of projects that can be taken up are expected to be decided in consultation with elected representatives and local communities as part of an overall plan for local development. But the substantive work of plan preparation, technical design and scrutiny of projects, as well as approval and financial sanctions for taking up projects are vested in the state bureaucracy.

The scope for leakages through malpractices was sought to be reduced by involving elected bodies and *gram sabhas* in selection of schemes, transferring funds to block and village *panchayats* based on progress of approved works, and arrangements for payment of wages to workers through post offices and banks. Detailed records are required to be kept on works carried out, muster rolls, employment sought by applicants and actually provided to them and payments made to beneficiaries. These are to be audited regularly, and also put on the net so that they are accessible to the public. Grievance redressal mechanisms are to be in place at all levels. Mandatory review of implementation of programmes by elected bodies and oversight bodies at different levels from village upwards, social audit by institutions independent of government, and bringing the entire programme within the purview of the Right to Information (RTI) Act are notable innovations meant to ensure public accountability.

Impact

That these have had a significant positive impact is undeniable: the response to the programme among the poor is both widespread and positive; it is providing work to as many as 45 million (as of last year); half or more of the beneficiaries are reported to be women and SCs and STs who are among the neediest groups; besides beneficiaries getting better wages, their bargaining power in local labour markets has increased; the system of paying wages to beneficiaries directly through post offices and banks helps reduce leakages. The scale and scope of evaluations and social audit of the programme performance has greatly increased. Together with the RTI Act, this has helped bring the shortcomings of the programme into sharper focus. It has created a legal and political space to demand fulfilment of the guarantee. This space is being used by civil society activists to articulate deficiencies in the programme and demand corrective action. But the potential beneficiaries themselves are too dispersed and unorganised to exert effective pressure.

At the same time, independent field surveys and first hand interactions with participants in the programme in numerous villages across various states highlight several persistent deficiencies. In most states the actual employment provided to those who register for work falls short of the 100 days guaranteed by the Act; norms of labour intensity are not always met; manipulation and fudging of muster rolls, underpayment and delayed payment of wages, widespread use of private contractors, and corruption in the procurement of material are widespread; works taken up are ill-planned and poorly executed; they do not meet the aim of providing the economic base for sustained increase in employment, and the incidence of these sources of corruption appears to be widespread. Though inadequate as a basis for assessing the overall presence of leakage and corruption in the programme, these findings are serious enough to cause concern.

Criticisms

These deficiencies are cited by the proponents of sustained rapid growth as the best and most effective solution to the employment problem and to argue that wage employment programmes are diverting resources from more productive, growth-promoting investments. The milder form of this critique alleges that, by increasing rural wage rates, the programme is adversely impacting upon agricultural and non-agricultural enterprises by making it difficult to get labour and raising labour costs. Such complaints from enterprises that depend on wage labour are to be expected. But they can and do adjust to rising wages in many ways: labour saving devices and substitution of family for hired labour. There is hardly any credible evidence to show whether and to what extent rising wage rates, which benefit the poorest and most disadvantaged segments of rural society, have impeded investment and productivity-augmenting technical progress in the rural economy.

The severest critics of the programme argue that the way the programme is conceived and implemented is very inefficient, wasteful and prone to corruption and that whatever additional incomes they generate are more or less doles to the poor. The huge and growing outlays on the programme increase the already unsustainable fiscal deficit and cut into resources needed for programmes for investments in productive enterprises and basic infrastructure. Some even attribute the current food price inflation to increased incomes and attendant increased food consumption among the poor segments!

These arguments are specious. In the first place, outlays on the employment programme constitute only eight per cent of the total public sector plan outlay. And the additional wage incomes it generates (assuming no leakages) is less than two per cent of the GDP. To suggest that this puny tail is wagging the inflation dog is preposterous. Second, waste and corruption are by no means unique to wage employment programmes. They have become endemic features of all public sector programmes. Nearly half the public sector plan outlay is on irrigation, industry, energy and transport all of which are notorious for delays, cost escalations due to poor preparation and design, and corruption. Third, the magnitude of explicit and implicit subsidies on food, irrigation, fertilisers, energy and urban infrastructure contributes far more to the fiscal deficit.

While these arguments against large-scale wage employment programmes are untenable, some supporters of the programme are concerned that insistence on taking up schemes based on integrated plans for overall development of local economies for providing the base for sustained increase in employment may compromise the primary objective of employment guarantee. In the absence of such plans, it is argued, wage employment programme must not be burdened with the responsibility for overall development and that its primary aim should be to take up works that give employment to the needy. To insist on generation of employment as the overriding aim is far too short-sighted. But the large magnitude of resources being spent on the programme can be put to greater effect for providing sustained increase in employment by using them for investments that would augment the production potential of local resources and provide easier access for the rural population to markets for their produce and opportunities for employment outside their villages. The focus should therefore be on strengthening the capacity for regional planning, identify activities that will augment production potential and improve the quality of project preparation and implementation.

Deeper Causes

Deficiencies in the programme arise in part from the way the programme is structured; in the distribution of resources, authority and responsibility between the centre and the states, between elected representative bodies at different levels and the bureaucracy; the manner in which its planning and implementation is organised; and the lack of effective mechanisms to ensure accountability.

That the programme is a significantly large source of central funds is a strong motive for states to participate in it. This does not however mean that they are committed to implement the spirit of the programme. Effective implementation depends on the priority that state governments attach and the effort they put into popularising the programme among the target groups and mobilising them to take advantage of the opportunities it offers, as well as gear the administration to implement it. Their calculations and priorities in this respect are shaped by local compulsions which can differ even when the same party is in power at the centre and the states. Differences are likely to be far greater when states are ruled by different political parties or coalitions with varying ideologies and/or support bases, and are engaged in competitive electoral politics to consolidate or acquire power. That the needed commitment and effort is highly uneven across states is evident in published data on the scale of expenditure and the number of beneficiaries. In fact, states in which the need for the programme is greatest (e.g., UP, Bihar) turn out to be the most laggard in this respect. This unevenness is probably even more pronounced at the district and lower levels but these data are not readily available.

Central plan allocations for the programme are put into a fund but releases every year are linked to the actual expenditure on ongoing projects and the projected budget of employment under the programme. The release of funds to the districts and lower levels is done by the states on the same basis. While this acts as a check on abuse, the mechanisms and procedures of NREGA cannot eliminate them. Committees comprising officials, elected representatives and non-officials to decide the kinds of works to be taken up, review performance and report to legislatures have not been set up or are not functional in several states. Elected local bodies are entitled to suggest projects to be taken up under the programme through consultations with communities and elected representatives in their respective domains. There are reasons to doubt whether these consultations and suggestions emerging from them are taken seriously in the choice of works.

Planning and management of employment programmes is done through line departments organised by sectors that operate independently of each other. There is no organisational locus with the mandate and expertise for integrated planning of regional and local development. Because of this, district and local plans prepared by the bureaucracy are merely collections of schemes with fragmented perspectives and unmindful of varying local conditions. This results in considerable overlap in content between wage employment, other poverty alleviation programmes and the core development programmes. The need for convergence between programmes to avoid wasteful duplication and enable available resources to be used to greater effect is recognised. But this rhetoric has not made much of a difference in the way schemes are selected and implemented at the ground level.

The centre monitors states' compliance with the programme guidelines, actual performance in terms of outlays and employment generated, and provisions for ensuring accountability mainly through periodic reports sent by the state governments. The centre does not attempt nor is it equipped to verify the accuracy of these data and publishes an annual report based on them. Concurrent evaluations based on surveys of selected districts, reports of the Comptroller and Auditor General and social audit reports highlight extensive violations of the guidelines. They all show large interstate variations in all these respects. Apart from bringing these deficiencies to the notice of states and exhorting them to take corrective action, the centre does not have any effective means to enforce compliance.

Political Factors

The political compulsions that led to the launching of NREGA were shared by all political parties. But many had several qualifications and reservations on its design and modalities of implementation. These reservations were not confined to opposition parties. There were considerable differences even within the UPA and with the Left parties at the national level and between the centre and states, irrespective of party affiliation. A major point of contention was the role of elected *panchayats* at the district and sub-district levels.

The idea of entrusting the responsibility for planning and managing local development works according to their specific needs and potential to democratically elected *panchayats* was mooted by the Balwantrai Mehta and Ashok Mehta committees appointed by the Central government in 1957 and 1977 respectively. One of the problems was that the local bodies in most states were not political in character but agencies that executed the programmes of the state government. Even after the Ashok Mehta committee reported, this situation altered for the better only in states with a commitment to decentralisation. The authority for financial sanctions and technical approvals was vested with the bureaucracy. This gave huge scope for decisions on what projects were taken up, where and who would be given contracts at the district and lower levels to be manipulated to the advantage of parties in power. Over the years, the system has been used as a convenient and highly effective means for ruling parties to sustain a system of distributing spoils to the acolytes and local functionaries of ruling parties.

Efforts made during the nineties to achieve effective decentralisation of governance through a constitutional amendment that gave formal recognition to *panchayats* and empower them to plan and implement local development schemes had already been frustrated by strong and determined opposition from the elected representatives in Parliament and state legislatures as also upper tier politicians across all parties and the bureaucracy. Constitutionally mandated elections to these bodies and reservations for Scheduled Castes and Tribes and women are a major step forward. But their structure, functions and role in developmental activity was not only restricted but also in many respects left to the discretion of the state governments. The role of Panchayati Raj Institutions (PRIs) in NREGA is also severely limited.

Under NREGA, elected local bodies have neither the authority nor the means to take the responsibility for local development planning. Their formal role in project selection and implementation is limited. The authority for all substantive decisions on design, scrutiny and approval of projects, modalities of implementation and release of funds are vested with the bureaucracy. However local Members of Legislative Assembly (MLAs) and Members of Parliament (MPs), representatives of elected local bodies and other local politicians can and do influence decisions on what projects are to be taken up, when, where and by whom. Elected bodies are required to ensure maintenance of proper records of applicants, works taken up, muster rolls and wage payments; make them available for public scrutiny and to review performance based on audit reports. But they are ill prepared and ill equipped to handle these tasks. Support staff, mostly provided by the state government, is inadequate and answerable to their parent departments rather than the elected bodies. Under these conditions, there is much scope for collaboration and collusion between influential members of the local political class and the local bureaucracy. By all accounts this tendency is widespread and is a major reason for the use of private contractors in violation of guidelines, for leakages and corruption, as well as the ineffectiveness of mechanisms for ensuring accountability

Based on experience with earlier centrally sponsored poverty alleviation programmes, the political classes in the states knew they could manipulate the way the programmes were designed and managed to serve their interests. The fact that such schemes had a significant component of subsidies and comprised a large number of spatially dispersed construction works, gave politicians in power and the bureaucracy who managed them, much discretion in deciding the content of the programmes and the modalities of their implementation. Multiplicity of schemes implemented through bureaucracies of parallel agencies made effective monitoring extremely difficult. Under these conditions, parties in power and their functionaries could have a significant role in choice of locations, size and content of schemes, selection of beneficiaries and award of contracts at all levels to the benefit of their parties and to their personal advantage.

Under these conditions, it is impossible to devise effective mechanisms for monitoring operations of numerous, diverse and far-flung projects of local level development, ensuring efficiency and effective public accountability. Local communities are best placed to assess the specific felt needs of their members, ways in which they can be met and balance the claims of different segments and resolve conflicts. But it is crucially important that tasks are handled by democratically elected representatives with periodic elections and appropriate local level organisations and procedures (transparency of operations, accounts and rigorous audit) to ensure their accountability to the community. Periodic elections are constitutionally mandated although there may be 'defaulters'. In all other respects observance of prescribed procedures leaves far more to be desired.

The NREGA design, regrettably, is based on the presumption—which is shared by a significant and influential segment of academics and activists—that *panchayats* do not have the experience or the expertise to manage these tasks and that they are prone to huge corruption. These presumptions are exaggerated and in any case it is possible to correct them. The more important argument is that, given the huge social and economic inequalities in villages and the fact that *panchayats* are controlled by upper castes and large landholders, they cannot be expected to function democratically and in ways that serve the interests of the poor and socially disadvantaged segments. Hence, the opposition to entrusting the responsibility for local level development generally and of NREGA in particular to elected *panchayats*.

The stereotype of elected representatives as illiterate and not competent to take active part in local development is quite outdated. For long the only role they could play was to bring local problems to the attention of government and try through lobbying or agitation to get these attended to. But with growing institutionalisation of *panchayat* elections, the pool of people exposed to developmental issues and the social base of elected leaders has greatly broadened. Even under the existing, severely constrained, Panchayati Raj (PR) regime, numerous elected *panchayats* have shown the willingness and the ability to decide on projects appropriate to local needs, mobilise local resources for such projects and to take the responsibility for implementing government sponsored projects. Works taken up by them have been found to be completed faster, better and cheaper than those of the government agencies. A significant and growing number are keen to get more actively involved in development but are frustrated at the limited role given to them. There is also resentment about the way upper tier politicians control developmental activity and use it in corrupt ways to serve their personal interests and maintain their dominance in their party machinery by severely limiting local level leaders' entry into higher tiers of state and national politics. Tensions between the local and upper tier politicians are palpable, widespread and growing. Its dimensions and significance as a potentially creative force that would open up wider space for development of political leadership is not sufficiently recognised.

Apprehensions about the upper castes-large landholders' dominance in *panchayats* and about their lack of interest and commitment to employment and poverty alleviation programmes cannot be dismissed lightly. Nor, however, should it be exaggerated. The social composition of elected representatives has broadened significantly to include underprivileged sections. The configurations of local power are changing, though not everywhere and to the desired extent. There is ample evidence that the underprivileged are increasingly assertive of their interests. Debates and contestation in local bodies over attempts to bias allocation of resources and projects in favour of the well-to-do, and over corruption will intensify, though not uniformly. But for this to happen, it is essential to empower elected local bodies to have greater control over these decisions and ensure that their staff are answerable to them.

Elected representatives need not themselves have the technical expertise in managing development projects. Such expertise in any case can always be acquired by hiring staff with the needed skills. Currently the state bureaucracy provides staff support to elected bodies at the district and block levels, but is not answerable to these bodies. Such support is not available to village *panchayats*, who do not have staff even to carry out their limited oversight functions. There are serious questions whether, given their background, structure and traditions, the state development bureaucracy has the knowledge and resilience needed to design and implement programmes adapted to varied local conditions. In any case, the problem is not merely one of having qualified staff but ensuring that they are answerable to the elected bodies at all levels. This is not only precluded under the programme guidelines but the conflation of authority for design, scrutiny, approval, financial sanctions and performance review with the bureaucracy makes effective accountability extremely difficult.

All said, democratically elected, representative *panchayats* are a far more effective means for containing (though not eliminating) corruption and ensuring accountability than is generally recognised. If decentralised planning and implementation leads even to a modest reduction in waste and leakage—from the current, and widely quoted 85 per cent to, say, 50-60 per cent—there will be a dramatic improvement in effectiveness in all aspects of the programme. As for corruption, misuse and misappropriation of public money by elected local leaders are far more visible to their community than those by outsiders. That they have to seek re-election periodically to continue in office is the strongest inducement to check, though not to eliminate, corruption in the choice and implementation of local programmes. Therefore, ensuring the regular conduct of *panchayat* elections and empowering the elected representatives with the authority and the resources to implement EGS, and indeed all local development works is critically important.

This may be too radical to be implemented everywhere and soon. A beginning could however be made by persuading at least some states to agree to let the NREGA be implemented entirely by elected *panchayats* in one or two selected districts for a period of five years with the support and assistance of non-governmental organisations (NGOs) and relevant technical expertise from within government or outside. This will give an opportunity to demonstrate that *panchayats* can and will take up works appropriate to local conditions and implement them better, faster and at lower cost. By doing so it would help allay misplaced apprehensions about the capacity of the *panchayats* and also to better understand the problems involved, thereby creating a climate for a full-fledged decentralisation of local development.

References

Dandekar, V.M. and N. Rath (1971). *Poverty in India*. Pune: Indian School of Political Economy.

Minhas, B.S. (1972). "Rural Poverty, Land Distribution and Development Strategy Policy", *Indian Economic Review*. Reprinted in Srinivasan and Bardhan (1974).

Perspective Planning Division (PPD), Planning Commission (1962). *Perspective of Development 1961-1976: Implications of Planning for a Minimum Level of Living*. Reproduced in Srinivasan and Bardhan (1974).

Raj, K.N. (1957). *Employment Aspects of Planning in Underdeveloped Economies*. Cairo: National Bank of Egypt.

Srinivasan, T.N. and Pranab Bardhan (eds.) (1974). *Poverty and Income Distribution in India*. Calcutta: Statistical Publishing House.

5 Private Sector in Education

Supplement to or Substitute for the State

The role of the private sector in India's education is currently a hotly debated issue. But for the most part it centres on higher level professional education. The recent explosive and unregulated expansion of private institutions in engineering, medical sciences and management has sharpened differences between those who support the trend on the ground that the public sector is not in a position to expand the capacity of its institutions to meet the rapid growth in the demand for qualified professionals in these and related fields and those who are concerned at the proliferation of profit motivated entrepreneurs, the lack of any regulation of admission criteria or fees, and its adverse impact on affordability and equitable access to professional education for the lower income classes and socially underprivileged segments of the population. But the process of privatisation in education is not confined to professional education; it is characteristic of all segments of the educational system. The causes and consequences of the process are of much wider significance than professional education and therefore need to be viewed in a much broader perspective. This is what I shall attempt to do.

Trends

Private sector involvement in education is not a new phenomenon. During the colonial era the government took but limited interest in education. Religious and philanthropic organisations played a significant and pioneering role in establishing modern educational institutions. The scale and reach of both segments was however very limited. The situation changed dramatically with the advent of independence.

Achieving universal elementary education and expansion of educational facilities at higher levels came to be accepted as the primary responsibility of the State and important among the central goals of public policy. This led to a massive expansion in the publicly funded school system both in terms of the number of institutions and student enrolment. Most of the expansion in school education was in institutions set up, funded and managed directly by the government and local bodies. At the same time the government also provided financial assistance to selected private institutions, especially in the high school and collegiate levels. Categorised as 'private-aided institutions', these had to observe government guidelines regarding the fees to be charged, appointment and remuneration of teachers, and curricula. Enrolments in this sector increased substantially. Recognised but unaided private institutions also seem to have grown in this period despite lack of any state support. But this segment in all likelihood must have played only a marginal role at that time.

Estimates of enrolment in different categories of schools compiled from school records by the All India Educational Surveys (AIES) (Table 5.1) suggest that the role of private sector had become significant by the late seventies and that the bulk of this enrolment was in aided schools and that unaided schools had only a marginal presence. Subsequent surveys showed that, while the share of private sector as a whole changed but marginally, the unaided sector, which was not subject to regulation in matters of admission and fees, gained rapidly at the expense of the aided segment. While the actual magnitudes of these changes as reported in the AIES may not be wholly reliable, the broad direction and patterns of change are corroborated by more comprehensive information on actual enrolment obtained through household surveys conducted by the National Sample Survey (NSS) in 1995-1996 and 2004-05 (Table 5.2).

This period has witnessed a significant increase in total enrolment at all levels, the pace of increase being highest (90%) in the general collegiate stream, followed by secondary school (50%) and then the elementary stage (35%). In all stages, enrolment in private institutions has increased in absolute terms more or less at the same rate as in the public system. The overall share of private institutions has therefore not changed much at any level. However, within the private sector, enrolment in unaided institutions has increased much faster than in aided institutions. Their share in total private sector enrolment has increased at all levels, dramatically so in the secondary and higher education (general stream) levels than at the

Table 5.1

Growth of Enrolment in Different Categories of Schools at Different Levels in India

Category of school	1978		1986		1993		2002	
	Number in million	Per cent	Number in million	Per cent	Number in million	Per cent	Number in million	Per cent
Primary								
Govt. & local body	57.9	85.0	71.3	83.0	78.8	80.9	93.4	76.0
Private aided	8.6	12.6	10.2	11.9	10.3	10.6	11.1	9.0
Private unaided	2.1	3.1	4.4	5.1	8.3	8.5	18.4	15.0
All	68.6	100.0	85.9	100.0	97.4	100.0	122.9	100.0
Middle								
Govt & local body	9.6	53.6	15.9	58.2	19.7	57.9	25.2	53.8
Private aided	7.4	41.3	9.1	33.3	10.5	30.9	13.0	27.8
Private unaided	0.9	5.0	2.3	8.4	3.8	11.2	8.6	18.4
All	17.9	100.0	27.3	100.0	34.0	100.0	46.8	100.0
Secondary								
Govt & local body	3.2	36.0	6.2	41.3	9.2	44.4	12.8	38.6
Private aided	5.4	60.7	7.9	52.7	9.6	46.4	13.7	41.3
Private unaided	0.3	3.3	0.9	6.0	1.9	9.2	6.7	20.1
All	8.9	100.0	15.0	100.0	20.7	100.0	33.2	100.0

Source: Enrolment as estimated by various *All India Education Surveys*. The figures are from Kingdon's 2007 paper available on the net.

Table 5.2

Estimated Number of Students Attending Educational Institutions, and Proportions Attending Private Schools at Different Levels, India, 1995-96 and 2004-05

	1995-96			2004-05		
	Total in million	% in private	Unaided as % of total private	Total in million	% in private	Unaided as % total private
Primary	85.2	22.5	55.1	116	24.6	70
Middle	38.6	29.7	29.3	53	29.4	50
Secondary/higher secondary	30.6	39.3	19.8	45.6	40.6	35
Higher total				15.3	47.9	40.2
General	6.5	42.5	16	11.1	44.8	33.3
Technical graduates+	na	na	na	1.71	54.3	49.5
Technical graduates -	na	na	na	2.48	57.2	58.6
All	161	28.3	36.7	230	30.5	53.4

Sources: 1995-96 NSSO Report No. 439—Attending an educational Institution In India: Its level, nature and cost 2004-05 NSSO Report No. 517—Status of Education and Vocational Training in India 2004-05.

elementary stage. A similar pattern is observed in both rural and urban areas, the tendency being more marked in rural areas in the elementary stage and at the secondary and higher stages in urban areas (Table 5.3).

Table 5.3

Students Attending Private Schools as Percentage of Total Attending Different Stages of Education in Rural and Urban India 1995-96 and 2004-05

	1995- 96				*2004-05*			
	Rural Total Pvt. as % of Total Pvt.	*Pvt. unaided*	*Urban Total Pvt. as % of Total Pvt.*	*Pvt. unaided*	*Rural Total Pvt. as % of Total Pvt.*	*Pvt. unaided*	*Urban Total Pvt. as % of Total Pvt.*	*Pvt. unaided*
Primary	13.8	58.7	50.5	51.9	17.0	71.2	52.7	70.0
Middle	21.1	27.5	48.9	51.5	22.1	48.4	50.1	52.9
Secondary/ higher secondary	32.6	17.5	50.0	22.2	43.6	24.1	54.2	40.0
Higher total					46.1	43.0	50.1	38.9
General	38.7	17.3	44.7	15.2	42.6	30.8	54.9	31.9
Technical graduates+					55.0	59.6	56.2	48.9
Technical graduates-					57.1	59.0	57.8	57.4
All	19.2	37.0	49.6	36.7	22.3	52.9	52.1	54.5

Source: Same as in Table 5.2.

Current Position

By 2004-05 an estimated 220 million persons, or roughly half the population between the ages of 5 and 29, were attending educational institutions in the country. Nearly 70 per cent of them were attending educational institutions run by government and local bodies, and 30 per cent private institutions. Private institutions accounted for a fourth of the total enrolment in primary schools; this proportion increases progressively thereafter to 29 per cent in middle schools, 40 per cent in high schools and 48 per cent in higher education (which covers all post-secondary stage education).

Within the Private Sector

- Unaided institutions play a larger role in the primary and middle stages than aided institutions.
- The majority of students attending private high schools and higher educational institutions are in aided institutions.
- Within the higher education sector, private unaided colleges account for somewhat less than half of the students in private institutions in the arts, science and commerce segment, but for over 55 per cent in the technical/professional segment.

There are significant differences in these respects between rural and urban areas.

- The proportion of children and youth attending educational institutions in rural areas is much lower than in urban areas.
- The proportion of students attending private institutions in rural areas is much lower than in urban areas, both in the aggregate and in all stages of education.
- The difference in this respect is largest in the primary stages and declines at higher stages.
- Unaided institutions account for a much larger proportion of enrolment in primary and higher education in rural areas.

The role of the private providers of education is however much larger than the above estimates of enrolment suggest. The NSS elicits information on those "...attending any government or private educational institution including those registered for any regular correspondence or distance education course for a stipulated period at the end of which the person would be allowed to appear for examination for that course." There is reason to doubt whether and to what extent they capture students enrolled in open universities and distance learning courses (whose number, according to the Ministry of Human Resource Development (HRD) website, is over 3.3 million).

But more importantly they do not cover part time students in unrecognised private institutions that offer training in a variety of vocations and intensive coaching for competitive examinations as well as those taking private tuitions. The number of candidates appearing for entrance examinations for IITs, IIMs and civil service examinations conducted by Union Public Service Commission (UPSC) alone exceeds 1.2 million. Several times that number takes entrance examinations for other courses; for jobs in state government and public undertakings the number is several times larger. Coaching for these is a huge and thriving industry.

In 1995-96, household expenditure on tuitions in the country was nearly half the amount spent on tuition and other fees paid to educational institutions. (NSS report No:439). A subsequent sample survey conducted by the NSS in 2001-02 estimates that there were some 4.2 million persons engaged in own account enterprises and establishments in the unorganised sector providing educational services, and estimates their annual gross earnings at over Rs 13,000 crore (NSS Report No. 483).

Private Expenditure on Education

Another relevant indicator is the level of private expenditure on education. The NSS education survey of 1995-96 estimates private expenditure on education at Rs 14,000-15,000 crore; its latest household consumption survey estimates the expenditure in 2004-05 at Rs 29,000-39,000 crore. But sample surveys of households are known to have difficulties in getting the top 10-20 per cent households (which account for the bulk of enrolment in higher education) to respond fully and provide accurate information on expenditures on various items of consumption. It is believed that response biases in this class are sizeable. Estimates are sensitive to reference periods.

Moreover, the last decade has been a period of rapid expansion in higher education generally and technical and professional education in particular; this has also been the period of accelerated growth in private institutions providing professional education and in the fees that they charge. Estimates of total private expenditure on education (covering fees and costs other than fees) in 2004-05, based on official enrolment data is rather patchy—information on the distribution of enrolment between public and private institutions and the fees charged by them are much higher at Rs 60,000 crore per year than the estimates from household consumption surveys (Table 5.4). On the basis of NSS estimates of attendance in higher

Table 5.4

Estimate of Private Expenditure on Education based on Official Enrolment Figures and Annual Fees per Student, 2003-04

	Enrolment			Unit Cost		Total		
	Total	Govt. & Private Aided	Private Un-aided	Govt. & Private Aided	Private Un-aided	Govt. & Private Aided	Private Un-aided	All
	Million	Million	Million	Rs Pa	Rs Pa	Rs Mill	Rs Mill	Rs Mill
Schools[1]								
Primary	115							87600
Middle	54							73400
Secondary/higher secondary	46							111000
Higher education[2]								
BA	3.825	3.44	0.038	4000	6000	13770	228	13998
BSc	1.614	1.45	0.016	4000	7000	5800	112	5912
BCom	1.613	1.452	0.161	4000	10000	5808	1610	7418
MA	0.427	0.385	0.042	8000	10000	3080	420	3500
MSc	0.237	0.213	0.024	8000	15000	1704	360	2064
MCom	0.141	0.127	0.014	8000	12000	1016	168	1184
PhD	0.065	0.059	0.006	8000	6000	472	36	508
Engineering/ technology	0.772	0.154	0.618	10,000	50000	1540	30900	32440
Medical	0.223	.089	0.134	20000	150000	1780	20100	21880
Others	1.09	0.505	0.505	50000	100000	25250	50500	75750
Total	10.007					60220	104434	164654
Other costs 1.5 times the fees[3]						90330	156651	246981
Fees + Other costs						150550	261085	411635
Indians studying abroad	0.12			50000[4]				60000
Competitive entrance test (CET) coaching etc.[4]	1+							30000
Total education								610000

Notes: 1. Estimate for schools based on NSS estimate of total enrolment at each stage in 2004-05, its distribution between different categories of schools and the average cost per student based on NSS estimates of cost per student in 1995-96 adjusted for subsequent inflation.

2. In the case of higher education enrolment in different categories are based on official statistics published by Ministry of HRD. Distribution between government institutions and private institutions are guesstimates. It is assumed that 90 per cent of enrolment in all non-technical courses, 80 per cent in engineering, 40 per cent in medicine and about half in all other technical courses are in private institutions.

   Assumptions of tuition fees are based on the government notifications regarding the fees that different categories of institutions are allowed to charge. This information is available for several states and indicates ranges that are quite wide, especially in the case of technical and professional education. The estimates have to be taken as very rough approximations.

3. The ratio of other costs to fees (which includes tuition and other fees) is an assumption based on NSS estimates for 1995-2006 (NSS report No. 439) when the non-fees expenditure to fees (of all kinds) in higher education was 1.8 in rural areas and 1.2 in urban areas

4. Cost per student studying abroad assumed at around $10,000 per year. No. of students from CET coaching estimate taken from an article in the web.

education, which are much higher than official figures (Table 5.5), the estimated expenditure is even higher at Rs 96,000 crore. Though these estimates are based on inadequate data and gross assumptions—and these obviously call for close scrutiny—they do strongly suggest that private expenditure on education is much higher and growing much faster than suggested by estimates of the national income accounts and those based on household surveys.

Table 5.5

Comparison of Official and NSS Estimates of Enrolments in Higher Education

(Thousands)

	Official		*NSS*	
	1995-96	*2003-04*	*1995-2006*	*2004-05*
Arts	3160	4252		
Science	1220	1851		
Commerce	1120	1756		
	5500	7859	6526	11100
Engineering/Architecture	390	773		
Medicine	190	223		
Education	100	115		
Others	380	974		
	1060	2085	na	4178
All	6560	9940	na	15278

Source: Official figures from UGC website and NSS estimates from Reports 439 ad 517.

What Encourages Privatisation?

School Education

The Constitution mandates universal elementary education as a major objective of state policy. The State is formally committed to establish a public school network to achieve universal coverage of children in the 5-14 age group. While this is yet to be achieved, private schools have entered the field and are expanding rapidly. Somewhat surprisingly this trend is much more pronounced in the primary stage, both in rural and urban areas. Several factors have contributed: poor and deteriorating functioning of public schools; reluctance of upper castes to send their children to study along with children of lower castes especially scheduled castes and tribes; and the desire of parents with higher ambitions for their children to get better education often equated with English medium education. The first and the last factor are much more pronounced in urban areas but are significant in rural areas as well.

The tendency for privatisation becomes more pronounced in the high school stage. Performance in the school leaving public examinations is an important factor determining access to higher education and the courses that students can choose. Admission to professional courses requires high standards in science and mathematics and knowledge of English. The medium of instruction, quality of teaching, and laboratory and library facilities in high schools are seen to have a significant bearing on performance in public examinations and also in entrance tests, both of which are extensively used to decide on admissions to professional courses.

The quality of public schools varies. There are government schools—like the Central schools and Navodaya schools—which are well equipped and staffed but these account for a relatively small segment of the public system. For the most part government high schools suffer from much the same problems as government elementary schools—namely, poor physical infrastructure, severe shortage of resources for teaching aids, laboratory equipment and libraries, and indifferent quality of teaching compounded by lack of good quality textbooks in mother tongues. These are the mainstay of students from lower socioeconomic strata, both in rural and urban areas. The proportion of students from these strata, that enter high school after completing the elementary stage is much smaller than from the better-off sections of the population. And a large proportion—perhaps the large majority—of those who manage to get into high school cannot afford private schools and have to study in the government schools. Children of this segment thus suffer from a double disadvantage of low access to high school education and getting education of lower quality.

Private schools have an edge in all these respects. Though far more expensive, the demand for them has grown rapidly with the expansion of employment, especially in lucrative professional jobs.

Private aided schools, run by charitable trusts and missionaries, have long had a significant presence in high school (and collegiate) education. A sizeable part of their costs is met by government grants subject to restrictions on the fees they can charge. Increases in government grants for private aided schools were inadequate for them to cater to the growing demand. Their ability to raise resources for expansion by increasing fees was also severely limited. Many of them could and did get around the restrictions by collecting donations and various special charges to meet rising costs. Enrolment in this category of schools also increased but could meet only a part of the growing demand. This left the field wide open for the entry of private entrepreneurs to set up schools without any government grants.

They could mobilise resources to invest in providing much better facilities than the rest of the school system. They availed themselves of the opportunity of acquiring land at low cost and tax concessions. There were no restrictions on the fees they could charge. The burgeoning demand for, and the willingness to pay for perceived quality, gave them ample room to levy high fees and make profits. Profitability of investment in this category of schools was surely a major impetus for expansion of supply!

Rural-urban differences both in overall access and the importance of private sector for high school education remain significant. Compared to urban areas, the proportion of children and youth attending high/higher secondary school is much smaller in rural areas. The proportion of rural children going to private schools, especially private unaided schools, as well as the fees they have to pay in these schools are lower than in urban areas. The cost incurred per rural student at school level (overall and in terms of fees) is therefore considerably less.

An interesting feature is that a sizeable proportion of students in rural and urban areas report taking coaching classes and substantial amounts are spent for this purpose at all stages. This perhaps reflects an attempt to correct for deficiencies in quality of teaching in the elementary stage and a measure of the extra effort considered necessary to perform well in school leaving examinations and increase the chances of securing admission to preferred higher education courses. This phenomenon is much more widespread in urban areas.

Higher Education

The forces driving privatisation of higher education as well as its features are broadly similar to those operating in the school segment. Higher education comprises two distinct streams: the general and the professional. The former, consisting of undergraduate and postgraduate degree courses in humanities and in social, physical and natural sciences, accounts for the larger part of higher education in colleges. In the early phase of the post-Independence era, graduates in these categories were absorbed in a variety of white collar jobs in government service and the private sector, as teachers in schools and colleges and as self-employed professionals. A small fraction obtained higher level managerial positions in government and private sectors.

Opportunities of employment for graduates of the above categories grew fairly rapidly in the initial phase of the post-Independence period when the public sector was expanding. But growth in this source of demand for general graduates decreased with the slowdown in public sector expansion. Private sector demand continued to grow albeit at a slow pace relative to the growth in the number of graduates. Declining standards of collegiate education aggravated this imbalance and contributed to relatively high levels of unemployment and attendant frustrations among educated youth.

As the economy has grown and diversified, the requirements for persons with specialised professional education in engineering, technology, medicine and management increased rapidly. Initially many, in fact most, of the institutions for training such personnel were set up by the government. But over the years, and especially in the last two decades, as the process of growth and diversification accelerated, both the magnitude and the range of requirements for professionals have also undergone a sea change. The pace quickened in the wake of internal and external liberalisation of the economy since the early nineties and the explosive growth of the IT and related sectors, financial services as well as opportunities for employment abroad. This process also led to an unprecedented increase in both job opportunities and salaries for professionals as well as for the better performing graduates from the general stream.

The resulting surge of demand for trained professionals could not be met by the public system which had neither the resources nor the capacity and flexibility to provide the kind of quality training that was in demand. Government increased the number of professional colleges/universities in engineering/medicine/management and also the intake. But these have proved insufficient to meet the growing demand for education at all levels both in quantity and quality.

Public expenditure on higher education has no doubt increased manifold. Much of it however has gone to meet increased salaries of teachers and other staff and of the education bureaucracy. The remaining funds have been inadequate even for proper maintenance of existing facilities, not to speak of their expansion and improvement by increasing the number of qualified teachers, libraries, laboratories and other physical facilities in step with increasing enrolment and for new and specialised courses. Selected publicly funded colleges/universities have been allowed greater autonomy to adjust intake in conventional courses in arts, science and commerce and start courses in new subjects that are in demand in the market and have also been freed of restrictions on admission criteria and fees. But far too little has been done to improve the curricula, course content and pedagogy of the mainstream courses.

These constraints have been aggravated by deterioration in the quality of public institutions responsible for managing and regulating the higher educational system. The principal regulatory authorities of higher education—the University Grants Commission (UGC), the All India Council for Technical Education (AICTE), professional associations, the National Assessment and Accreditation Council (NAAC) and the National Board of Accreditation (NBA)—have not been able to ensure compliance with the norms they have set regarding the governance of universities and colleges, their autonomous functioning, the minimum standards (physical infrastructure, staff, admissions and evaluation of student performance) for recognition and sanctions of intake capacity. The standards they seek to enforce run the risk of being at variance with the obligations cast upon the universities by state governments, which in turn are sometimes the result of political interference and sometimes the consequence of the need to promote social justice through positive discrimination and other similar policies. The less desirable dimensions are the powers that state governments give themselves in respect of appointment of vice chancellors and the composition of governing bodies of universities. In addition, there is the near complete dependence of state level universities on the government for finance and inadequate autonomy relating to expenditure. There is a distressing trend towards 'politicisation' of higher education, which erodes university autonomy. A major adverse repercussion is that intellectual inquiry gets stifled.

Teachers' trade unions have shown little interest in these matters. Their main focus has been to press demands for higher pay and better service conditions. That a sizeable and increasing section of teachers are more interested in giving private tuitions than teaching regular classes is now common knowledge but not mentioned or protested against in public forums. No government has shown either the willingness or the ability to take corrective measures to arrest these trends.

The problem is exacerbated by the fragmentation of academic communities by class, caste and religion, reluctance of teachers to reform themselves and the systematic resistance from the political classes to loosen their control over crucial aspects of management of educational institutions. The social and political pressure for reform of the public system has become weaker and weaker as more and more of the rich and the burgeoning middle classes switch to private schools, which are perceived to be better equipped and better run. That they also teach in the English medium is an added attraction to parents with high ambitions for their children.

As the involvement of the elite in the public system declines, so does their interest in reforming it. They are far more interested in influencing government policy to expand higher and professional education facilities and on conditions of access to such education. They are strong supporters of allowing the private sector to fill the gap between demand and the capacity of the public sector to meet it. This pressure for privatisation is strongest in the sphere of professional education, especially in courses that have opened rapidly increasing opportunities for lucrative jobs. An added reason is that intake in highly subsidised public institutions is far less than the overall demand and therefore intensively competitive. Moreover, being subject to quota restrictions, large sections of aspirants with the means and/or the ability, who cannot make it to the public system, are for allowing private institutions to enter the field and are willing to pay the much higher fees charged by them.

Besides allowing existing unaided institutions to expand, a new class of educational entrepreneurs (mostly from the political class or those with strong political connections with little or no experience in education and motivated mainly by the prospects of private profits), have entered the field in a big way. They were able to get governments to permit, aid and abet their growth. But this was done by executive action without any serious public deliberation of the role of the private sector in education in Parliament or the legislatures. There is no clear and explicit statement of state policy in the matter. Surprisingly there is not even a reference to the private sector and its growing role in the educational system in any of the five year plans or in the national educational policy.

Governments have been proactive in allowing and facilitating the setting up of new private unaided colleges and expanding intake in existing ones. As the demand for professionals with specialised training in such fields as computers, IT, finance, tourism and hotel management increased, existing recognised private institutions in these fields (like NIIT and Aptech) expanded rapidly and many new ones were established. Some of the new institutions—of which Amity and ICFAI are notable examples—have grown huge in terms of the number of campuses they have, enrolment and the range of courses offered. Many of the private institutions have now been recognised as deemed universities. More and more foreign universities are showing interest in investing in higher education in the country. There is in fact a strong lobby favouring liberalisation in this sector.

The rapid growth of unaided private institutions has been facilitated not merely by a liberal policy in permitting them to be set up and granting recognition, but by active state help in acquisition of land, granting them the status of not-for-profit institutions and tax advantages that go with that status; and allowing them to charge very high fees. Land grants and acquisitions are the prerogative of state governments. Hardly any information is available in the public domain about the extent of land acquired/given to unaided institutions or the terms of such acquisition/grants. But it is widely known—several concrete instances are reported in the media from time to time—that the private institutions obtain extensive areas of land on highly favourable terms. Most of these institutions have been set up by persons belonging to the political class and those with close connections to influential members of that class. Political patronage and corruption are believed to be widespread in these deals.

Recognition, approval for starting courses and intake capacity are decided by the UGC in the case of arts/science colleges and deemed universities, and by statutory bodies (like AICTE, Medical Council of India (MCI), Nursing Council, Pharmacy Council) in the case of professional colleges. However, as urged earlier, these bodies are not fully effective in the discharge of their primary regulatory functions.

The fees charged by private unaided institutions for admission and annual tuition are notorious for being exorbitant, if not extortionate. The fees are supposed to cover costs whose scope and content are spelt out in guidelines set out by the regulatory body concerned. Capitation fees are not permitted. In the absence of an independent institutional mechanism, these institutions are left free to charge what they like. It was only after the Supreme Court's judgment in the Unnikrishnan case that states set up quasi-judicial committees to recommend fee structures after scrutinising the audited accounts of individual institutions. Their reports however do not give details of the data submitted by the institutions or comment on what modifications were made in arriving at their recommendations and the wide range of variation in rates suggested by them.

Admission procedures and criteria to be followed by private institutions is another contentious issue. These institutions want to conduct their own entrance examinations to decide on admissions, seek a substantial proportion of admissions to be left to the management to decide; and of course not be subject to quotas for SC/ST/OBCs. The courts seem to have upheld the right of private institutions to hold their own entrance tests despite doubts about whether they will be as transparent and strict as the tests conducted by government.

Consequences and Impact

The expansion of educational facilities has of course widened access to education across regions and socioeconomic segments. The class and caste composition of students in attending public institutions at all stages has undoubtedly widened. Disparities in overall attendance between males and females, rural and urban areas, and the poorest and richest quintiles of the population have narrowed. Attendance in high school and higher education institutions has increased in both absolute terms and as a proportion of the relevant age groups, faster in rural than in urban areas. But disparities in all these aspects remain large.

Thus in 2004-05, a little over 45 per cent of rural youth (5-29 years) reported attending educational institutions compared to 53 per cent among urban youth. Only 8 per cent of rural youth report attending high school compared to 12.4 per cent in urban areas. The disparity in access to higher education is much greater with only 1.4 per cent of rural youth in this category compared to 5 per cent in urban areas. These figures also highlight rural-urban differences in elementary and higher education in rural India.

Per capita educational expenditure of urban households is about three and a half times that of rural households in absolute terms and about three-fourths higher as a proportion of their total consumption expenditure. Disparities in all these dimensions between the poor and the well-to-do are much wider. In rural areas, the top 20 per cent of households spend about 4.8 times what the bottom 20 per cent do in absolute terms and about three times as a proportion of their total consumption expenditure. The disparities between the top and the bottom quintiles of the urban households is even greater: six times in absolute expenditure and about three and a quarter times as a proportion of total expenditure (see table 5.6).

Table 5.6

Inequality in Access to and Private Expenditure on Education Rural and Urban India, 2004-05

All Persons		*Rural*	*Urban*
	1. Monthly per capita expenditure (mpce) total Rs/30days	559	1105
	2. mpce education Rs 30 days	14.9	53
	3 Education/Total percentage	2.67	4.80
	4. % of 5-29 attending education institutions	45.5	53
	5 % of 4 in high schools	17.3	23.4
	6. % of 4 in higher education	3.1	9.4
Bottom 20%			
	1. mpce total Rs/30days	219.00	394.00
	2. mpce education Rs/30days	3.04	7.98
	3 Education/total percentage	1.39	2.02
	4. % of 5-29 attending education institutions	45	46
Top 20%			
	1. mpce total Rs/30days	1044	2394
	2. mpce education Rs/30days	42.14	155
	3 Education/total percentage	4.04	6.47
	4. % of 5-29 attending education institutions	54	62

Source: Estimated from NSSO Report 508—Level and Pattern of Consumption Expenditure 2004-05.

Being more expensive, only the better-off and more influential segments can afford private schools. Those with relatively high incomes send a much larger proportion of their youth to better equipped English medium private schools, which groom students to do well in CET for higher education. Urban households send a larger proportion of their children to private schools than their rural counterparts and also spend much more on special private coaching for various entrance tests. But intra-urban and intra-rural disparity in this respect is almost certainly much greater.

Cumulatively these differences show that the rural population and the poorer and socially less privileged segments of society are at a great disadvantage compared to their urban counterparts and the richer segments in accessing higher education and the growing opportunities for skilled and professional job opportunities that require such education. These disadvantages are mitigated by reserved quotas for SC, ST and OBCs in admissions to government institutions of higher learning, but only to some extent. There is a valid apprehension that the benefits of reservation as it presently operates go mostly to the emerging middle and upper income classes in these groups. However, since it is the groups that are ready to absorb the opportunity offered that do so, too much should perhaps not be read into this, although steps are required to keep it in check.

The higher educational system is increasingly becoming job-oriented. Training to equip youth in knowledge and professional skills needed to secure employment is no doubt important. But the educational system is also meant to enable youth to acquire a broad based background and knowledge of liberal arts, humanities as well as basic and social sciences and to give intensive and specialised courses in these fields to interested students. Universities have an equally important role to serve as centres of learning, scholarly research and vibrant intellectual activity and to produce teachers for higher educational institutions. As the educational system becomes increasingly commercialised its ability to perform this role is set to diminish at an alarming pace.

Concerns about the quality of education in both public and private sectors at all levels persist. There are of course some institutions in both sectors, which have achieved and maintained standards that have earned a high rating in national and international job markets. But worrisome is the decline of universities as centres of learning and scholarship due to the commercialisation of higher education and its inability to attract and retain high quality faculty with a commitment to teaching and research. This is evident in the marked decline in the number and quality of students interested in pursuing research and academic careers in the country and their increasing preference to go abroad for further studies or for jobs.

The importance of highly specialised courses is increasing in response to the demand for professionals with specialised skills in the rapidly growing traditional and more importantly in the new 'sunrise' sectors. Specialisation is essential in a modern economy, but so are courses that impart knowledge and skills of broader scope and perspective. The declining interest in, and quality of, the latter is a matter of concern.

There are also indications of growing disjunction between the areas in which students are trained and the jobs that they do. Thus the software sector hires engineers from all branches at salaries much higher than in other sectors, notably manufacturing, where their specialised training is required. Another example is that of management professionals concentrating on finance and marketing rather than production. The extent of such mismatches or their impact is not known but needs close watch.

The Way Forward

Current debates on educational reform are far too preoccupied with higher education especially professional education, the role of private sector and caste based quotas in admissions to higher education. Several protagonists, including the Knowledge Commission, emphasise the need for a huge quantitative expansion and institutional reforms in higher education to improve its performance. Opinions on reservations are sharply divided. The issue has triggered heated debates, polarised the polity and has led to violent protests for and against. The quality of education, privatisation and ensuring equitable access to education are important issues that are germane to the entire education system and not just higher education. They therefore need to be considered in a much broader perspective.

Public policy must serve two basic objectives: (1) expand the coverage and improve the quality of educational facilities; and (2) promote greater equality of access to educational opportunities at all levels to different segments of the population and especially to those who are socially and economically disadvantaged. Reconciling these two objectives in a context where the public system is in disrepair, the State is short of funds and an unregulated private sector is mushrooming adds up to a formidable challenge.

Universal access to good quality elementary and secondary education is socially desirable in itself in modern societies: people need to be educated in order to function in a complex economy; enabled to participate in politics and civic society activities; and for nurturing innate talents and abilities of children of all classes and giving opportunity for them to flower. It is also an essential precondition for achieving a level playing field to all segments in accessing higher education, which necessarily has to be selective.

We Need to Start at the Base: The Schools

As in most democracies in the world, a uniform public school system for elementary and high school education based on the neighbourhood principle and managed by local communities would be ideal. But this may be unrealistic in our current context given the state's resource limitations and the fact that a differentiated public system and a large private sector have been allowed to establish themselves. The focus has to be on redressing the deficiencies of the public system in terms of coverage and quality, and better regulation of private schools.

Improvement in the public school system calls for a three-pronged strategy to raise more resources, enable and encourage communities to play a larger role and take greater responsibility and make teachers accountable for their performance.

Larger government funding is necessary, but given the severe constraints on governments' resources, emphasis should be on more effective use of resources by rationalising the design and delivery of schemes for free tuition, scholarships and subsidised supply of books, uniforms and transport to make sure that they reach the really needy; and to raise the fees for the better off.

Community stake and responsibility in better management of schools needs to be increased by encouraging them to supplement government grants through donations and contributions in cash or kind; creating mechanisms for community monitoring of various aspects of public school functioning along with a mechanism for liaison with government to redress deficiencies, especially those relating to regularity of attendance and teaching; allowing communities to invest in improving their physical facilities and extra-curricular activities; and to hire their own teachers at least in elementary schools to meet shortages from inadequacy relative to needs.

Improvement in teachers' performance in public schools calls for much greater transparency in appointments and transfers; giving greater weight to qualifications and aptitude as against caste and community in selections, while not ignoring the claims of social justice; and improving the quality of teacher training. Teachers in public schools should be freed from responsibilities for duties unrelated to school teaching and school activities even as observance of norms relating to the latter are strictly enforced. Proactive engagement with teachers' unions is essential to address the problem of non-conduct and irregular conduct of teaching; to evolve and enforce codes regarding private tuitions. The system of periodic inspection of schools, which has become lax and ineffective needs to be revived. Devising a system for rating schools based on their performance in annual public examinations and making the publication of ratings mandatory is desirable to generate an atmosphere of healthy competition for quality improvement.

The role of private schools needs to be reviewed. The runaway expansion of this sector has been facilitated by state support and encouragement through numerous but hidden subventions, leaving them near-total freedom in matters of admissions and fees, and calculated laxity in imposing and enforcing conditions of state support. This has led to a growing differentiation even within the public educational system and more glaringly between institutions serving the rural and urban areas, and those serving the rich and the poor. In every respect this process has worked to the disadvantage of rural areas and the poor, thereby aggravating their disadvantages in terms of access to and performance in all levels of education.

While realistically we have to be reconciled to continued expansion of private schools, building a strong and good public school system must be recognised and accepted as the principal claim on the state's resources and support, and its primary responsibility in education. The state can contain their growth and check undesirable features in their functioning by drastically cutting down its direct and indirect support to them (especially in the form of land allocation on a liberal scale, gratis or at highly subsidised rates), stricter scrutiny of their not-for-profit status, subjecting the fees they can charge to independent regulatory review; and devising ways in which class composition of admissions can be made more broad based.

Regrettably the systemic issues relating to school education and the importance of reforms to address them have received far too little attention, both in and out of government. Efforts to mobilise public opinion to exert pressures for reform have been very anaemic. This is in sharp contrast to the current attention given to higher education. The deficiencies in higher education and remedial strategies have been extensively discussed and debated by the Knowledge Commission as well as several scholars.[1] The World Bank too has produced a special report on the subject.

All of them stress the need for a rapid quantitative expansion of higher education and measures to improve quality. The Knowledge Commission for instance suggests that, by 2015 the number of universities should be increased from the present 300 to 1500, gross enrolment rate in higher education from 9 per cent to 15 per cent and public funding for this sector from the present 1.5 per cent of GDP to 6 per cent. All speak of the need for relaxation of direct involvement of government in the functioning of higher educational institutions; substantial increase in the proportion of total costs of public institutions met out of student fees; greater autonomy for these institutions both in academic matters, tapping non-government sources of funding and in the use of funds; and measures to improve quality.

There are however strong differences about the role of the private sector in expanding higher education. There is an influential lobby advocating allowing the private sector to expand and even encouraging foreign universities to enter into collaborations with indigenous institutions or set up their own campuses. Those opposed to privatisation—and this opposition is widespread among the public—are against commercialised education motivated by profit, and draw attention to the fact that the high cost of education in private institutions has already resulted in accentuating inequalities in access to higher education between the largely urban socioeconomic elite and the vast majority of the rest of the population. In

1. Kapur and Mehta (2004); National Knowledge Commission (2006).

order to correct this tendency, public policy should be focussed on expansion and improvement of the public universities and colleges. The extent to which this can be done however depends on the ability of the government to increase financial allocations for higher education and to carry out radical reforms in the structure and functioning of the public system for improving its quality.

Finance is, and will remain, a major constraint for the public sector. Governments have been struggling to contain and reduce fiscal deficits. A good part of the growth in tax and non-tax revenues and borrowings will go to meet growing non-development expenditures and maintain developmental facilities (including education). The volume of resources available for new investment for expansion and improvement will no doubt increase. But so will the claims of numerous development activities in the public sector. There are reasons to doubt whether the overall allocations for education can be increased to the extent needed to achieve the constitutional directive of universal elementary education and expansion and improvement of the public school system (in the face of continuing rise in costs) and still be able to increase allocations for higher education of the magnitude envisaged by the Knowledge Commission. There are serious limits to the extent to which *inter se* allocations for different levels of education can be changed in favour of higher education.

Recognition of these constraints is the rationale for suggestions that public educational institutions at all levels should be permitted to tap extra budgetary sources (community contributions, donations from alumni, charitable trusts/foundations and corporates) and for increasing the contribution of tuition fees to cover at least 20 per cent of the recurring costs in higher education. These measures, together with greater freedom and flexibility for institutions in the management of their finances, are necessary to ease the financial constraint. The potential for attracting donations from alumni is believed to be large, provided they are allowed to be given directly to institutions of the donors' choice without having to be routed through or being subject to conditions imposed by the government. While there is considerable optimism about the scope for mobilising funds from non-governmental sources, it is necessary to ensure transparency and regulations to avoid backdoor private control.

Improvement in the quality of education in public universities and colleges requires major changes in law to reduce drastically the scope for political and bureaucratic interference in their governance, in academic matters as well as financial management. Monitoring and assessment of functioning based on clearly defined norms must be vested with independent regulatory bodies and made transparent. The academic environment cannot be improved without radical changes in the processes of appointments and promotion of teachers and introduction of transparent mechanisms for accountability of performance. Under the present regime—marked by strong union pressures, mandatory caste quotas and politicisation of appointments, promotions and transfers—it is difficult to ensure that those with the aptitude, interest and competence to be good teachers are chosen. Teaching is indifferent and often classes are not held; automatic promotions have created a perverse incentive structure, which does not even penalise delinquent teachers let alone reward the conscientious and able ones. Both the teaching community in public institutions and the political class are strongly opposed to any change in this regime.

At the same time it needs to be appreciated that a large proportion of students in high schools, and even colleges, come from relatively poor classes with little or no home support or help in learning. They deserve the best teachers available to stimulate their interest in learning and give them good quality education. Teachers and their unions, as well as the political class, have to be made to understand the long-term societal implications of continuing 'business as usual' and getting them to recognise and cooperate in introducing needed reforms.

Under these circumstances the public sector may not be able to meet the growing demand for educated professionals, both quantitatively and in terms of quality. The pressure for expansion of the private sector will therefore continue to be strong.

Private aided institutions, run by charitable trusts and missionaries, have long had a significant presence in both school and collegiate education. They are required to observe regulations laid down by the government. Of late however selected institutions in this category as well as government institutions have been given greater freedom in academic matters, starting self-financing courses and on admissions and fees charged for such courses.

This autonomy deserves to be expanded to give them, as well as other government funded institutions, scope and encouragement for innovation in curricula, teaching and assessment procedures.

The pressures for allowing wholly private institutions to grow will also increase. There is need for clearer enunciation of public policy on the spheres where they will be permitted, the conditions that they must fulfill and the norms for recognition and accreditation, admission policies, and fees. As noted earlier, though some of these elements and regulatory mechanisms to enforce them are formally in place even now, they are ineffective in checking gross abuse because of their pervasive politicisation and corruption. Correction of these deficiencies is imperative. On the whole there is need for proper regulation of the working of the private sector in education.

The penchant for unrestricted entry of foreign private investment and universities is neither desirable nor necessary. A review of international experience of this aspect shows that a majority of the leading developing countries such as China, and also Japan have either disallowed them or insisted on their entry only in collaboration with indigenous colleges and universities and being subject to all the regulations applicable to local institutions.

There is near unanimity in recent assessments of the higher education scene, with widely different views on the role of the private sector, about the crucial importance and the imperative need to make the regulatory system effective. This calls for strengthening accreditation and assessment agencies for higher education by introducing a transparent process of selecting personnel, who command credibility for their professional competence and objectivity. They must be free to decide and enforce their decisions in all matters entrusted to them without any government and political interference. It would be necessary to lay down clear norms regarding the constitution and role of governance bodies and put in place effective mechanisms to ensure that the academic management of autonomous institutions is not controlled by a close group of non-academics; that its functioning is transparent and accountable, both for academic performance and financial matters; that there is full disclosure of its academic activities and financial accounts; and that these are subject to strict periodical scrutiny to verify their 'not-for-profit' status and that they are not making profits for the promoters' benefit.

But current discussions are far too preoccupied with quantitative expansion of higher education. More institutions, better physical infrastructure, are necessary but they are not sufficient to produce desired results in terms of quality of graduates turned out by the system. The outcomes in this respect depend crucially on its ability to attract and retain competent and motivated teachers. The supply of such teachers is getting increasingly scarce as those who do well in postgraduate courses prefer going abroad for further studies or take to lucrative non-teaching jobs within the country. There is concern about the inadequacy in both the number and quality of PhD candidates in science subjects and those choosing a research career within the country. The problem is much more serious in humanities and social sciences: the number of applicants for doctoral studies are getting increasingly fewer.

None of the recent reviews recognise that inadequate supply of good quality teachers may well prove to be a serious constraint on achieving the quantitative targets of enrolment and, more so, quality improvement. The attraction of teaching as a profession is set to decline further unless the academic environment of educational institutions at all levels, and especially in higher education, is vastly improved and the huge and growing differential between teachers' salaries and those in alternative occupations is reduced. To what extent this can be done by the public system faced with severe financial constraints or for that matter by the profit-centric private sector is uncertain. It also depends on whether and by what means the resulting increase in costs will be met.

Raising the contribution of student fees to cover a substantially larger proportion of costs, along with measures to raise non-governmental funding, acquires greater urgency in this context. But raising student fees will meet strong resistance from students and their parents. There are ways to mitigate the adverse impact on students from the poorer strata by offering them scholarships and educational loans on liberal terms, and by cross-subsidising them by charging higher fees from students belonging to the better-off segments. Implementing such schemes however is not an easy task from the political viewpoint. These constraints are far less in the case of private institutions catering to and supported by the affluent segments of the population. The chances are that the differences between the public and private institutions, as well as the caste-class inequalities in access and quality, will get further aggravated. These issues are conspicuously missing in current debates on higher education.

The Issue of Equity

Educational inequality exists at all stages of education and in varying degrees between regions, between men and women, between rural and urban areas and between different social groups. It reflects differences in the availability and quality of accessible educational facilities; differences in the cost of availing of the facilities; and the capacity to meet the costs. Apart from inadequate schools and teachers, socio-cultural attitudes have contributed significantly to differential progress between gender, caste and community groups. Inequalities in all these respects exist even at the elementary level and get accentuated at the secondary school level and become far more pronounced in higher education. This progressive increase in educational inequality is associated with a steep decline in enrolment rates (as a proportion of relevant age groups) and increasing bias in access towards upper socioeconomic strata from lower to higher stages of education. Surprisingly the persistence of considerable caste-class inequalities in school education and the importance of redressing them are conspicuously missing in the current controversies on inequality in higher education. Moreover, by focussing exclusively on the merits of caste based reservations, these debates distort the issues involved by pitting merit versus equality, and looking at equality purely in terms of caste.

No discussion of educational reform can ignore the issue of caste based quotas for admissions to higher education. The Constitution, through the first amendment enabled reservations in education for the scheduled castes and tribes and 'socially and educationally backward classes of citizens' (Article 15[4]). Reservation in employment in the state sector was already present under Article 16(4). The aim was to provide for positive/protective discrimination in favour of those groups that suffered from the handicap of birth leading to other disadvantages such as poor education, unremunerative employment and poverty. These handicaps are particularly true of the scheduled castes and tribes and are reflected in lower enrolments even in elementary schools, higher dropout rates and below average performance. Those who manage to complete high school are ill-equipped to perform as well in public/entrance examinations as the upper castes and therefore cannot gain admissions in higher education. These disadvantages are also faced, though not in the same degree, by several lower caste groups collectively and loosely referred to as 'other backward castes'. Strong political pressure from these groups has led to legislation providing for an OBC quota in higher education and jobs; and to a progressive increase in its scope and magnitude.

The quota regime in higher education has been operative for a fairly long time. There have been controversies and some tension over the rationale for quotas, but they remained manageable till recently. During the last decade and a half, as the increase in demand for professional education outstripped the intake capacity it led to increasing competition for admissions. With competition for admissions to highly subsidised public institutions, which were subject to quotas, becoming more and more intense, opposition from those who were adversely affected by quotas also grew. Attempts to increase the magnitude of the OBC quota aggravated social conflicts over this issue, which spilled over into street violence and demands for judicial intervention.

The protagonists of reservations see caste based quotas as essential to achieve equality of access in higher education. Opponents argue that merit based on performance at public examinations/entrance tests must be the sole basis for admissions and that special treatment based on caste violates the principle of equality and leads to deterioration in quality. Both positions are open to contest. But neither protagonists nor opponents of caste quotas in higher education (many of whom belong to the upper socioeconomic stratum) recognise the fact that unequal performance in public/entrance examinations is the result of entrenched and chronic inequalities in the school education. Neither of them has shown substantial interest in pressing for measures to address the causes of inequality at the school level.

It is significant that the agitation against quotas was spearheaded mainly by the medical students and doctors with some support from those in engineering and management schools. Their concern for merit as the primary criterion for access is touching. But success in entrance tests for professional colleges is hardly a reliable indicator of 'merit' because the field of competition through these tests is far from level.

It is only fair that a society committed to democracy, social justice and equality of opportunity must take special measures at least to mitigate this disadvantage. This is the basic and irrefutable rationale for affirmative action. It does not however follow that reservation based exclusively on caste as the criterion of backwardness is the best instrument for this purpose. While reliable data are lacking, there is widespread agreement that benefits of reservations have been largely cornered by the better-off segments, the so-called 'creamy layer' of these castes. Income has thus become a key factor in access in these groups as well.

It is therefore important to find a way to relate eligibility under the quota to the economic status of the aspirant's family combined with measures to create a more level field in selection based on competitive tests. Since admissions to higher education generally and professional education in particular can accommodate only a small fraction of high school graduates, the focus of special and preferential treatment for SC,ST,OBC and other chronically disadvantaged social groups should be on students who despite their multiple handicaps have done well in the public examinations. Such students deserve to be given the opportunity for special coaching at public expense to better equip them to compete in entrance tests. And those who perform satisfactorily in the entrance tests should be enabled to join and complete the courses by giving them financial assistance from public funds to meet the costs.

Judging the functioning and impact of the present quota system as well as a reformed system of affirmative action in higher education calls for reliable information on caste/income distribution of those who appear for entrance tests, their performance in them, as well as the proportion of students from underprivileged categories who do well, appear for the examinations, become eligible for admissions at higher levels and join and complete the course. Such information is simply not available now. It is important to ensure that this information is collected by independent agencies and that it is placed in the public domain so that its effectiveness in achieving greater equality of access to higher education across socioeconomic groups can be assessed in a fair and objective manner.

Summing Up

The principal thrust of the arguments advanced here can be summarised in the following form. The phenomenon of privatisation of education is not confined to higher education but is pervasive in all parts of the country's educational system. The process is accelerating partly because of the inability of the public system to cope with the growing demand and the increasing deficiencies in its functioning. It has been facilitated by fuzziness of state policy regarding private schools and its lax implementation. Private unaided institutions motivated by profit are becoming increasingly important at all levels, more so in higher education, especially professional education. There is hardly any regulation of private schools. The State has set norms for higher education institutions and a regulatory system to ensure their observance, but these are violated widely and with impunity. Cumulatively these have greatly increased the inequality in access to and quality of educational opportunities at all levels and not just higher education. Improving the overall quality of education and reducing inequalities therefore calls for measures to expand and improve the quality of the public systems at all levels. At the same time we need a clear enunciation of policy regarding the role of private institutions and the conditions under which they have to function, backed by strong regulatory mechanisms independent of government to ensure compliance with these conditions. The main elements of the needed reforms to improve the quality of public systems and narrow the gap between public and private systems are fairly clear. Given the magnitude and complexity of the task, a concerted effort on the part of experts to work out the specifics, anticipate difficulties and ways to solve them is necessary to generate an informed discussion, to mobilise public opinion in support of the reform and to ensure its implementation.

References

Agarwal, Pawan (2006). *Higher Education in India: The Need for Change.* New Delhi: ICRIER.

Agarwal, Pawan (2007). "From Kothari Commission to Pitroda Commission", *Economic and Political Weekly* 42(7), February 13.

Anandakrishnan, M. (2007). "Critique of Knowledge Commission", *Economic and Political Weekly* 42(7).

Department of Commerce, Trade Policy Division (2006). *Trade in Education Services: A Consultation Paper on Higher Education in India and GATS.*

Kapur, Devesh and Pratap Bhanu Mehta (2004). *India's Higher Education Reform: from Half-baked Socialism to Half-baked Capitalism*. Centre for International Development at Harvard University.

Kingdon, Geeta Gandhi (2007). *The Progress of School Education in India*. Accessible at *http://www.gprg.org/*

National Knowledge Commission (2006). *Recommendations on Higher Education*. GoI. November.

NIEPA (2005). *Report of the CABE Committee on Financing of Higher and Technical Education*.

III

Finance and Banking

6 Commercial Banks

Has Growth Widened Coverage?

Organised financial institutions in India have expanded at an unprecedented rate in terms of numbers, variety, geographical spread and volume of business. They include, besides scheduled commercial banks (SCBs), several other entities including regional rural banks (RRBs), mutual funds, non-banking financial companies (NBFC). All of them have grown in number and scale of operations since the 1980s as a result of a proactive government policy of expanding and diversifying the financial system. The focus of this paper is SCBs which are expected to mobilise deposits, provide credit and offer a wider range of banking services needed to support and sustain rapid economic growth. Besides encouraging their expansion, government policy has also been concerned to extend their reach to different parts of the country and to a wide group of users especially from the rural areas and sectors (like agriculture, small scale enterprises) whose growth prospects are constrained by difficulty in getting credit at reasonable rates.

The growth of this sector during the last three decades has been truly phenomenal: The number of their outlets has grown some two and half

Table 6.1

Growth of the Commercial Banking System, 1982–2009

		1982	*1990*	*2000*	*2009*
Outlets	000	32.4	59.8	65.4	80
Deposits number of accounts	Million	158	333	412	763
Amount outstanding	Rs Billion	451	1659	7514	39220
Loans number of accounts	Million	24	53	55	110
Amount outstanding	Rs Billion	297	1043	4601	28476

Source: RBI, *Handbook of Statistics of the Indian Economy 2010-11*.

times during the last three decades; their deposit accounts have grown about five fold and loan accounts by nearly five times; the magnitude of deposits by eight times and loan outstanding have grown nine times (Table 6.1).

This paper examines whether and to what extent this expansion has fulfilled the policy objectives of the government and Reserve Bank of India (RBI):

- Bring banking facilities within easier reach of population and enterprises, mobilise deposits and provide credit, especially in rural areas and smaller towns.
- Broaden and deepen the flow of credit to different productive and consumptive uses and to different categories of borrowers.
- Efficacy of the policy of earmarking a defined proportion of credit flow to 'priority ' sectors, especially agriculture and small scale industry.
- The extent to which it has achieved wider financial inclusion.

Expansion Facilities

The pace of branch expansion has been uneven over this period and across rural and urban areas. The first big phase of expansion in fact occurred during the seventies in the wake of bank nationalisation: the number of branches increased eight fold during that decade. It nearly doubled again during eighties. The pace has since greatly slowed down: the increase during the subsequent two decades is less than 35 per cent. Expansion in the branch network has been faster and more sustained in urban and metropolitan centres than in rural and semi-urban areas. The process has

Table 6.2

Growth of Banking Facilities in Rural and Urban Areas, 1980-2009

	Outlets (000)				*Deposit accounts (million)*				*Loan accounts (million)*			
	Rural	*Semi-urban*	*Urban*	*Metro*	*Rural*	*Semi-urban*	*Urban*	*Metro*	*Rural*	*Semi-urban*	*Urban*	*Metro*
1980	15.1	8.1	5.2	4	41.5	46.2	36	32.5	11	8	3	1.5
1990	34.8	11.3	8	5.6	102	92	76	63	28	15	7	3
2000	32.7	14.4	10	8.2	125	114	90	83	25	15	8	7
2009	39.6	19.1	15.5	13.9	200	170	142	151	34	25	15	37

Source: RBI, *Handbook of Statistics of the Indian Economy 2010-11*.

been quite uneven in rural branches: after more than doubling during the eighties, their number actually declined during the nineties. Though the trend has been reversed since, the number of branches at present is barely 10 per cent more than in 1980. Practically all towns and cities now have multiple bank branches. By contrast only a fourth of semi-urban area and barely 6-7 per cent of villages have them (Table 6.2). The proportion of settlements having bank branches varies from 2 per cent in villages with less than 2,000 population, 46 per cent in villages with population between 5,000-10,000 and 96 per cent of those with more than 25,000.

The number of accounts give an idea of the reach of the banks in mobilising deposits and in providing credit. The following features are noteworthy:

- The number of deposit accounts per branch is highest in metropolitan cities and least in rural branches; this index shows an increase over time, but its extent is greater and more sustained in rural and semi-urban areas than in urban areas. According to data reported by banks to RBI, the number of both deposit and loan accounts per household in rural areas is less than half compared to urban areas. The reported number of 'agricultural loans works out to one per every three operational holdings. However, according to information from NSS household surveys less than six per cent of rural households seek bank loans.
- The number of loan accounts is invariably much smaller than that of deposits in all settlement categories in absolute terms; relative to deposit accounts, rural and semi-urban areas have more borrowers than in urban areas; for reasons that need to be investigated, this index did not change significantly in either rural or urban areas till the last decade, which shows a sharp rise in urban areas but not in others.
- The value of both outstanding deposits and outstanding loans have grown much faster than the number of accounts (Table 6.3). Overall Deposit-GDP ratio has risen from around 24 per cent in 1982 to 5 per cent in 2009. Credit-GDP ratio is consistently lower but also has recorded a steep rise over this period from 17 per cent to 43 per cent.

Table 6.3

Growth of Outstanding Deposits and Outstanding Loans, 1982-2009

	Outstanding deposits (Billion Rs)				*Outstanding loans (Billion Rs)*			
	Rural	*Semi-urban*	*Urban*	*Metro*	*Rural*	*Semi-urban*	*Urban*	*Metro*
1982	63	105	115	175	38	52	65	172
1990	262	364	424	609	255	176	224	388
2000	1205	1020	1890	3499	594	648	796	2563
2009	3639	5298	8229	22054	3096	3110	4986	17284

Source: RBI, *Handbook of Statistics of the Indian Economy 2010-11.*

- Urban areas account for more than three-fourths of SCB deposits and as much as 80 per cent of their outstanding loans. That rural areas contribute barely a fifth of deposits and one-sixth of their loan portfolio underscores their limited reach. Banks have done far better in increasing the number of depositors and borrowers than in mobilising deposits or in disbursing credit. Their share in total deposits has in fact declined over the period (from 14% to 9%). That their share in credit, though still small, has increased (from 12% to 15%.) shows that they have played a significant role in expanding the flow of credit in rural areas.

Trends in Scheduled Bank Credit 1990-2008

Access can be assessed in terms of: (a) the number of entities that have loans outstanding relative to the total number of potential borrowers of different categories; and (b) the magnitude of loan outstanding relative to the requirements again of different categories of borrowers. RBI collects and publishes detailed data on the number of loan accounts and the total quantum of outstanding loans of all scheduled loans and its distribution by sectors as well as by different types of organisations as of end March in each year.[1]

1. These are available in the Bank's annual publication, *Basic Statistical Returns (BSR) of Scheduled Banks in India*. There have been significant changes in coverage and concepts over time. Data based on comparable classifications of borrowing sectors and entities are however available since 1990. The data for earlier years have not been used because the figures from the BSR are at variance with those reported in the Bank's *Handbook of Statistics*.

Differences in Reach of SCBs to Different Users

Currently (2008), the number of outstanding loan accounts of SCBs is reported to be around 110 million. More than three-fourths of it consists of loans to agriculture and personal loans for durables, housing and other consumption. Only a fourth are loans to productive activity in non-agricultural sectors. Within this group, the number of loans is largest for trade, followed by professional services and manufacturing; a large part is categories as other loans whose break up is not available.

The number of outstanding loans has doubled since 2000.[2] This would suggest that the reach of bank credit has widened and deepened. But it must be noted that the bulk (over 90%) of this growth is accounted by agricultural and personal loans. Loans to non-agricultural activities have increased by somewhat more than 50 per cent, but they account for less than a fifth of the increase in the total number of loans. Another notable feature is that the number of loans for professional services, trade and 'others' have increased much faster than others. The near stagnation in the number of loans to manufacturing is striking.

Table 6.4

Growth in the Number of Loans (in Millions) for Different Purposes 2000-2008

	Agriculture	*Personal*	*Manu-facturing*	*Trans-port*	*Professional Services*	*Trade*	*Finance*	*Others*	*Total*
1991									
2000	19.8	16.2	4.7	0.6	1.7	5.4	0.04	3.7	52
2008	38.2	44.0	4.1	0.73	5.7	6.5	0.2	7.5	107

Source: BSR of scheduled commercial banks.

Since the same borrower can have more than one loan with the reporting bank and/or with more than one reporting bank, the number of borrowers availing of loans will be less than the number of loans. This makes it difficult to establish a one to one correspondence between loan accounts and borrowing entities. The phenomenon exists in all sectors. Its incidence is likely to be particularly high in the case of agricultural and

2. Figures for 1991 reported in BSR (3-2 million) is much lower than those cited in the Bank's *Handbook of Statistics on the Indian Economy*.

personal loans. Because of this, the number of entities availing of loans is likely to be smaller than the number of loans. In the absence of any scrutiny of the veracity of reported data, there is also scope for overstating the number of loans to meet norms of lending for priority sectors like agriculture. Moreover, in so far as loans have longer maturities, the number of outstanding loans at a point of time includes those who have taken the credit earlier. This is especially important in the case of housing and durable good loans. Because of these reasons, reported number of loans tend to overstate the actual access to potential borrowers. The reach of SCBs to entities within each sector is also very unequal.

This is corroborated by independent surveys of access of agriculture to institutional credit: for instance, relative to the number of holdings, farms with less than 1 ha have far fewer loans (10 million loans outstanding against a total of 70 million holdings) than those with holdings >1 ha (24 million out of 31 million). About three-fourths of outstanding loans are for holdings with more than 1 ha, and about half for those with more than 2 ha. The Economic Census of 2005-06 estimates the number of unincorporated and own account non-agricultural establishments at 36 million of which only 1.4 million establishments reported having loans from financial institutions. The number of loan accounts for non-agricultural enterprises reported by SCBs is around 4.7 million.

Distribution of Loans across Sectors

Of greater importance is the volume of credit obtained by different sections of borrowers. This is also marked by inequality but of a very different pattern. Of the total quantum of outstanding SCB loans as of end March 2008, about one-fifth is for financing durables, housing and other personal loans, which are presumed to be for consumption. The balance 80 per cent gives a measure of credit given to productive sectors. Of this, about 14 per cent is for agriculture; nearly half for mining and manufacturing, utilities and construction; 11 per cent for trade and around 9 per cent each for finance and professional services. The significant differences between the share of loan accounts and that of loans outstanding across these segments are a reflection of differences in the average size of loans: personal loans and that of agriculture are much smaller than in other sectors, while in industry and finance they are several time larger than average.

Significant changes in the distribution of loans across different sectors have occurred during the last two decades (Table 6.5).

1. The share of commodity producing sectors (i.e, agriculture, manufacturing, utilities and construction) in SCB loans has come down progressively from 67 per cent in 1996 to 48 per cent in 2006. Though the trend has since been reversed, the current (2008) share of around 50 per cent is well below the 1996 level. The share of loans to services sectors has increased, though not in a sustained fashion. The share of personal loans has increased rapidly from 9.2 per cent in 1996 to 23.4 per cent in 2006 but has since come down slightly to 20 per cent currently.
2. Among the commodity producing sectors, agriculture's share is more or less constant at around 11 per cent; the proportion going to infrastructure (electricity, gas and water and construction) has increased progressively from 2.3 per cent in 1996 to 10.8 per cent in 2008. The more striking feature is the decline in the share of loans to manufacturing from nearly 46 per cent in 1996 to about 29 per cent in 2006. Though the share increased in the subsequent two years, at 34 per cent, it remains well below the level at the beginning of the period.
3. Among services, the share of transport operators is more or less stagnant; and that of trade has declined progressively from nearly 14 per cent in 1996 to less than 9 per cent in 2008. The big increase is under professional services and finance whose share in total outstanding loans has risen progressively to double the level of 1996.
4. Personal loans explicitly for durables and housing shows the largest increase, their current share being more than three times the 1996 level. Including the share of 'other personal loans', in total loan outstanding (LO) it increased from a little over 9 per cent in 1991 to over 23 per cent in 2006 but has since come down to 20 per cent in 2008.

Table 6.5

Distribution of Loans Outstanding by Sector 1995-96 to 2007-08

Rs Billion

	1991	%	*1996*	%	*2001*	%	*2006*	%	*2008*	%
Agriculture	83	8.6	288	11.3	517	9.6	1727	11.4	2741	11.3
Manufacturing	540	55.7	1164	45.7	2179	40.5	4348	28.7	6651	27.6
Electricity, gas and water	9	0.9	24	0.9	120	2.2	363	2.4	807	3.3
Construction	18	1.9	35	1.4	65	1.2	833	5.5	1807	7.5
Transport operators	31	3.2	46	1.8	87	1.6	237	1.6	447	1.8
Professional services	23	2.4	90	3.5	192	3.6	819	5.4	1873	7.7
Personal (durables/ housing)	37	3.8	80	3.1	289	5.4	1889	12.5	2555	10.6
Other personal	34	3.5	156	6.1	371	6.9	1643	10.9	2298	9.5
Trade	140	14.4	353	13.9	895	16.6	1502	9.9	2125	8.8
Finance	28	2.9	90	3.5	265	4.9	951	6.3	1706	7.1
Others	35	3.6	220	8.6	404	7.5	708	4.7	1138	4.7
Total	969	100.0	2547	100.0	5384	100.0	15128	100.0	24170	100.0

Source: RBI, *Handbook of Statistics of the Indian Economy 2010-11.*

Distribution by Institutional Categories

The period has witnessed significant shifts in the distribution of credit to different categories of borrowers: In 1991, private corporate sector was the largest borrower accounting for about 39 per cent of outstanding loans; proprietary and partnership enterprises accounted for 29 per cent; of the total: about one-sixth went to households and individuals; and the share of public sector undertakings stood at 14 per cent. By the end of the decade, the share of private corporate sector and that of government undertakings increased to their peak levels, only to decline during the subsequent eight years. Cooperative institutions, which borrowed very little from the banking system earlier now account for nearly 5 per cent of its total loan portfolio. The most striking change is the near doubling of the share of households and individuals reflecting the growing importance of lending to agriculture and for housing, durables and other consumption. The share of loans going to non-agricultural sectors has declined substantially during this period. The continued decline in share of bank finance to unincorporated enterprises, which comprise the most disadvantaged segment of the economy, is obviously a matter of concern.

Table 6.6

Distribution of Outstanding Loans by Institutional Categories 1991-2008

	1991		*2001*		*2008*	
	Million	%	*Million*	%	*Million*	%
Government undertakings	136	14.2	863	20.0	3488	16.6
Cooperatives	14.6	1.5	67	1.6	1100	5.3
Private companies	378	39	2029	47.0	8595	41.1
Proprietary/partnerships	280	29.2	868	20.1	2762	13.1
Households and individuals	159	16.5	463	10.7	4768	22.8
Others					54	0.2
All	960	100	4321	100	20860	100

Source: *Basic Statistical Returns*, RBI Website.

Credit Relative to Production

The ratio of LO relative to output of various production sectors is generally used as a rough index of the extent to which the banking system meets the credit requirements of various sectors. Table 6.7, which summarises the estimates based on BSR data for broad sectors of the economy, highlights significant and persistent differences in this index of access across sectors. Currently, this is lowest at 16 per cent in the transport sector; ranges between 25 and 35 per cent in mining, finance, trade and agriculture and 45 to 50 per cent in construction and services. It is highest in manufacturing (85%) and more than 100 per cent for utilities.

The fact that the ratio of credit to GDP has risen progressively during the last two decades suggests that SCBs are meeting an increasing proportion of the credit needs of the economy. Much of this increase has however taken place since 2001. This pattern is also evident in all sectors, except transport and finance (in which the ratio declined during the 90s and recovered thereafter) and trade (in which the ratio shows a progressive, though small, decline). Among others, the increase in ratio is least in manufacturing (which had a very high ratio to begin with) and largest in utilities. SCB credit to GDP ratio in agriculture has increased six fold and 2-3 times in others.

Table 6.7

Trends in Credit-Deposit Ratios of Major Sectors

(Rs in Billion)

	1991			2001			2008		
	GDP	LO	LO/GDP	GDP	LO	LO/GDP	GDP	LO	LO/GDP
	Rs	Rs	%	Rs	Rs	%	Rs	Rs	%
Agriculture	1508	83	5.5	4572	517	11.3	7836	2741	35.0
Mining	138	11	8.0	457	65	14.2	1174	303	25.8
Manufacturing	860	529	61.5	3004	2214	73.7	7851	6671	85.0
Utilities	110	9	8.2	462	120	26.0	761	807	106.0
Construction	277	18	6.5	1120	65	5.8	3762	1808	48.1
Trade	653	213	32.6	2809	895	31.9	7182	2125	29.6
Transport	270	31	11.5	1162	87	7.5	2784	447	16.1
Finance	599	170	28.4	2540	265	10.4	5940	1705	28.7
Services	735	110	15.0	3165	596	18.8	6715	3010	44.8
Total	5156	1174	22.8	19302	4824	25.0	43208	19617	45.4

Note: GDP at current prices
Total LO excludes personal loans for durables, housing and others
Utilities: electricity, gas, water
Services: community, social and professional services, including communication

Source: CSO national income estimates based on BSR data.

More than two-thirds of SCB loans go to government undertakings and private corporations, which are relatively large in scale and constitute the bulk of the organised sector. In 1991 they accounted for close to 75 per cent of LO for mining and manufacturing, 89 per cent in utilities and practically all loans to financial institutions. The proportion is lowest in transport; professional services and agriculture, which consist predominantly of unincorporated and owner operated enterprises. It ranges between 55 and 60 per cent in construction and trade. This feature has become much stronger since. By 2006, the government and corporate sectors' share has increased in all sectors, and exceeds 60 per cent in most sectors (and as much as 95 per cent in some). This bias towards corporates is the least in agriculture and remains more or less unchanged at 30-31 per cent.

Table 6.8

Share of Government and Private Companies in Loan Outstanding of SCBs 1991 and 2006

(Rs in Billion)

	1991			*2006*		
	Total LO	*Companies**		*Total LO*	*Companies**	
	Rs	*Rs*	*%*	*Rs*	*Rs*	*%*
Agriculture	83	26	31.3	1726	517	30.0
Mining	11	8	72.7	163	138	84.7
Manufacturing	567	437	77.1	4201	3398	80.9
Utilities	9	8	88.9	481	461	95.8
Construction	18	10	55.6	818	629	76.9
Trade	213	122	57.3	1501	936	62.4
Transport	31	5	16.1	237	156	65.8
Finance	170	166	97.6	951	903	95.0
Professional services	83	22	26.5	817	444	54.3
Others	28	12	42.9	709	467	65.9
Total	1213	816	67.3	11604	8049	69.4

Note: * Government undertakings and private corporations.
Source: RBI, *Handbook of Statistics of the Indian Economy 2010-11*.

The unorganised sector which constitutes the bulk of economy has clearly not benefited much directly from credit provided by SCBs. The above figures also show that the extent to which they have benefited from the huge expansion of bank credit has declined significantly. This is corroborated by Table 6.9, which shows the credit–NDP ratios for organised and unorganised segments of different sectors in 2005-06. (This is the only year for which this break up of NDP is currently available.) In most sectors (except mining and community services), the LO-NDP ratio of the unorganised segment is lower by large margin than in the organised segment. Dependence of the unorganised sector on non-bank institutions whose terms are more onerous is not only large but also growing.

Table 6.9

Output and SCB Loan Outstanding in Organised and Unorganised Sectors 2005-06

(Rs in Billion)

	NDP Rs[1]			*SCB LO Rs*[2]			*SCB LO/NDP per cent*		
	Total	*Organised*	*Unorganised*[3]	*Total*	*Organised*	*Unorganised*[4]	*Total*	*Organised*	*Unorganised*
Agriculture	5766	530	5236	1726	538	1188	29.9	101.4	22.7
Mining	795	712	83	163	138	25	20.5	19.4	30.2
Manufacturing	3964	2692	1272	4201	3299	902	106.0	122.6	70.9
Electricity, gas and water	278	263	15	481	461	20	173.0	175.3	133.2
Construction	2573	1088	1485	818	629	189	31.8	57.8	12.7
Trade	5260	1015	4245	1501	762	739	28.5	75.1	17.4
Transport & communications	2248	807	1441	237	131	106	10.5	16.2	7.4
Finance, real estate, busness services	3982	2270	1712	1770	1104	666	44.5	48.6	38.9
Community services	4102	2953	1149	707	162	545	8.7	3.1	19.1
Total	28969	12341	16628	11604	7224	4380	40.1	58.5	26.3
Non-agriculture	23203	11811	11392	9880	6888	2992	42.6	58.3	26.3

Note: 1. CSO National accounts statistics
2. Excludes personal loans
3. As defined by NAS
4. Assumed to be equivalent to Lo of 'other enterprises' and individuals.

Caveats

However, the data on both the number and the volume of L0 for different sectors reported by banks, as well as the ratio of LO to GDP in different sectors based on them, have to be interpreted with caution. For several reasons: in the first place, the level of output (or other appropriate indicators) of the potential credit requirements are not reliable basis to judge differences in access to bank credit across sectors and categories of borrowers. GDP is not a satisfactory index of requirements. We need more refined measure of requirements, distinguishing between for working capital and investment needs and matching them with the term structure of loans. The reported figures tend to be biased upward in some cases and downwards in others. There are strong grounds to suspect that reported number and volume of outstanding of SCB loans among rural households, and business establishments in the unorganised sector is vastly exaggerated.

Apart from evidence from independent sample surveys of these segments, a substantial and increasing part of the reported figure of loans to agriculture consists of loans to input suppliers, marketing, processing and other activities that are supposed to be supporting agriculture. Moreover, loans (cooperatives plus banks) to agriculture are not only implausibly high in relation to the working capital and private investment in the sector, and their growth is accelerating even as agricultural growth seems to be stagnating, if not slowing down.

SCBs are mandated to provide a specified proportion of their lending to designated 'priority sectors' including agriculture. Given their limited geographical reach (they have only 5,000 branches in villages and semi-urban areas), it is difficult to believe that about a third of all rural households have got loans from them on a scale that amounts to nearly a fifth of the sector's total GDP. RBI as regulator does not attempt an independent check of the veracity of the figures even on a sample basis.

SCBs, though by far the largest, are not the only source of credit from organised and regulated financial institutions (FIS). Cooperative credit societies and urban cooperative banks, non-bank financial institutions (NBFIs) and NBFCs provide substantial amounts: on a rough estimate the loans are currently of the order of Rs 5,000 billion. These are lent to agriculture and diverse non-agricultural activities as well as for housing, durables and other consumption expenditures. Most of their loans are to enterprises in the unorganised sector and to individuals. Details of their break up by sector of use and categories of borrowers are however not available.

Since borrowed funds are fungible, the purposes for which they are actually used may not be the same as the purposes for which they are given. The scope for such divergence is significant in the case of loans to agriculture, small industry and individual loans for unspecified purposes. Since lending rates of SCBs and cooperatives for agriculture and small industry are lower than the rates charged on other loans, there is a strong incentive for arbitrage by borrowing in the name of agriculture and using the proceeds for investing in other profitable avenues and/or on-lending at higher rates to the unorganised sectors who cannot access credit from institutions. The way credit cooperatives function, gives ample opportunity for locally influential sections of the population to take advantage of this opportunity by manipulating the disposition of loan funds for themselves and their supporters. Dysfunctional mechanisms of supervision and audit, reinforced by intrusive role of politicians and the bureaucracy has allowed this process to continue unchecked.

Financing Credit Needs of the Unorganised Sector

Total SCB outstanding non-agricultural loans to this segment is around Rs 6,100 billion of which about Rs 1,500 billion is for housing and community development (CD). The balance includes a large (Rs 1,600 billion) amount of personal loans. Assuming optimistically that all of it is available/used for productive purposes, SCB credit available for unorganised non-agricultural activities is barely Rs 5,000 billion. This is *prima facie* very small, at any rate much smaller than for the organised sector. But actual availability of institutional credit for this sector GDP ratio is much larger when we include loans for non-agricultural purposes from other FIs. A rough estimate of the latter pieced together from various sources is estimated at over Rs 5,000 billion.

Very little information on the sectoral distribution of these advances and the characteristics of borrowers is available. Given the fungibility of resources raised by loans, the purpose for which loan is reported to be taken may not, and in many cases does not, be the purposes for which it is actually used. The requirement to meet priority sector lending targets tends to distort reporting. Furthermore, the structure of interest rates leaves ample room for arbitrage for influential and relatively well to do borrowers to access relatively cheap priority sector loans and relend it at much higher rates for other borrowers. Given the fungibility in its use as well as complex relations between banks and other FIs and between both and the informal segment of the credit market, we need to know a lot more about the sectors which use credit from both SCBs and from other FIs, as well as interrelations between the two segments, than is available in current reporting.

The declining share of credit going to commodity producing sectors is paralleled by their decline in GDP. In the case of agriculture, the level of reported bank credit relative to its contribution to GDP is relatively high. But there are strong reasons to doubt whether all of it really is used for increasing agricultural production. Shortage of credit is surely not the critical constraint that accounts for the stagnation and possibly even decline in the growth of agriculture.

In the case of manufacturing, SCBs are not the only source of finance. Industries, especially the organised sector has access to finance from other FIs both domestic and foreign. The extent to which the availability of credit is cause and to what extent it is the effect of relatively slow growth in commodity production sectors is a moot question. But there is little doubt that the growth of unorganised sectors is impeded by their declining relative access to bank credit. There are in any case legitimate concerns about the pace of growth in consumption credit being provided by SCBs and its impact on the health of the financial system.

That access to bank credit for unincorporated enterprises and individuals is quite limited is well known, but its extent is far greater than generally appreciated. The Census of Establishments 2005 estimates the number of establishments (excluding crop and animal husbandry) at some 42 million: over 60 per cent of them are own account enterprises whose loans are likely to be classified as loans to individuals. The remaining 15 million undertakings employ one or more hired workers probably corresponding to the 'unincorporated enterprise' category in the BSR institutional classification. Out of these, only 1.5 million enterprises reported being financed by FIs, which compares with a figure of 1.1 million outstanding loan accounts of 'other private enterprises' reported by SCBs. A National Sample Survey (NSS) survey of unorganised manufacturing enterprises conducted in 2005-06 estimates the number of undertakings employing one or more hired labour at 2.5 million. Most of them are proprietary or partnership concerns. The number of outstanding scheduled bank loans to the non-public sector undertaking (PSU), non-corporate manufacturing enterprises was less than 300,000. The census of small scale industries conducted in 2001-02 estimated that out of 4.4 million, barely 700,000 reported having outstanding loans to banks.

Access to finance from SCBs and other FIs is thus far less extensive than the banking statistics suggest. Exclusion is more acute in rural areas and for small enterprises both in agriculture and non-agricultural activities. Mandated targets of lending to agriculture and small enterprises, designated as priority sectors, have been effective only to a limited extent.

Current initiatives on financial inclusion are mostly focussed on measures to deepen and widen access to modern financial services provided by commercial banks by extending their branch network and encouraging them and microfinance institutions (MFIs) to use business correspondents and business facilitators to facilitate people to open and operate bank accounts and avail of remittance and other financial services; and to increase the coverage and magnitude of institutional credit to the unorganised sectors of the economy.

Expansion of the branch network of commercial banks is, and will continue to be, constrained by high operational costs and risks involved in managing a large number of small accounts, especially in the rural hinterland. Encouraging no-frill accounts and the use of business correspondent/facilitator model may well bring a larger number of people to have deposit accounts thereby getting them used to dealing with banks and also facilitate wider use of financial services. How wide and deep this process will be remains to be seen.

While there is some indication of a positive relation, across major states, between the number of deposit accounts and those of loan accounts, the latter is invariably only a fraction of the former. The policy of mandated lending to priority sectors has led to larger lending to agriculture and, to a smaller extent, enterprises in the unorganised sector. But how much of it actually goes to and is utilised by the target sectors is an open question. So is the quality of this segment of the banks' portfolio in terms of prompt and full recovery of dues. Doubts that are reinforced by the fact that government policy on lending rates for agricultural loans creates huge opportunities for interest arbitrage and the fact that credit discipline has been eroded by periodic restructuring/waivers of interest and principal repayments at public expense.

Private, for-profit MFIs, many of them set up and funded by SCBs, other FIs and foreign organisations, have been proliferating. Reliable and comprehensive data on the characteristics of their borrowers, their geographical spread, the purposes for which loans are given and used, and the interest rate charged are not available. Available information suggests that interest rates are as high as 36 per cent—about three times the average lending rate of banks. The huge differential between the cost of funds in developed countries and market rates of interest in India is a major driving force behind this trend. There is considerable pressure for allowing more of them to be set up and expand their operations without any attempt to limit the interest rates they can charge or subject them to regulation.

The self help group (SHG) model seems much more appropriate to address these problems. They are growing rapidly in number and volume of lending. They are, however, concentrated in a few regions and account for a relatively small fraction of total institutional loans. (The concept of lending to small farms and non-farm enterprises based on the concept of group liability has not made much headway.) For the most part they comprise of women from poor and disadvantaged segments. Loans are for consumption, retiring existing debt and, to a lesser extent, for income augmenting activities. Lending rates, which are decided by group members, are relatively high (as much as 24% in several cases). The margin over costs is substantial in the case of well-managed groups. Unlike MFIs, this surplus is viewed as the common savings of the group to be shared by members or used for their common benefit. Discipline in the use of credit and in repayments is uneven, especially in the government sponsored/subsidised groups. The spillover effects on other segments of programme are feared to be quite significant. It is important to have an independent assessment of the growth and performance of different segments of this movement: the government sponsored programme, the bank linked SHGs and those sponsored by MFIs and non-governmental organisations (NGOs).

SHGs are informal, miniature cooperatives based on the concept of mutuality with thrift and credit functions going hand in hand. This is indeed the basis on which the rural cooperative credit system has been actively encouraged and supported for over a century. Currently (2007), there are nearly 100,000 rural cooperative credit societies, (roughly one for every six villages on the average) serving 48 million borrowers (nearly twice the number of agricultural loan accounts of SCBs). At present, no other institution has comparable range of physical reach in rural areas. They account for a substantial but declining share of institutional credit to agriculture with total loan outstanding of Rs 586 billion (compared to Rs 1,400 billion by SCBs).

The system, however, has not developed and functioned as self-reliant, democratic institutions that encourage members' thrift, enforce strict credit discipline on their borrowing members and manage their resources prudently. Their phenomenal expansion is based mostly through public FIs at the behest of government. They have come to depend entirely on funds provided by public FIs and lend at rates prescribed by governments. Intervention by state governments in practically every aspect of their functioning is intrusive and pervasive leading to laxity in providing loans and in ensuring their proper use. Instead of checking these tendencies, government policy has compounded the problem by condoning postponement and granting outright waivers of loan and interest payments at public expense. As a result, the system has been impaired in governance, managerial and financial fronts. Its chronic financial state, reflected in poor recovery, huge accumulated losses has worsened to a point that despite government pressure and huge amounts of funds made available to them, their borrowing membership has come down from 64 million in 2003 to 48 million currently. The rate of expansion in their disbursements has come down sharply relative to that of commercial banks. Consequently, their share in total rural credit flow has come down from over 60 per cent in the 2002 to barely 38 per cent currently.

Concerned about this state of affairs, the Central government appointed a special task force to suggest ways for revival of the rural cooperative credit system. It argued forcefully that 'reviving and revitalising the cooperative credit system (CCS) is essential, both on functional and ideological grounds'. Functionally cooperatives have a wider and deeper reach in the countryside than other FIs which mostly serve the better off segments of borrowers and are reluctant to cater to small and marginal farmers and underprivileged segments' on grounds of high costs and risk. They further argued that mutual thrift and credit cooperatives are '...the only form of organisation by which economically disadvantaged groups and individuals could, through voluntary collective action overcome their disadvantageous position in unequal markets and promote their well being.' They also underscored the potential of such societies in reducing costs of administration, risks of default and prudent use of credit.

While recommending that the government would be justified in providing financial assistance to wipe out accumulated losses and non-performing assets (NPAs), it made such assistance strictly condition on the implementation of major legal and institutional reforms to make coops democratic, member driven, autonomous and self-reliant institutions free of state interference and political manipulation. The Central government accepted all the recommendations and took the extraordinary initiative of organising a series of high level consultations with state governments. Cooperation being a state subject under the Constitution, states' consensus on the proposed reforms was essential. That the process culminated in endorsement and acceptance of all key elements of the proposed reform package is a landmark event. A mechanism to oversee the implementation of the reforms was set up and has been functioning for the last three years. Practically all state governments have signed formal memorandum of understanding (MOUs) spelling out their commitments for legal reform and the Centre's commitments for financial assistance. Several have also made required changes in law through legislation or ordinances. Audit of societies is progressing and initial instalments of Central assistance have been released.

Even as this process got underway, the decision to waive farm loans on a massive scale has undercut the incentive to pursue these reforms seriously. There are in any case strong entrenched political interests cutting across party lines in controlling coops as instruments of power and patronage. This adds to doubts whether, once the financial package is delivered, the reform part of the package will be implemented in its true spirit. The leverage of the Centre to induce state to implement the reforms, already eroded by its decision to waive loans, will be further reduced. The implications of all this for realising the immense potential of revitalised coops for financial inclusion do not seem to bother even the Central government, let alone states.

Nor for that matter the Reserve Bank, which is spearheading the movement for financial inclusion; its strategy is focussed almost entirely on extending the reach of commercial banks and other institutions in the organised sector through various intermediaries. RBI's efforts in the cooperative sector are limited to improving the health of urban cooperative banks. The concern, understandably, is on ensuring that they are managed efficiently and prudently from the regulatory perspective rather than promoting inclusion. The Reserve Bank could and should play a more proactive role in highlighting the critical importance of credit cooperatives of all types (including SHGs) for successful financial inclusion and the consequences of failure to implement the programme for legal/institutional reform in letter and spirit. It needs to take more serious note of the several hundred successful and vibrant rural mutual thrift and credit cooperatives under the MCA model, highlight the impediments under existing laws that make it difficult to set up new societies or allow existing societies to migrate to that pattern, and create public opinion to remove those impediments. Together with National Bank for Agriculture and Rural Development (NABARD), it could also be proactive in identifying and supporting NGO and civil society initiatives to organise such societies in different parts of the country.

7 Consumption of Gold in India

Trends and Determinants

Trends in Consumption: An Overview

India produces hardly any gold; but it is the second largest consumer of the precious metal in the world. The only important gold mine in Kolar has been contributing a miniscule proportion of total annual absorption. Practically the entire demand is met from imports and recycling of previously accumulated stock and scrap generated from it.

The country has long been importing substantial amounts of gold: Between 1831 and 1931, imports averaged 37 tonnes per annum. The 1930s—the period of the great depression—were marked by an exceptionally large net outflow of gold averaging around 140 tonnes a year. This tendency

Table 7.1

Net Import of Gold into India

(Tonnes)

Period	*Total Quantity*	*Annual Average*
1831-1931	3700	37
1931-1940	(-)1400	(-)140
1941-1950	311	31
1951-1957	653	93
1958-1963	520	87
1964-1967	720	180
1968-1973	815	136
1974-1980	160	23
1981-1990	1550	155
1991-1997	2792	399

Notes: (1) Figures for 1831 to 1940 based on official trade statistics. During this period import and export of gold was legal. The figures cited probably relate to undivided British India.

(2) Gold imports from late 1940s till 1990 are estimates of Consolidated Gold Field and Gold Field Mineral Services as cited in Sarma *et al.*, 1992. For subsequent years estimates of World Gold Council. Except for imports through officially approved channels (mainly facilitate exports of ornaments and jewellery), imports were illegally smuggled into the country.

Source: Sarma *et al.*, 1992: Tables 1 and 5. For the 1990s World Gold Council estimates (see Table 2).

was reversed during the following decade, when there was a net gold import of around 31 tonnes per annum. Thereafter, despite the imposition of a ban on gold imports in 1947, net imports (practically all of it illegally smuggled) increased progressively to 80-90 tonnes per annum during the 1950s, and close to 150 tonnes per annum during the 1960s and early 1970s. After a sharp decline in the 1970s, gold imports surged again during the 1980s and, following the lifting of the ban and permitting of imports in 1992, the rate of imports increased sharply in the 1990s (Table 7.1).

A rough[1] picture of overall gold consumption and sources of supply during the 1990s is given in Table 7.2. There was a big spurt (about 80%) in estimated consumption following the liberalisation of gold imports in 1992. Consumption seems to have remained around 400-425 tonnes in the next couple of years before resuming the rising trend. Estimated consumption in 1998 was more than thrice the level recorded in 1990 and nearly 70 per cent higher than in 1992. Domestic gold scrap is estimated to have met nearly a fourth of the demand in 1990. The scrap supplies, according to trade estimates has remained more or less stable in the past. Allowing for a 3 per cent annual increase in scrap availability—in the present state of knowledge this can be no more than a guestimate[2]—an increasing share of the demand has been met by imports.

Till 1991, practically all these imports were obtained by smuggling. But with liberalisation, the share of smuggled gold has progressively declined, both in absolute terms (from an estimated 290 tonnes in 1992 to 94 tonnes in 1998) and even more so in relation to total consumption (from over 70% in 1990 to less than an eighth in 1998). This decline is the direct result of progressive liberalisation of gold imports, (subject to payment of a 15% duty) and a considerable narrowing in the margin between international and domestic price of gold. This margin in 1998 was close to the import duty on gold. Note, however, that the volume of smuggling (90-100 tonnes a year)

1. There is room for further refinement in these estimates by: (a) disaggregating total consumption by end use between exports ornaments, and gold held as bars and (b) more reliable estimates of scrap availability. Given the extreme sensitivity of the matter, it is difficult to get reliable direct data on these aspects. But efforts to disaggregate, even if roughly, by end use is important for analysis.

2. 'Scrap' availability depends in part on the stock of ornaments. In the case of rural population, gold stocks seem likely to be affected by fluctuations in output and terms of trade. But little is known about these aspects.

remains quite large: a smuggler who successfully escapes the customs net still stands to make a substantial profit!

Economic Impact of Gold Imports

Gold, by itself, does not add much to production or productive capacity. However, the foreign exchange used for importing it, in effect, reduces the availability of this resource for other imports (including raw materials, intermediates and capital equipment) needed for current production and expand productive capacity. In the Indian context, the magnitude of foreign exchange expended on gold imports has been large and growing. In 1970, India's imports at the prices prevailing in the world market at that time would have cost 2.2 billion US dollars, equivalent to about one-eighth of merchandise exports and eight per cent of merchandise imports. The corresponding figures for 1997 being 7.5 billion US dollars (equivalent to about a fifth of exports and one-sixth of imports).

Prior to 1992, gold imports, being illegal, were financed by the proceeds of under-invoicing of exports, over invoicing of imports, earnings of migrant workers remitted through hawala channels, and smuggling of silver and contraband drugs. These transactions did not figure at all in the country's trade or payments statistics. After 1992, the value of legal gold imports cleared through the customs are included as part of merchandise imports in the balance of payments data (but not in trade statistics), an equivalent amount being recorded as transfer receipts under 'invisibles'. The nature and sources of the latter are not indicated for lack of information. Clearly they, as well as the resources needed for the still substantial smuggled gold, must have been derived from one or the other of the extra legal sources cited earlier. Possibly their relative importance has changed. In effect the hawala market continues to operate but with indirect legal sanction given by the gold import policy.

The magnitudes involved are large in relation to the size of the country's foreign trade and payments: the gold stock of the country at the end of 1997 was close to 10,000 tonnes valued at current prices on the world market at $120 billion: This is nearly four times the country's exports and official foreign reserves in that year. Their continued rapid growth can have significant consequences in terms of the scale and functioning of the hawala market, the availability of foreign exchange for other uses and the health of the balance of payments. The factors determining the demand for gold and the sources of finance for importing it therefore merit closer study.

The other characteristic of gold is that it is a highly liquid store of value. It represents command over resources, both at home and abroad, which can, in principle, be invoked whenever necessary. Its physical depreciation is negligible and it can be readily converted into cash by sale in the world markets for acquiring other resources, both at home and abroad. Though it does not earn any interest and though it is not any longer used as the standard for fixing currency values, the fact that there is a well developed world market for the metal and that its prices have until recently increased much faster than the general price level makes it a particularly attractive asset.

Insofar as gold is used as an ornament, it can be treated as a durable consumer good. But this function does not in any way dilute its advantages as a liquid, risk free asset. In any case, not all gold is held in the form of ornaments; a part (perhaps a large part)—no one knows how much—is held as hordes of bars. Altogether, from the country's viewpoint, gold holdings, whether as bars on ornaments, are no different from foreign exchange holdings. That the bulk of it is in the hands of private individuals who may or may not be willing to convert it into other assets is another matter, and does not detract from this feature. Of course it is important, in such a context, to understand why people prefer to hold gold and the conditions under which they will add to or reduce the stock of it in their hands. If accumulating gold, in principle, is no different from accumulation of foreign exchange reserves or investment in foreign financial assets, then they must properly be counted as part of the economy's savings. The more so because investment in gold is, in a real sense, a substitute for investment in other assets. It is significant that during the last few years, the value of additions to gold stock accounts for over 20 per cent of the private non-corporate sector's investment in financial assets. Also this proportion has been varying: from about 31-32 per cent in 1970, it fell to a low 2 per cent in 1979 but has since risen more or less progressively to reach 22-23 per cent in 1996-97.

Exclusion of gold from the estimates of domestic savings thus understates the household and overall domestic savings rate, and this bias has been increasing in the last 2 decades: thus during the early 1970s, the household savings including gold averaged around 12.2 per cent compared to 11.4 per cent as per official estimates; the difference is much narrower in the early 1980s, the respective rates being 14.1 per cent and 13.5 per cent respectively, but thereafter the divergence increased. During the mid 1990s (1994-95 to 1996-97), the household saving rate including gold averaged 21.6 per cent compared to 19.8 per cent excluding gold. This again emphasises the importance of including gold accumulations as part of domestic savings and focussing on the factors determining their level and disposition.

Factors Determining Gold Imports

Surprisingly there are few systematic studies of these issues. The only work that attempts to explore them, and is available in the public domain, is a paper published by the Reserve Bank of India in 1992 (Sarma *et al.*, 1992). Its primary purpose was to suggest ways in which, in the short run, 'gold already in the possession of the household sector' could be mobilised and used to 'release external constraints' and, in the long run, 'eliminate incentives for unofficial imports by narrowing the price differential between international and domestic markets' and to 'influence the asset preferences of households in favour of productive use of capital'. In the process, it provided a useful compilation of available data on production, imports and prices of gold; discussed the factors affecting the supply of and demand for gold and even attempted to empirically estimate supply and demand functions. The study identified the following major factors influencing demand: the price of gold, 'rural surplus' and rural income distribution, magnitude of 'black' income generated, rate of return on alternate financial assets and the general price level. The relevance of the price of gold and returns to alternative investments is obvious enough. Rural surplus not defined by the authors and income distribution were seen to be a function of irrigation and technological change. As the latter spread, marketed surplus and hence 'rural surplus' increases and generates 'a highly skewed income distribution'. All of which lead to higher demand for gold. Fertiliser consumption was used as a proxy for these factors in the estimated demand function.

The authors further argued that much of black income, which is an important source of demand for gold, 'looks like originating in the services sector rather than in commodity producing sectors'. Therefore, the income generated in the services sector was used as a proxy for black income. The general price level was expected to reduce the demand for gold by reducing the purchasing power for acquiring jewellery and reducing the real return on gold. These effects were, it was argued, likely to more than offset increased skewness of income distribution as a result of inflation.

Table 7.2

Trends in Gold Consumption after Liberalisation

(Tonnes)

	1990	*1991*	*1992*	*1993*	*1994*	*1995*	*1996*	*1997*	*1998*
1. Total demand[1]	236	260	454	424	415	477	508	737	770
2. Less:scrap[2]	60	70	70	70	70	71	75	75	76
3. New gold (1)-(2)	176	190	384	354	345	406	433	672	694
4. Official imports[3]	6	40	95	114	178	249	298	526	600
5. Non-official imports[4] (3)-(4)	170	150	289	240	167	157	135	146	94

Note: 1 Total demand figures from World Gold Council gleaned from newspaper reports. 1998 figure adjusted to annual basis using data for first three quarters and assuming fourth quarter demand to be slightly above the third quarter figures.

2 Sarma *et al.* (1992) give estimates of scrap for 1981 to 1990. The figure is more or less constant around 50 tonnes during the 1980s. The figure for 1990 is 60 tonnes. For other years, the difference between the World Gold Council estimate of total demand and total gold imports as given in Table 7.3 is taken to be met by scrap.

3 Figures of official imports from 1992 based on WGC estimates. 1990 official imports were negligible (6 tonnes); 1991 figures derived as difference between total gold import and unofficial imports.

4 Unofficial imports for 1990 and 1991 as given in Sarma *et al.*, (1992) (based on estimates of Consolidated Gold Field and Gold Field Mineral Services Ltd). For other years, derived as difference between total imports and official imports.

The econometric estimate of the demand function using the above variables yielded poor results: when fertiliser consumption and service sector income entered separately in the estimated equation, the coefficients were found to be significantly positive. But when both figured in the equation, the coefficients were not significant. Wholesale prices had a significantly negative coefficient in all specifications. The higher the wholesale price index (WPI), the lower the gold imports. The coefficient for gold price was significantly positive implying, contrary to expectation, that higher the gold prices, the higher the demand for gold. Returns to other financial assets were reported to have no significant relation to gold demand [Sarma *et al.*, 1992: 6-8, 38].

Table 7.3

Gold Imports and Related Macroeconomic Variables, India: 1970-71 to 1997-98

Year	Gold Imports (Tonnes)	GDPR Rs (10^9)	GDPN Rs (10^9)	GDSN Rs (10^9)	HHSN Rs (10^9)	HHFS Rs (10^9)	Price of Gold: Mumbai (Rs/10gm)	Price of Gold: London (Rs/10gm)	Gold (Value) Rs (10^9)	GDPDF	IDGP	IOSP	Gold Price Related to: GDPDF	Gold Price Related to: IOSP	MARG	HHSN/ GDPN	HHS/ GDS	HHFS/ GDPN	HHFS+G/ GDPN	RI
1970-71	217.00	904.26	431.63	67.83	48.73	12.7	184.96	88.71	4.01	44.10	12.20	62.60	27.66	19.49	1.08	11.30	71.84	2.94	3.87	7.60
1970-71	217.00	904.26	431.63	67.83	48.73	12.7	184.96	88.71	4.01	44.10	12.20	62.60	27.66	19.49	1.08	11.30	71.84	2.94	3.87	7.60
1971-72	176.00	913.39	462.57	75.08	54.77	15.5	200.16	113.22	3.58	46.50	13.10	59.50	28.17	22.02	0.77	11.80	72.95	3.35	4.12	6.10
1972-73	110.30	910.49	510.05	78.33	57.13	21.3	242.14	173.74	2.67	51.30	15.90	60.40	30.99	26.32	0.39	11.20	72.94	4.18	4.70	4.50
1973-74	63.60	951.92	620.07	114.32	85.62	36.1	369.23	290.50	2.35	60.00	24.20	71.80	40.33	33.70	0.27	13.80	74.90	5.82	6.20	2.60
1974-75	15.70	962.97	732.35	127.26	86.10	23.7	519.10	424.76	0.81	69.60	34.10	70.40	48.99	48.44	0.22	11.80	67.66	3.24	3.35	0.90
1975-76	26.20	1049.68	787.61	149.28	105.34	39.2	544.99	416.06	1.43	67.80	35.80	60.90	52.80	58.78	0.31	13.40	70.57	4.98	5.16	1.30
1976-77	33.80	1062.80	848.94	180.30	126.98	48.5	549.50	356.37	1.86	72.00	36.10	65.10	50.14	55.45	0.54	15.00	70.43	5.71	5.93	1.50
1977-78	40.50	1142.19	960.67	202.30	146.86	58.5	637.95	433.95	2.58	76.50	41.90	67.30	54.77	62.26	0.47	15.30	72.60	6.09	6.36	1.70
1978-79	45.20	1205.04	1041.90	241.38	177.47	66.6	791.22	550.21	3.58	77.90	52.00	81.70	66.75	63.65	0.44	17.00	73.52	6.39	6.74	2.00
1979-80	10.90	1142.36	1143.56	246.98	173.79	60.8	1158.75	1053.03	1.26	89.70	76.10	89.70	84.84	84.84	0.10	15.10	70.37	5.32	5.43	0.70
1980-81	8.30	1224.27	1360.13	287.86	218.48	86.1	1522.44	1485.31	1.26	100.00	100.00	100.00	100.00	100.00	0.03	16.00	75.90	6.33	6.42	0.60
1981-82	25.40	1298.89	1597.60	316.00	218.50	98.0	1719.00	1209.71	4.37	110.30	112.90	118.90	102.36	94.95	0.42	13.60	69.15	6.13	6.41	2.00
1982-83	60.00	1339.15	1781.32	337.80	230.40	127.9	1723.00	1250.36	10.34	119.10	113.20	110.40	95.05	102.54	0.38	12.90	68.21	7.18	7.76	4.20
1983-84	53.00	1448.65	2078.89	392.90	293.40	132.8	1859.00	1342.24	9.85	129.10	122.10	125.30	94.58	97.45	0.38	14.10	74.68	6.40	6.87	3.20
1984-85	94.50	1504.33	2313.43	421.80	317.00	181.0	1984.00	1294.19	18.75	138.80	130.40	136.00	93.95	95.88	0.53	13.70	75.15	7.82	8.63	5.60
1985-86	123.40	1565.66	2622.43	519.30	381.60	184.6	2126.00	1290.05	26.23	149.60	139.70	221.70	93.38	63.01	0.65	14.60	73.48	7.04	8.04	6.40
1986-87	88.40	1632.71	2929.49	548.00	415.60	233.1	2324.00	1577.73	20.54	159.90	152.70	230.60	95.50	66.22	0.47	14.20	75.84	7.96	8.66	4.70
1987-88	99.20	1703.22	3332.01	696.30	566.30	267.8	3082.00	1911.91	30.57	173.80	202.50	207.30	116.51	97.68	0.61	17.00	81.33	8.04	8.95	5.10
1988-89	135.00	1884.60	3965.93	846.70	682.50	271.1	3175.00	1959.88	42.86	187.90	208.60	247.50	111.02	84.28	0.62	17.20	80.61	6.84	7.92	5.90

contd...

...contd...

Year	Gold Imports (Tonnes)	GDPR Rs (10^9)	GDPN Rs (10^9)	GDSN Rs (10^9)	HHSN Rs (10^9)	HHFS Rs (10^9)	Price of Gold: Mumbai (Rs/10gm)	Price of Gold: London (Rs/10gm)	Gold (Value) Rs (10^9)	GDPDF	IDGP	IOSP	Gold Price Related to: GDPDF	Gold Price Related to: IOSP	MARG	HHSN/ GDPN	HHS/ GDS	HHFS/ GDPN	HHFS+G/ GDPN	RI
1989-90	172.50	2014.50	4568.00	1023.70	833.00	380.0	3229.00	2063.26	55.70	203.40	212.20	359.40	104.33	59.04	0.57	18.20	81.37	8.32	9.54	6.30
1990-91	170.00	2122.80	5355.00	1300.00	1096.00	497.0	3452.00	2164.26	82.85	225.60	226.80	500.30	100.53	45.33	0.59	20.50	84.31	9.28	10.83	5.10
1991-92	190.00	2141.60	6168.00	1412.50	1094.00	627.0	4298.00	2840.71	111.75	258.80	282.40	776.20	109.08	36.38	0.51	17.70	77.45	10.17	11.98	6.90
1992-93	384.00	2234.40	7059.00	1555.20	1248.00	657.0	4104.00	3331.20	186.32	280.80	269.60	1142.10	96.01	23.61	0.23	17.70	80.25	9.31	11.95	11.20
1993-94	354.00	2330.40	8098.00	1837.00	1407.00	950.0	4532.00	3767.20	192.16	307.80	297.80	1051.30	96.75	28.33	0.20	17.40	76.59	11.73	14.10	10.20
1994-95	345.00	2577.00	9537.00	2471.00	1954.00	1095.0	4667.00	3864.00	161.01	366.40	306.80	1537.30	90.50	19.94	0.21	20.50	79.08	11.48	13.17	7.60
1995-96	406.00	2761.00	11190.00	2830.00	2104.00	972.0	4958.00	4189.00	201.29	389.00	325.80	1189.60	88.92	27.39	0.18	18.80	74.35	8.69	10.49	8.70
1996-97	433.00	2968.00	12770.00	3382.00	2595.00	1334.0	5071.00	4284.00	219.57		333.20	1146.80	85.66	29.05	0.18	20.30	76.73	10.45	12.17	7.80
1997-98	672.00		14150.00	3679.00			4347.00	3776.00			285.60	1061.00			0.15					

Notes and *Sources*:

Gold Imports	Volume of gold imports up to 1990 as reported in Sarma *et al.*, 1992; for subsequent years World Gold Council estimates culled from newspapers. The figures relate to calendar years, e.g, 1970-71 related to 1970.
GDPR	Gross domestic product at factor cost (1980-81) prices as reported in National Income Statistics.
GDPN	Gross domestic product at current market prices.
GDSN	Gross domestic savings at current prices.
HHSN	Gross household savings at current prices.
HHFS	Ratio of household financial savings to gross national product
Gold Price	Average price per 10 gms in Mumbai and London as compiled.
Value of Gold	Value of imported gold in rupees at domestic price.
GDPDF	Implicit GDP deflator 1980-81 = 100.
IGDP	Index of domestic gold price 1980-81 = 100.
IOSP	RBI index of ordinary share price 1980-81 = 100.
Gold Price related to GDPDF	Ratio of index of gold price to implicit GDP deflator.
Related to IOSP	Ratio of the index of gold price to ordinary share price index.
MARG	Ratio of difference between domestic and foreign price of gold relative to foreign price.
HHSN/GDPN	Household savings as per cent of GDPN.
HHS/GDS	Household savings as per cent of total domestic savings.
R1	Value of gold/(HHSN+value of gold) 'gold consumption as a per cent of total hh savings (including gold).

The supply of gold, being almost entirely from smuggling, was seen as a function of the differential between its domestic and international price (reflecting the potential profit from smuggling), the premium in exchange rate prevailing in the hawala market relative to the official rate (reflecting the cost of acquiring the necessary foreign exchange through illegal channels), and the quantum of inflows in the form of foreign currency non-residents (FCNRs) deposits and remittances (presumed to be inversely related to the supply of foreign exchange in the hawala market) (ibid:12-13,39). The multiple regression of gold imports on the above variables covering the period 1970 to 1990 confirmed the expectation that, the higher the differential between domestic and foreign gold prices and the lower the hawala premium, the larger the gold imports. The coefficient for foreign currency deposits and remittances turned out, contrary to expectations, to be positive.

The above hypotheses regarding the determinants of gold imports as well as the manner in which they were tested leave room for improvement in several respects. In the first place, consumption demand for gold (as ornaments) depends not only on agricultural prosperity and the distribution of agricultural incomes but also on non-agricultural incomes and their distribution. It is possible that the preference of agricultural and non-agricultural population for ornaments differ, but little is known about this. Nor are any reliable time series of income distribution available. Under the circumstances, at the very least, it would be better to use overall real GDP rather than indirect and questionable proxies (like fertiliser consumption) for agricultural incomes alone.

Second, insofar as gold ornaments are viewed as durable consumer goods, the price of gold relative to the general price level would influence demand for (and therefore imports of) gold. One might expect that the higher the price of gold relative to prices of other commodities and services consumed, the smaller will be the demand for gold.

Third, insofar as gold is sought and held as asset, the demand for it might be expected to depend on the volume of savings. For a given level of GDP, the higher the savings rate, the higher is likely to be the demand for gold. Neither government nor public and corporate enterprises invest in gold. Therefore, household saving would be more relevant in determining gold demand than the overall domestic saving rate.

Savings can be used to buy gold, acquire other financial asset or invest in physical assets. The demand for gold for any given level of GDP and saving rate will therefore depend significantly on the allocation between these forms of assets. It seems more likely that investment in gold will depend on the magnitude of saving in the form of financial assets than of total savings. The allocation of financial saving between gold and all other kinds of financial assets depends, among other things, on the relative returns of these two categories of assets.

Financial assets differ in terms of liquidity, the extent to which they provide a hedge against inflation, the risks involved and the rate of return after adjusting for taxes and changing market price of assets. Gold is almost as liquid as currency, and much easier (and less costly) to dispose of than other financial assets. If gold prices rise faster than the general price level (and the prices of financial investments), investment in gold will be seen as a superior hedge against inflation and preferred for that reason.

Many financial assets (like currency or bank deposits or provident funds) offer little hedge against inflation. Some others (like ordinary shares) do. Where there is a well functioning market (as in the case of shares and securities) and volume of financial investments available in the market is large relative to the savings, the attraction of gold would be significantly influenced by behaviour of its price relative to that of securities.

Table 7.4

Estimated Multiple Regressions to Explain Level of Gold Imports in India

Period	*Functional form*	R^2	*Coefficient for*			
			GDPR	*HHFS*	*IOSP*	*MARG*
1970-90	Linear	0.775			+0.167 (2.83)	+208.8 (7.06)
	Log linear	0.728			+0.368 (6.50)	+.961 (2.08)
1970-96	Linear	0.890	.075 (1.75)	–28.4 (2.88)	+0.299 (3.28)	1.36 (3.28)
	Log linear	0.783	–1.34 (1.03)	–0.82 (1.30)	+1.47 (4.07)	.753 (5.17)

Note: Figures in brackets represent 'T' value of the coefficient.

Yet another relevant consideration could be that incomes from financial assets attract tax and are more difficult to hide them than gold. Though gold does not give any current income, it is easier to conceal from tax authorities. Where the incentive to evade taxes is higher (because of high tax rate and/ or lax administration), the attraction of gold is likely to be higher. The attraction would be stronger when gold prices move at least as fast as the market price of other financial instruments. This aspect however is difficult to quantify.

Financial assets are highly heterogeneous and their composition as well as market values are variable over time. It is therefore difficult to get a weighted index of returns to financial assets as a whole. Sarma *et al.*, computed the rate of return on representative financial assets, but the basis is not spelt out. Moreover, this specification does not take into account the level of market prices of the asset. For these reasons, the present analysis uses the market prices of ordinary shares (reflecting rate of return as well as extent of protection against inflation) as a proxy for the return to financial assets.

Fourth, Sarma *et al.*'s estimating equations include domestic gold price, the WPI, and 'rate of return on representative financial assets' among the explanatory variables. The impact of gold being a function of gold price relative to 'substitutes', it would seem more appropriate to specify price variables in the estimating equation as prices of gold relative to the general price level and to the ordinary share prices.

Fifth, from the supply side view point, the quantum of gold imported would depend (as Sarma *et al.* rightly argue) on the extent to which domestic price exceeds the price in the world gold market and, under a regime of fixed rates, the difference between the open market rate of exchange and the official rate. The former (which reflects the impact of changes in domestic and foreign prices as well as exchange rate changes) indicates the potential margin of smuggler's profit on imported gold. The latter, representing the extra cost he has to incur to get the needed exchange in the hawala market was an important factor till 1992 when exchange rates were left more or less free to be determined by the market and gold imports were legalised. Sarma *et al.*'s estimated equation for the period 1968-1990 includes the *hawala* rate, but yearwise data on these rates are not given.[3] After 1992, of course,

3. The omission of the hawala premium from the estimated relation would give biased estimates of the coefficients. This could be connected if the relevant data used by Sarma *et al.* were available.

the difference between the rate on the official foreign exchange market and the rate in the hawala market has been greatly narrowed, though perhaps not entirely eliminated. We have therefore had to omit this variable in the present exercise.

The logic of including accretions to FCNR deposits and remittances to capture the supply of hawala exchange is rather dubious. In any case the open market exchange rate already reflects the net effect of both demand and supply of exchange in that market. There is no need to introduce a variable to capture supply of exchange in the hawala market.

In view of these considerations, gold imports viewed from the supply side is postulated to be a function essentially of the margin between domestic and international prices. And since observed gold imports simultaneously denote the quantum absorbed by, and the quantum supplied in, the market, it is not meaningful to estimate supply and demand functions separately. Therefore, we use a reduced form combining elements affecting both side of the picture. Thus, gold imports

$$= f\left(GDPR, HHFS, \frac{GPRICE}{GDPDF}, \frac{GPRICE}{IOSP}, MARG\right)$$

Where,

GDPR – Total gross domestic product at constant price

HHFS – Ratio of household financial savings to gross national product

GPRICE – Domestic price of gold

GDPDF – Implicit GDP deflator

IOSP – Index of ordinary share prices

MARG – Difference between domestic and foreign price of gold as per cent of foreign price.

Estimation and Results

The above relation has been estimated in its linear and loglinear forms on the basis of data for the period 1970-1996. These data and their sources are set out in the Table 7.5. A clarification regarding gold import figures is in order. The figures up to 1990 are estimates of the Consolidated Gold Field and Gold Field Mineral Services reproduced in Sarma *op. cit.* (p.29). Thereafter, the estimates are taken from the World Gold Council, which is said to have started functioning in 1990. These are the best informed estimates of experts on the world gold trade. However, it must be noted that the basis for these estimates and the comparability of the pre-1990 estimates and those for subsequent years could not be ascertained.[4]

Since the policy regime affecting gold imports changed radically in the 1990s, the above relation has been estimated separately for the period 1970 to 1990 as well as for 1970 to 1996. The number of observations available for the post-liberalisation phase is too small to permit a satisfactory testing of difference in the underlying relations before and after liberalisation. Instead, comparison of the predicted values for 1991 to 1996 based on the regressions for the two periods with actual values is used to find out whether liberalisation made a significant difference.

The regressions were initially run using all the five explanatory variables included in specification in the equation on page 186. The coefficient for the ratio of the gold price index to the index of GDP deflator turned out to be statistically non-significant in practically all cases. This variable was therefore dropped and the regressions reestimated. The coefficients for GDPR and also HHFS were non-significant in both the regressions for the period 1970-1990 but significant in the linear regression for 1970-1996. Therefore, regressions for 1970-1990 were reestimated with only IOSP and MARG. All four variables were retained in regressions for 1979-1996. The results (summarised in Table 7.5) indicate the following.

The bulk of the variations in gold imports (upwards of 75% and in one case, as much as 89%) are accounted by the explanatory variables. The regression for the entire series (1970-1996) explains a higher proportion of variance in gold imports during this period than the regression for the period prior to liberalisation.

The coefficients for GDPR and HHFS are not statistically significant during 1970-1990. This implies that in this period, gold imports were not influenced by the level of real output or household financial savings. They were therefore dropped and regression reestimated using only IOSP and

4. According to Sarma *et al. op. cit.* (p.10), as against the Gold Fields Mineral Services estimate of 170 tonnes of imports during 1989-1991, the World Gold Council estimated the 1990 imports at 240 tonnes. This suggests that the assumptions and basis of the two estimates differ. To this extent the series for 1991-1997 is not strictly comparable to that for earlier years.

Table 7.5

Estimated and Actual Gold Imports, and the Contribution of Significant Explanatory Factors in Recent Decades, India

(Tonnes)

Period	Actual	Predicted Values Based on Multiple Regressions* for Different Periods: 1970-71 to 1996-97								1970-71 to 1990-91				
		Predicted Total	Mean Deviation (Per cent)	Estimated Contribution of: Constant	GDPR	IOSP	MARG	HHFS		Predicted Total	Mean Deviation (Per cent)	Estimated Contribution of: Constant	IOSP	MARG
1970-1980	750	703	82.4	252	860	236	689	-1274		681	67.7	-283	132	965
1981-1990	1021	1095	32.8	229	1239	675	711	-1758		1090	25.3	-377	377	1090
1991-1996	2112	2066	17.8	137	1126	2046	206	-1449		1232	35.7	-226	1143	315
1970-1996	3883	3864	49.6	618	3225	2957	1606	-4481		3003	45.5	-886	1652	2370

Note: * The linear form. Mean deviation = Mean of deviations between predicted and actual values during each period as per cent of actuals.

MARG. Both coefficients are strongly positive, corroborating the expectation that higher the difference between domestic and foreign gold prices and higher the ratio of gold to share prices, the larger will be the gold imports.

Estimates for the entire period show the coefficients for all four explanatory variables to be significant. The signs of the coefficients for GDPR, IOSP and MARG are positive as expected. But the negative coefficient for HHFS implies that higher financial saving by households goes with smaller gold imports. (The results are similar if we specify household financial savings to include gold acquisitions or use the total household saving rate instead of the financial savings rate.) This is against expectation.

The positive and highly significant coefficient for IOSP and MARG establish convincingly that gold imports tend to be higher when domestic gold prices rise relative to those of: (a) ordinary shares and (b) international gold price. The estimates further suggest that the effect of both these variables on gold imports was considerably less during 1970-1990 than the period taken as a whole.

The fact that the value (and in some cases the significance) of the coefficients estimated from the two series are markedly different suggest that the underlying relations may have undergone substantial changes between 1970-1990 and 1991-1996. This is illustrated by comparing the closeness of the predicted values estimated from the linear regressions for the two periods to the actuals. The results are presented in Table 7.5.

They show that the mean percentage deviation between predicted and actual values of gold imports during the period 1970-1996 is only slightly more when predictions are based on the regressions for the entire period, compared to predictions based on regression using 1970 to 1990 data. However, the picture is very different when we consider different sub-periods. The percentage differences between predicted and actual values during 1970-1980 and 1981-1990 are considerably less when predictions are based on the 1970-1990 series compared to those based on the 1970-1996 series; the opposite being the case in respect of the 1990s.

Another way of looking at it is to compare the total of predicted and actual gold imports derived from regressions for the two periods. By this criterion, the predicted imports of gold during 1970-1980 and 1980-1990 are roughly the same in both cases. But during 1991-1996, the prediction based on 1970-1990 regressions are 40 per cent below the actual, while those based on the 1970-1996 regressions are close to the actual.

The table further shows that, while variations in IOSP and MARG are major factors affecting gold imports in all cases, the influence of GDP and HHFS (which was weak during 1970-1990) become significant when we consider the period as a whole. Another significant point emerging from both projections is the increasing importance of IOSP and the decline in that of MARG in accounting for the changes in gold imports. Thus, the regressions based on 1970-1996 show that IOSP accounted for 33 per cent of the predicted gold imports during the 1970s, 62 per cent in 1980s and nearly 100 per cent in the 1990s. The corresponding figures for MARG being 98 per cent, 65 per cent and 10 per cent respectively.

The relative roles of these two factors need closer study. The 1970s were marked by an increase in IOSP and a decline in the margins. Though the former would have meant higher demand for gold, imports fell probably because the black market exchange rates were too high to make gold smuggling profitable. The 1980s witnessed a reversal with IOSP showing a falling trend even as MARG rose steeply. The margin of profit after allowing for cost of dollar in the hawala market might have been sufficient to attract gold imports. But during the 1990s, both have been falling; with gold imports legalised, the principal determinant is the IOSP whose decline seems to be the principal stimulant for a steep rise in gold imports.

Conclusion

In sum, it is clear that the price of gold relative to share prices and international gold prices are important determinants of gold imports. IOSP is emerging as an increasingly important factor, even as the margin between domestic and foreign of gold has dwindled largely as a result of changes in exchange rate and gold import policies. So long exchange rate and gold imports are allowed to be determined by the market, IOSP seems likely to emerge as the crucial determinant of gold imports. However, the results need to be confirmed by incorporating the hawala premium in the estimating equation. The role of aggregate income is not clearly established: it seems to be unimportant in the pre-liberalisation period but emerges as significant when we consider the period as a whole. Whether, and how far, this may be due to non-comparability of estimates for the pre-1990 and post-1990 period needs to be more closely examined. The strong, large and unexpectedly negative impact of household financial savings on gold imports is difficult to explain. The nature of the underlying relations, and their specification in the estimating equation, deserve deeper probing.

References

Sarma, A., A. Vasudevan, K. Sabapathy and M. Roy (1992). "Gold Mobilisation as an Instrument of External Adjustment", *Reserve Bank of India Discussion Paper*. DRG Studies. Mumbai: RBI.

IV

Political and Institutional Dimensions

8 Irrigation Institutions

An Evolutionary Perspective

Introduction

The functioning of all societies involves activities that are numerous, diverse and interrelated. They are carried out by different types of organisations in different spheres. The nature and objectives of these activities and the manner in which their pursuit is organised and managed are also varied. The social system as a whole can be viewed as a multilayered but interconnected web comprising numerous organisations. Their orderly functioning requires rules governing the domain and functions of organisations in different layers and their inter relations, the structure of their internal management, and the rights and obligations of stakeholders *inter se* and with the organisations that serve them. These rules have to be backed by mechanisms for monitoring/enforcing compliance and for settling disputes/mediating conflicts over their interpretation and observance. The basis on which rules are constructed, the locus of authority to make and enforce them and the forces (and in particular the role of 'power') shaping the manner in which the process in fact works are of obvious relevance to any study of social institutions.

It is important to recognise that authority to make and enforce rules operates in a material and social context comprising individuals and groups with divergent, competing and, at times, conflicting beliefs, goals and interests. It is necessary to have mechanisms for achieving a workable balance between the diverse and changing goals and interests of constituents and to resolve conflicts among them. Such mechanisms are built into the design of all social institutions but their functioning depends on those who design and control them. The manner and extent to which they cope with changes necessitated by internal and external factors depend both on their magnitude and the institutions' resilience to respond and adapt themselves to changing situations without unmanageable disruptions.

This paper explores the evolution of irrigation institutions in this perspective and the approaches to understanding the process. While the focus is on the Indian experience, the discussion is of wider relevance not only to irrigation in other countries but also for understanding the dynamics of a wider class of institutions.

Evolution of Irrigation in India

Irrigation plays an important role in India's agricultural economy. Vast variations in the productivity of land (and its growth), across regions are in large measure explained by differences in nature and extent of irrigation (and changes therein). The impact of irrigation depends on the extent to which it increases the overall quantum and reliability of water supply. These in turn are conditioned by agroclimatic conditions, the nature of the water source and the manner in which water distribution is managed. The impact is likely to be much greater in hot and arid areas where rainfall is low, highly variable within and across seasons compared to areas with relatively high, more reliable and more evenly distributed rainfall across the year. Small storages depending on local catchments are likely to contribute much less to increasing productivity compared to larger storages drawing their water supply from wider catchments. Regulating the distribution of water from surface irrigation works to match crop water needs is difficult both technically and managerially. In all these respects, characteristics of ground water are very different: its extraction and management are amenable to the preferences of individuals; control over timing and quantum of water use is easier; and, until recently, not subject to social control.

Water by nature is a renewable but finite resource, it is, therefore, important to ensure that its exploitation is kept within sustainable limits set by the volume of renewable supplies. It is also important to ensure a fair and equitable sharing of available supplies among different uses and users. Being a fluid common pool resource, the market mechanism cannot perform these functions. The conditions necessary for an effective market mechanism to mediate allocations (and in particular clearly defined and enforceable private property rights) are nearly impossible to fulfil. Entitlement to access (geographical and by use) to a given source (which could be a tank, a reservoir, a river basin, or an aquifer) as well as the sharing of the available supplies from that source among diverse claimants is therefore, everywhere regulated through social institutions.

The mammoth flood control works of ancient China, extensive canal deltaic irrigation systems in Mesopotamia, the Nile, and the Cauvery are some notable examples of early attempts to construct and manage large scale water control and irrigation systems. These are associated with the emergence of prosperous agrarian civilisations that sustained centralised empires holding sway over wide areas. Many, but not all, of them went into decline due to a variety of factors including physical deterioration of works, major changes in climate, internal upheavals and external invasions.

Before the 20th century, irrigation in India was mostly from small scale tanks and diversion of local stream flow constructed by village communities and from shallow dug wells. Though widespread, they benefited only a very small proportion of cultivated area.

Over time, the local surface systems went through a process of expansion and integration covering several contiguous communities. This process, of which there are well-documented accounts for India, as wells as China, Japan, and Indonesia, is the result of a combination of local level interest in exploiting potential for increased production through expansion of irrigation as well as encouragement and support from regional chieftains interested in expanding their domain and revenues. The latter seem to have played basically a facilitating role.

These systems have undergone several changes over time. Unsettled conditions during the early phases of British rule and changes in the traditional system of land tenure led to a deterioration of the physical facilities due to neglect of maintenance and repair of major damages caused by natural calamities and local military conflicts. The state took over these responsibilities as well as that of regulating water management in some of the larger multicommunity works. However, many of them had elaborate rules, sanctioned by long standing conventions, regarding the rights of different communities, scheduling of water and sharing it in times of scarcity, as well as mechanisms for monitoring, enforcement and conflict resolution among users. These were left undisturbed. Maintenance and management of water allocation in other smaller works were left to be handled by local communities. Entitlements to and allocation of water from these local works were regulated and disputes were settled locally by the concerned communities based on traditional conventions and informal negotiations.

The government's role in rehabilitation and improvement of existing works and also construction of new minor irrigation works at public expense has increased progressively. So has the scope and need for involvement of extra/supra-local centres of authority. This trend has intensified further in recent times as traditional local institutions weakened. This weakening is the result of major changes in the social composition of land ownership, growing conflicts between uses and users of water, and changing configurations of local power, increased contacts with the outside world (through for example migration, integration with wider markets and spread of education), and incursion of extra-local institutions and centres of power (state government and its bureaucracy, political parties and the judicial system) in community affairs.

Most of the expansion in irrigation over the last century has come from large scale surface irrigation systems and exploitation of ground water. This trend has been facilitated by advances in civil and hydraulic engineering technology that have made it possible to construct large storages and extensive canal networks. The growing pressure of demand for water for increasing food and fibre production has been a strong impetus for their increasing importance. The resources and organisation needed to implement them are far beyond the capacity of local communities. The state has, therefore, taken the responsibility for planning, construction and management of these systems as part of national development plans. Their development has become central to the strategy for promoting rapid agricultural growth. Massive amounts of public funds have been invested in them.

These systems serve large areas, numerous uses and a huge number of users. Balancing the competing claims of different regions, uses and users and managing the continuing task of regulating the distribution of water requires huge, complex, multitiered organisations managed by a professional bureaucracy based on formal rules and procedures. The state specifies regulations concerning the structure, composition and role of these organisations and procedures and mechanisms for dispute settlement. The mechanisms and personnel to handle most of these functions are manned by officials appointed by and answerable to the state.

By contrast, ground water, though a common pool resource in a given aquifer, can be easily tapped from wells and tube wells and lifting devices that are within the capacity of individuals and can be adjusted, within limits, to their water needs. Exploitation of ground water is therefore mostly in the private sector but usually subject to government regulation. The extent of ground water irrigation was relatively limited until the advent of energised pumping which greatly reduced costs by making it possible to tap deeper aquifers and lift much larger volumes per unit of time. Improvements in agricultural technology (notably the introduction of high yielding varieties) and the spread of electricity to rural areas gave a strong fillip to expansion of ground water use in recent decades. The process has been actively encouraged and supported by the government leaving the actual construction and operation of wells and tube wells to farmers.

Changes in agricultural technology through the introduction of new crops and varieties and non-traditional inputs, reinforced by a policy of providing most inputs, including water, at subsidised rates have increased the returns to irrigated agriculture. This has led to a huge surge in demand for irrigation even as demand for non-agricultural uses is growing rapidly. With demand outstripping the increase in supplies from public systems, unauthorised and illegal tapping of surface water have increased and become widespread. Extraction of ground water in many regions is already more than renewable recharge and is reaching the limit in more and more areas. Conflicts over water between uses, users and regions have intensified.

At the same time the expansion and imprudent use of chemical fertilisers and plant protection chemicals have led to increasingly widespread pollution of water sources. These trends are the result of complex and intricate interactions between the characteristics of water, technological, institutional and economic factors and policies that seek to manage them. Containing these trends has become a major problem but efforts to address it have been both inadequate and ineffective.

Current academic research and policy analysis tend to focus on particular aspects: the major ones are—the impact of irrigation on agricultural growth, equity in access to and use of water, user participation in management, issues relating to water pricing, adverse social and environmental impact of large reservoirs, expansion of ground water and the depletion of that resource, the nature of water related disputes and conflicts and the efficacy of mechanisms to resolve them. Researchers tend to view each of these aspects individually and at specific locations from fragmented disciplinary perspectives, exploring the interconnections between different facets of the resource and their management calls for a wider multi- disciplinary perspective that is rare. Studies of the dynamics of change are even rarer. The rest of the paper tries to address this lacuna based on extant research on various aspects available in the literature and on my own research over the years to understand the structure and functioning of irrigation institutions and their dynamics.[1]

Framework for Study of Institutions

The literature on irrigation institutions highlights the diversity of their forms, structure and functioning, and to some degree their historical evolution. It is rich in description but rather less so in throwing light on the factors underlying variations in these respects and in their effectiveness. Collective action theories help in exploring the working of community level institutions to some extent. But they are inadequate when local institutions are part of a wider network of institutions and more so for studying organisations managing large irrigation systems.

Much of the discussion of these aspects tends to view them from a management perspective and focus on particular issues such as the technical design of systems, ability to ensure proper maintenance of facilities, pricing policies, monitoring and enforcement of rules, and corruption. Much is also written about the relative merits of centralised versus decentralised management, bureaucratic versus self-managed systems, and markets versus public regulation. These provide useful partial perspectives but are inadequate to comprehend differences in structure and functioning of networks of inter-related institutions and large organisations.

Irrigation institutions share certain common characteristics with other institutions in that their functioning is governed by a framework of rules and regulations defining the domain of their activities, the goals they are

1. see Vaidyanathan, (1999), (2001), (2006), (2008).

expected to pursue, the structure of the organisation and its management, and mechanisms for accountability of performance. However given the common pool nature of water and the multiplicity of functions it performs, they are required to balance multiple objectives (efficiency, equity and sustainability of water use) and are open to state intervention and political forces to a much greater degree than private enterprise.

While there is no unified theory applicable to public systems, the basic concepts and insights of institutional economics can be used to understand better the way water institutions are structured, and how they function and change, and for the differences in these respects. In doing so it is important to bear in mind that the working of irrigation institutions, as well as their overall outcomes are significantly influenced by agroclimatic conditions, technology for harnessing and use of water for agriculture, and the socio-economic and political environment.

Small Scale Local Systems

Consider, for example, the relatively simple case of an irrigation tank in Tamil Nadu. Typically it serves a section of farmland within the village. It is considered to be the common property of the village community. Access to and use of the water is expected to be governed by customary rules and conventions. Originally—often several centuries back—these were constructed under the leadership of local temples, prominent landowners or local chieftains with contributions of material and labour by members of the community.

The rules for maintenance of the physical infrastructure and management of available water to ensure that it is distributed in a fair manner among the users are based on an implicit social contract in the communities. Typically they spell out the contribution expected of members of the irrigation community to the maintenance and upkeep of the tank and its distribution network and for appointment and remuneration of its functionaries. The notion of equity is also fuzzy sometimes focusing on head to tail allocations; sometimes on fair sharing of available supplies in times of scarcity; but rarely of equal access to different classes of farmers. In all these respects actual practice, if not the rules, change over time.

The authority to make and change rules, as well as to enforce sanctions for non-compliance, is, in theory, vested with the community. In fact, however, the exercise of this authority is in effect delegated to leaders. They have traditionally been drawn from the relatively well-to-do landowners belonging to the dominant caste/s in the community. The realisation of the overall yield impact (both overall and for individual irrigators) depends on the proper observance of obligations for maintenance and the rules of water allocation; non-observance entails the risk of not realising the yield potential. For this reason irrigators collectively have a strong shared interest and individuals have the incentive to ensure that rules are observed. There are designated functionaries to attend to monitoring and enforcement. Within a small community getting reliable and timely information on rule compliance is relatively easy and inexpensive.

The economic and social position of the dominant users gives them the power to enforce compliance if need be through coercive means. Their personal interest is not always harmonised with that of other, less well-endowed members or of the community as a whole. In that event, the dominant group is in a position to use its authority and power to manipulate the rules and their application in its favour. That, by virtue of their position and experience, they may be better informed about the intricacies of functioning of the system also makes it possible for dominant groups to manipulate the use of such information to their advantage.

This does not mean that everyone will be satisfied with the way the system is managed or with all decisions of those in authority. Nor does it mean that there are no conflicts over water among users. Nevertheless the disaffected are content to acquiesce in the situation so long as the attitudes and responses of those in authority to different contingencies are predictable. Conflicts are not pushed to the brink of breakdown because there are also costs to defying the authority and because members of the irrigation community are inter-related at several levels and in diverse ways and have to maintain long-term relationships with each other. So long as the local power relations are stable, the interpretation and enforcement of 'rules' under different contingencies is predictable, the system does not get disrupted and manages to maintain more or less orderly functioning.

The picture is more complicated in the case of local systems serving several communities like the system tanks and tank cascades in south India, and the 'melons on vine' of China. Often they evolved by expanding and integrating pre-existing local systems through a process of trial and error and mutual negotiations among the concerned communities with the support and active encouragement of supra-local authority (chieftains, kings). The institutions to manage them are more complex than those works serving single communities. They are known to have evolved elaborate conventions concerning the rights of different communities, scheduling of water and sharing it in times of scarcity, as well as mechanisms for monitoring, enforcement and conflict resolution.

Authority and power do play an important role in formulating and implementing the rules but are more diffused than in a single community. Built-in containment mechanisms are much weaker than within individual villages. Consequently constituent communities put in more effort to monitor each other's activities in relation to the system and rely more on mutual accommodation through negotiation. The relative power of leadership of constituent communities has an important role in the process but cannot always handle conflicts amicably without external intervention. Institutions of governance at higher levels have to intervene by laying down a framework in which local institutions are to function and, therefore, their involvement in the settlement of disputes is greater. The extent of this involvement and intervention has vastly increased in recent times.

These institutions have had to adapt to physical deterioration of their systems, reduction in water availability, changes in irrigation and agricultural technology, competition from other uses, and changes in social structure of communities. The process has been uneven and not always conducive to smooth and efficient functioning. Large numbers have gone out of use due to neglect, encroachment and pollution; traditional institutions have weakened because of internal social changes. Nevertheless, a large number of systems of this category have been able to remain functional over long periods. They have also adapted to changing conditions but only to a limited extent.

Large Scale Systems

The picture is very different in the case of large surface irrigation works most of which have been constructed, financed and managed entirely by the government. Time was when fresh investment in such works (except protective works in famine prone areas) was made only when there was an assurance that it would earn a net return in terms of government revenue. There are instances of the government taking up less viable projects on condition that the beneficiaries contributed a substantial part of the investment. Management was vested with the bureaucracy with practically no user participation. Neither efficiency (in terms of output impact) nor equity in distribution was the central consideration. The focus was on ensuring that users paid their dues. Political considerations and pressures did play a role but not in the degree and manner observed currently.

The state's role in developing water resources for irrigation and other uses increased dramatically in the post Independence era. The expansion of irrigation was essential for raising agricultural production and thereby incomes and employment in rural areas and for supporting faster growth in the rest of the economy. The scope for increasing irrigation from small scale local works and dug wells being very limited, harnessing river flows by constructing large reservoirs and canal networks, and utilising ground water resources became imperative. While technology rendered both these possible, the resources and effort needed to exploit the potential they opened up reached unprecedented levels in scale and complexity. As a matter of policy, the government decided to take exclusive responsibility for planning, construction and management of all large-scale surface water projects.

The task has however become much wider and more complex than expansion of supplies. It has to deal with the problem of defining and enforcing the basis to determine entitlements of various users and uses across and within basins; regulation and pricing of water for different uses; minimise adverse effects caused by displacement of people and loss of productive land and forests and provide adequate corrective measures to address them; contain and reduce pollution of water sources; and regulate the exploitation and use of water to ensure efficiency and long term sustainability. These problems have grown in importance over the years. Since these objectives are not all mutually consistent, this balancing is inherently difficult.

In principle these issues can and ought to be decided on the basis of clearly laid out priorities to different objectives; careful, transparent and public consideration by independent experts of alternative feasible patterns of exploitation and use; their implications in terms of costs and the impact on different objectives and trade-offs among them. But this is not the way the system works. While the rhetoric of policy pronouncements express commitment to all these aims, little has been done to define the priorities clearly or to set up institutional mechanisms to work out and implement a coherent programme of action to realise them.

The plethora of laws and regulations tend to see different problems and their solutions in fragmented perspectives. They are quite fuzzy, riddled with loopholes and do not take cognisance of the conflicts and complementarities between measures to address different objectives; they tend to rely mainly on penalties and hardly on incentives. In any case they cannot be implemented because implementing agencies are also fragmented and have neither the personnel nor the authority to enforce them. Recourse to courts has increased but this has made very limited impact because of delays in getting decisions and difficulties in having them implemented.

The growing demand for water and the surge of grassroot pressures for increased water supplies has overwhelmed the claims of other objectives. Political necessity and expediency drives policy makers to attach greater importance to satisfying the mounting grassroots pressures for increased water supplies than to ensuring other objectives (efficiency, equity and sustainability) which are more disparate and whose solutions are more complex and call for long term action. Moreover, those concerned about these aspects are neither organised nor equipped—in terms of knowledge and resources—to articulate their interests effectively with the government directly or in the political space.

Preoccupation with expansion of supplies also serves the interests of politicians. They are naturally concerned with retaining power, or wresting it from opponents, both at a personal level and for the party/group to which they belong. Given the widespread clamour for water, all parties use promises of larger investments in water projects in their competition for electoral support. This propensity is stronger when politics is in a fluid state, and tenures are short and uncertain.

Moreover with the government undertaking to finance the entire cost, the demand for starting irrigation projects soared. Their potential as a means of cultivating and expanding electoral support made elected governments eager to accede to these demands. This led to promises to launch far more projects than could be accommodated with available funds.

More and more projects have come to be based on inadequate investigations and are poorly designed. Pressures for relaxing and diluting the appraisal processes have grown.

Many projects have been taken up without prior technical approval or financial sanctions. The fund raising potential of construction contracts for politicians and bureaucracy further distorts the programme and erodes procedures for technical and financial audits to the point of nullity. Countervailing forces to check these trends have been deliberately weakened. For much the same reason, the policy that irrigation projects should bring a reasonable net return on investment was given up soon after independence.

It is not that there are no institutional mechanisms to keep these propensities in check. Project proposals are supposed to be scrutinised by independent experts to evaluate their technoeconomic viability before being cleared for implementation; there are procedures for award of contracts based on open, competitive bids; statutory public audit reporting to parliament and the legislatures are mandatory; regulatory bodies are supposed to review and approve pricing decisions. Civil society has numerous organisations that track the weaknesses of polices and their implementation, educate public opinion and seek corrective action through protests, regulatory agencies and the courts.

But these are not effective. Under the existing regime the decisions on projects to be taken up, appraising them, awarding contracts and monitoring their implementation are all made by agencies controlled by the government. These agencies, including independent regulatory bodies, lack the autonomy and independence to ensure objectivity and transparency in deciding these matters. Oversight agencies like CAG as well as courts and other adjudicatory institutions have not been effective in checking illegality and corruption in government and adjudicating disputes over sharing of water among riparians of interstate rivers. Failure to provide full and free public access to information on executive decisions and their rationale severely impeded the capacity of stakeholders, interest groups and civil society organisations to exert countervailing pressure on state agencies to check and correct these tendencies.

Under these conditions the expansion of water supplies through public irrigation systems has turned out to be incommensurate with the magnitude of resources invested in them, and much below the targets. At the same time, the policy of subsidising canal water and of energy for lifting ground water has led to demand for water growing much faster than supplies from public systems and also in relation to renewable ground water resources. This has led to extraction and use of water by farmers and other users on a huge scale without any authorisation from government. Governments have been unable and unwilling, for reasons of political expediency, to check this trend and the attendant increase in scale and spread of conflicts over water.

These features spill over into the continuing management of water projects. In the case of surface systems, delineation of the area commanded by each system is decided at the time of design on the basis of expected water availability to the system, estimates of irrigation requirements of various crops taking into account local rainfall and losses in conveying water from source to field, and crop patterns that would serve as large an area as possible with the available supplies. These in turn form the basis for formulating rules regarding scheduling of water and conditions for permissible crop patterns.

These estimates suffer from inadequate and unreliable information of most key parameters. Assumed crop patterns are often dictated more by political compulsions to accommodate claims to extend the command area than any realistic assessment of the feasibility of achieving the assumed crop patterns. Because of this, engineering design of systems, the patterns of use and the objectives they are meant to achieve and the rules and procedures to implement them are seldom coherent and internally consistent. They are certainly not capable of ensuring that available water is used efficiently and equitably. The spread of conjunctive use of surface and ground water in areas served by canals has been beneficial to a limited but uneven extent.

These inadequacies and resulting inconsistencies surface once the systems become operational. Actual water availability to individual systems depends on the rainfall in the basin of which they are part and on usage by other systems (whether authorised or unauthorised). Rainfall is variable and the allocation of available flows between different systems and users in the basin is neither rule based and effectively regulated by the state. On the other hand, actual crop patterns invariably turn out to be very different from design assumptions. All these are prone to unpredictable variations over time in direction, timing and magnitude.

System managers have the authority to adapt to changing conditions in these respects. But this flexibility is not exercised on the basis of objective study of the factors responsible for wide divergence of reality from design assumptions and experienced changes in the nature and extent of temporal variations in the availability of and demand for water in the system. Key decisions that affect the water available to different systems are made by the government, rather than the system managers. They tend to be ad hoc and non transparent in terms of the data and the principles on which they are based. This is also characteristic of the way the allocation and use of water to users within systems are managed.

Entitlements of users within the command of systems are defined in terms of area that each can irrigate and not in terms of volume, duration and timing of supplies. Entitlements for irrigators and other uses are also liable to be changed at the discretion of government and its functionaries. Supply to the system is also variable. The ability to regulate the distribution of quantum and timing of supplies to different segments of the command is constrained by the design and conditions of the distribution network. Actual crop patterns chosen by farmers and their requirements of irrigation water invariably turn out to be very different from those assumed in the design. Given the enormous number of holdings dispersed over wide areas and growing diverse crops, it is difficult to ensure that water deliveries match crop water requirements of all users and sections of the command. Violations of crop pattern restrictions and unauthorised use of water are therefore widespread.

Under these conditions, system managers are more preoccupied with responding to coping with pressures from different segments of users to get adequate volume of water. Violators are far too numerous and widespread to permit rigorous monitoring; they are also in a position to prevent enforcement of penalties by persuasion and bribery of system functionaries and pressuring government through political channels. The policy of supplying water at highly subsidised rates has had huge perverse effects on the prospects of ensuring efficient, equitable and sustainable use of water. Besides weakening users' incentives to conserve water and improve the efficiency of its use, pricing policy for water has led to the growth of its demand outstripping the expansion of supplies from public systems as well over exploitation of ground water.

Unauthorised extraction of surface water from canals, storages and river beds has grown enormously even as the level of utilisation by public systems is reaching close to the limit of exploitable resources. That unauthorised and illegal use of surface water by direct tapping of canals and pumping from river beds has become extensive is neither acknowledged officially nor is any attempt being made to assess its magnitude and consequences. Governments have done little to track the volume of water being used for various purposes even from public systems.

The scale, spread and intensity of conflicts and disputes have increased. Mechanisms for resolving them remaining inadequate and ineffective, these conflicts continue to fester and have become a serious source of social and political tension. Little has been done to learn from experience and adapt programmes, policies and their management to rapidly changing technology, cropping patterns and patterns of water demand. Altogether water resource development and management is best described as a functioning anarchy but one which is worsening by the day.

Remedying the situation calls for massive improvements in rehabilitation and modernisation of distribution networks and regulatory devices, restructuring of water resource management with effective user participation; establishment of regulatory agencies and dispute settlement mechanisms autonomous of government; radical changes in pricing policy combined with stringent action to induce more efficient use of water and proactive measures to enforce deterrent penalties for checking unauthorised use of water and pollution of water sources. The importance of these reforms has been strongly advocated by academics, civil society organisations and external agencies. Rehabilitation and modernisation of existing works are beginning to get greater attention and resources in recent plans. The concept of participatory irrigation management is now widely accepted as national policy. Some states are in the process of implementing larger structural changes in water institutions. But these are limited, piecemeal efforts and implementation is fitful and hesitant in the face of opposition from established interests. Given the fluidity of politics, the attendant insecurity and shortness of tenure of governments, expediency and populism continue to inhibit any major reforms and serious efforts to implement them. The prospects of significant change in these attitudes are therefore far from bright.

By Way of Summing Up

Water by its very nature is a finite, limited common pool resource that is used for irrigation and several other uses and sought by numerous users. The volume of surface water flows and underground aquifers effectively available for use is invariably much smaller than requirements. Matching supply and demand and allocating available supplies between competing uses and users cannot be mediated through the market mechanism. Besides measures to augment supplies, their fair distribution between claimants and ensuring efficient and sustainable use of the resource calls for social regulation. At the ground level, this is done through informal community based institutions in the case of small local works, complex organisations based on formal rules and managed by a professional bureaucracy for large canal systems and regulated private extraction of ground water. But, they are subject to the state's laws and regulations; modern surface water systems are managed entirely by government officials; the others are open to government intrusion in varying degrees. The performance of all of them in almost all important aspects is strongly influenced by state directives and policies.

The functioning of institutions and their outcomes are invariably quite different from their mandate at all levels for a variety of reasons: The state's preoccupation with expansion of water supplies to the neglect of all other important aspects; the lack of credible and effective mechanisms for sharing limited water resources between different claimants and managing growing water related conflicts; the dominance of government control over all key functions of development and regulation of water resources; and policies for financing of investments and pricing of water that are inimical to its efficient and sustainable use are systemic features that condition the functioning of individual systems. System managements are further constrained by inadequacies in engineering design and maintenance of facilities, non transparent rules and lack of accountability for efficient and equitable use of water compounded by conflation of authority for these functions with the government bureaucracy open to pervasive intrusion by higher levels of government in checking violations of rules for access and use of water. All this also severely impedes the ability of systems to make improvements in physical infrastructure and adapt their rules and modes of functioning to changing use patterns and technologies for more efficient, prudent and sustainable use of water.

Lacuna, disjunctions and dysfunctions evident in irrigation and water management are common features of several other social, political and public institutions. Assessments of the efficacy of social institutions in achieving their intended objectives must therefore focus not merely on whether they conform to the framework (formal or informal) of laws, rules and regulations in which they are supposed to function. Given the vastness and diversity of the country, public institutions addressing particular issues must be adapted to varying regional conditions and needs. At the same time, it needs to be recognised that they are not wholly autonomous but part of a multilayered, interconnected network functioning in and influenced by conditions in the wider socioeconomic context and of government policies shaped by the unraveling of politics at various levels. The extent to which institutions can adapt their functioning to address emerging location specific problems is also a function of changes in the wider socioeconomic context and of political responses to them. A proper understanding of the performance of public institutions therefore calls for studies in a wider evolutionary perspective, sensitive to the complex and intricate ways in which they are shaped by material conditions, social and political configurations and the economic context.

References

Vaidyanathan, A. (1999). *Water Resource Management: Institutions and Irrigation Development in India*. New Delhi: OUP.

———. (2001). *Tanks of South India*. New Delhi: Centre for Science and Environment.

———. (2006). *India's Water Resources: Contemporary Issues in Irrigation*. New Delhi: OUP.

———. (2008). "Understanding Common Property Resources and their Management", in Pranab Bardhan and Isha Ray (eds.), *The Contested Commons: Conversations between Economists and Anthropologists*. Malden Ma, US: Blackwell Publishing.

9 The Political Class and Development in India

There is a widespread public perception—reflected in the popular mass media—that politics is the bane of society; and that unbridled corruption, venality, cynical and manipulative use of power by politicians for private gain rather than the public good is the root cause of all that is wrong in society. Better informed observers of society also note and comment on these unsavoury features of the way politics and politicians function. But they can hardly be the sole cause of the sad state of our polity. Instead of demonising them, it is important to take a detached look at their role and functioning.

Politics and Politicians

To begin with we need to distinguish politics from politicians. Politics in its broad sense refers to the mediation, balancing and resolution of competing interests of different segments of society—regions, religions, castes, and classes—and conflicts arising from them. This is an important function essential for orderly working of society. The mechanisms and processes by which this function is handled vary widely in form and complexity.

Politicians are persons who participate in the political process individually or through political formations. They perform an essential social function by articulating concerns and interests of citizens and interest groups and seek to influence state policies and their implementation directly (by gaining control over governance) or indirectly (by exerting pressure on those who control governance). They have, however, to function within a framework of rules and laws that define the mechanisms and procedures by which people can come to hold political office; the powers they can exercise and responsibilities they have to shoulder; and norms of justice, fairness and due process that they have to observe in making and implementing decisions.

In India this framework is defined by the Constitution. Its basic features—universal adult franchise, separation of powers between legislature, executive and judiciary, and a federal structure of government—are too well known to need elaboration. It provides for an elaborate system of checks and balances—comprising a guaranteed set of fundamental rights to all citizens, a set of directive principles of state policy, and a variety of autonomous watchdog and regulatory authorities of which, besides the Judiciary, the Election Commission, the Comptroller and Auditor General (CAG) and the Public Service Commissions are the most important. It also leaves sufficient flexibility to interpret and adapt the provisions in the light of evolving experience and situations. The responsibility for exercising this adaptive flexibility is left to the judgment and wisdom of the constitutional functionaries.

Taking a broad view, and keeping in mind the experience of other newly independent countries of the third world and even the functioning of constitutions in countries with a long democratic tradition, our structure has performed well in several respects. Free and fair elections have been held regularly with high voter turnout; the Judiciary, the Media and civil society have intervened at critical junctures to check legislative and executive excesses; the polity has shown remarkable resilience to manage many difficult situations within the framework; the multi-party system has also played an important role in this respect by enabling the regional and social diversity to find political expression and to check any tendencies for the emergence of authoritarian regimes; and the electorate's rejection of the Emergency in 1977 by a massive margin has shown that people will not tolerate attempts to suspend democracy.

Politicians and the Constitution

However, the manner in which the polity actually functions is hardly consistent with the spirit of the Constitution. There is legitimate concern over serious violations of the spirit of the Constitution reflected in stuffing of electoral rolls, booth capturing and buying of votes; increasing presence of corrupt persons and persons with dubious antecedents in different organs of the state; widespread and large-scale corruption in public institutions; lack of accountability of government and its agencies for fair and efficient discharge of their functions; failure of watchdog institutions to be vigilant in monitoring the functioning of government agencies and taking effective action to correct wrongdoing; and inability to contain and to resolve growing conflicts between regions, communities and classes. The situation in all these respects has been deteriorating.

These deficiencies are also manifest in the performance of governments in the economic sphere. Revenue collections have not kept pace with the growth of GDP due, in large measure, to laxity in assessment and collection; they have been outstripped by uncontrolled growth of the revenue expenditure (salaries and benefits of staff, interest on public debt and explicit and implicit subsidies); public debt is soaring; public enterprises as a whole are deeply in the red; the public sector is unable to expand and improve basic social and economic infrastructure needed to sustain rapid economic growth; and effectiveness of public spending on development, social welfare and poverty alleviation is severely impaired by huge waste, corruption and inefficiency. This state of affairs is in many ways and to a large extent due to the commissions and omissions of the political class.

The Constitution leaves a great deal of room for the legislature and the executive to decide eligibility criteria and devise independent institutions and transparent processes for appointments to the watchdog institutions, the bureaucracy and various public bodies. The political elite have systematically misused these powers to manipulate appointments to public office and to influence their functioning. Politicians in power, irrespective of party, are in a position to delay appointments, to get favourites and loyalists appointed or to prevent appointment of others whom they do not favour. They are also in a position to affect their functioning through allocation and release of funds to them. Internal mechanisms within public institutions to maintain high standards of probity and integrity have become weaker. Under these conditions, the interest of watchdog bodies and, more importantly, their ability to perform their constitutional functions with independence and objectivity have been seriously compromised.

The growing proliferation and ascendance of political parties and fragmentation of their political base by region, caste and community have progressively eroded the hold of national parties at the regional and eventually the national levels. The emergence of coalition governments has made politics more fluid, and the prospects of gaining and retaining power more uncertain. The cumulative result has been to shorten the time horizons of the political class which has come to be guided by expediency and survival rather than the pursuit of coherent long term vision. In the sphere of economic policy, this has led to a competitive populism eroding the capacity of the governments to provide basic amenities and infrastructure of a scale and quality needed to sustain rapid overall growth. Populism as a tactic to woo the support of one or other interest groups is not unknown to democracies. India is no exception. But the political class—irrespective of hues and ideology—has taken it far beyond reasonable limits by proliferation of poverty alleviation programmes with scant regard for their efficient management and indiscriminate expansion of subsidies.

Poverty Alleviation Programmes

One of the most significant achievements of our democracy is to bring latent and deep seated socioeconomic inequities and conflicts into the open thereby forcing the polity to confront and deal with them. Positive discrimination has made some difference to the conditions of the least privileged segments of society. Successive elections have made the underprivileged groups—Scheduled Castes and Tribes, backward classes and minorities—increasingly articulate and assertive in voicing their grievances and demands. This has led governments at the Centre and the states to launch a variety of special measures and poverty alleviation programmes to help augment employment, productive assets and income earning opportunities for different segments of the poor and underprivileged.

Besides affirmative action, we now have a wide variety of poverty alleviation programmes including:

- Earmarked allocations for education and welfare of scheduled castes and tribes and for special development programmes in tribal areas.
- Schemes to ensure a minimum standard of education, health care and safe drinking water to every one.
- Special programmes for developing production potential of hilly tracts, deserts and drought prone areas.

- Programmes (like the erstwhile Integrated Rural Development Programme (IRDP), Development of Women and Children in Rural Areas (DWACRA), Training of Rural Youth for Self Employment (TRYSEM and their later versions) designed to help poor segments to acquire or add to their productive assets and enable them to make more productive use of such assets.
- Various special programmes to provide additional employment to the rural poor culminating in the National Employment Guarantee scheme backed by law (now titled Mahatma Gandhi National Rural Employment Guarantee Act (MGNREGA)).
- Various forms of direct transfers (by way of pensions, insurance cover against disability and death) to the aged, disabled and widows; state funded school feeding, nutrition programmes and supply of textbooks and uniforms for children.

That these programmes are given not merely in the rhetoric of party manifestos but are backed by large financial allocations (on a rough estimate Rs 40,000 crores, accounting for nearly a fifth of total public sector plan outlay in 2004-05) shows that the political class has come to recognise that, by sheer weight of their numbers, these classes have a crucial role in determining electoral outcomes, and have found it necessary to go beyond slogans to demonstrate the credibility of their concern for the 'downtrodden'. At one level this shows the efficacy of democratic pressure in influencing priorities in favour of the poor. But the picture is different when we look at how these priorities operate at the ground level.

In concept, the programmes reflect a welcome recognition that the poor and the underprivileged are a heterogeneous group requiring different interventions. Problems however arise from the tendency with every change in the party in power to announce schemes without adequate preparation, resulting in proliferation of schemes with similar objectives under different names and packaging. To make matters worse, in far too many cases, separate agencies are set up to execute the programmes. There are examples galore of the same functional activity being undertaken under these programmes by different agencies with parallel hierarchies, each acting independently of others. There is no mechanism to track what each one does, where, how efficiently and with what effect. Records of actual expenditure and works taken up and completed under different schemes in different locations do not exist or are incomplete. There is no independent assessment of the veracity of reported achievements. And since the records of implementing agencies at the ground level are not accessible to the public, civil society criticisms, though based on first hand, local knowledge, are easily dismissed for want of hard, documented evidence.

All this cannot be attributed to mere administrative failure. The political class has shown scant interest in addressing these aspects. One reason is that most of these programmes are sponsored and funded by the Centre often with rigid specifications of their content, priorities and procedures. States do not have a sense of ownership for these programmes and tend to view them primarily, if not exclusively, as a source of funds. It is not uncommon for them to divert these funds for other purposes. Knowing that these practices are widespread and that reported achievements by the concerned state level agencies are unreliable, the Centre has chosen not to undertake or insist on independent validation of such reporting. This despite ex post evaluations of some programmes highlighting these deficiencies.

This indifference of the political class to transparency and accountability has much deeper and not so edifying reasons. Programmes for the poor and the underprivileged cover wide areas, numerous villages and towns and a huge number of potential beneficiaries. Many of the programmes also have sizeable loan and subsidy components. Detailed administrative monitoring is inherently difficult. Since elected *panchayats* have no role in making or implementing decisions, or do not know what is done, there is no local mechanism to ensure accountability.

Under these conditions, there is a great deal of scope for parties in power to give their elected representatives and local cadres a significant say in decisions regarding where and who should be given the loans or subsidies, who should be given contracts, and also for party and its functionaries to benefit personally from cuts and kickbacks. This scope has been systematically exploited by all political parties to create, over time, a widespread and institutionalised network for political patronage and corruption. This is a public secret. Everyone knows it but no one speaks publicly about it.

The poor feel cheated and there is widespread cynicism, rapidly turning into anger, at the huge waste and inefficiency and corruption in these programmes. This is palpable in any encounter with village level leaders. Their views are receiving increasing, though still anaemic, attention in public discourse and in the reports of some governmental committees. But this has not as yet made any dent on the political classes' attitudes or behaviour.

Burgeoning Subsidies

The other key element of the electoral stratagem used by the political class is to provide a variety of goods and services by or through the public sector at below cost prices and a deliberate policy of keeping prices, charged to users, unchanged or not raising them in step with rising costs. In some cases—electricity being a prime example—rates have been in fact reduced with some states opting for free power for some sections. The deficit between costs and recoveries has increased nearly six fold during the decade 1987-1998. There is of course a strong case for free school education, basic public care services, water supply and sanitation, social welfare expenditures and poverty alleviation programmes on larger social considerations. Leaving these aside, the magnitude of implicit subsides on 'non-merit' goods (which include among others fertilisers, canal irrigation, electricity, higher education) have been soaring. By 1998-99—the latest year for which estimates are available—they are estimated at a whopping Rs 1,33,000 crore constituting eight per cent of the GDP, almost equal to the fiscal deficit, and about 80 per cent of public sector plan outlay of the Centre and the states in that year. The situation has undoubtedly become much worse since.

The unabated increase in implicit subsidies is a major reason for the high and increasing fiscal deficits of the Centre and the states, and the inability of governments to fund much needed investments in expansion and improvement in infrastructure. More important, but less widely recognised, is the fact that subsidised provision of goods and services encourages their wasteful and inefficient use. Besides raising costs of production, it leads to excessive use which in turn causes or aggravates environmental degradation and resource depletion. Thus, underpricing of fertilisers and water has contributed to increasing incidence and intensity of pollution of water sources, water logging and salinity. Low prices stimulate larger demand and faster growth of demand. When the supplies are short of (in relation to) demand, conflicts over access to limited supplies and inducement to theft increase: overexploitation of renewable resources leads to resource depletion and degradation. These problems have already assumed serious proportions in the case of water, electricity and forests. The political class is quite aware of them but none of its constituents is willing to act or even to consider action.

Compulsions of competitive electoral politics in an era of governments based on unstable coalitions and uncertain tenures are usually cited by politicians as the reason for their unwillingness and inability to take 'tough' decisions. While there is considerable force in this alibi for inaction, it does not quite explain why governments continue to yield to pressures for more and more concessions of one kind or another to appease sectional interests. The usual justification for such concessions that they are meant to help the poor and vulnerable segments is totally specious.

The fact of the matter is that only a small fraction of the total usage of products (like canal water, electricity for pumping ground water, fertilisers, technical and higher education) that are so heavily subsidised out of public funds is accounted for by the poor. The bulk of the use is by the well-to-do. Thus, only half the rural cultivating holds have access to irrigation. Holdings of <0.5 ha with irrigation account for barely 10 per cent of all holdings and account for 6-7 per cent of both surface and ground water irrigated land. Holdings with more than 2 ha having access to irrigation account for a fifth of total holdings and over 60 per cent of irrigation from each source. Fertiliser use is similarly concentrated in the larger holdings. Theft of electricity—estimated at about a fourth of total consumption—is mostly by industrial and commercial establishments and affluent households. Similarly, the majority of youth getting higher education (college plus) are in urban areas and in the households belonging to top 10-20 per cent of the population.

Despite the fact that subsidies are strongly biased in favour of the top 20 per cent of the population, the political class, including those who profess to be socialist, is unwilling even to consider seriously, let alone implement, measures to reduce the subsidy burden. The needed measures are obvious: improving the efficiency of public agencies and enterprises to reduce the costs of providing services and improving their quality; raising the prices that users are charged to cover costs at reasonable levels of efficiency; stricter, fairer governance to check thefts, and ensure proper assessment and full collection of user charges and dues.

Politics and Public Sector Inefficiency

Improvement in the efficiency and accountability of public systems and enterprises is crucial to improve tax and non-tax revenue collections, derive more per unit of public expenditure and generate more resources for development. This calls for major changes in the way public sector organisations are structured and managed to permit more streamlined and flexible deployment of their work force and also incentives to induce better performance. Trade unions in the organised sector oppose these reforms. However, the organised private sector has managed for quite some time to circumvent the existing laws and the opposition of the unions. The private sector has succeeded in reducing the workforce and increasing productivity by adopting stratagems that are not feasible for the public sector. Their hands are tied and in the bargain they get blamed for inefficiency!

The strongest and staunchest opponents of any change in labour laws are the public sector unions. They also exert strong pressure to extend guaranteed lifetime employment to those appointed for specific works. Being crucial for the smooth functioning of the state, they are strategically placed to stall major reform. Recent attempts by a few states to take a hard line proved unsuccessful and all have had to backtrack by restoring the *status quo*. The decision to constitute the Sixth Pay Commission does not augur well for the prospect of much needed restructuring of public enterprises and public systems for more efficient and accountable performance. (Central and state governments are wrestling with the consequences of the recommendations of the Commission.)

Union pressure is, however, not the only reason for the current state of the public sector. The political class has contributed to it significantly in several ways: (1) Using the power of appointing chairpersons and directors of public and even quasi-public undertakings (like cooperatives) to reward their party functionaries. This practice has become nearly universal, resulting in the Indian equivalent of the 'spoils system'. (2) Disabling or dismantling internal check and control mechanisms to ensure that public funds are spent for approved purposes, without corruption and in an efficient manner. This has led over the years to widespread political interference in government administration at all levels and emergence of a pervasive system of corruption in government and public agencies marked by growing collusion between political functionaries in positions of power and sections of the bureaucracy. (3) Using the executive's power of appointments to public service commissions, judicial officers, vigilance commissions, members of tribunals and inquiry commissions and other watchdog institutions to 'pack' them with party favourites. This has considerably weakened their independence and integrity. (4) Denial of information, selective use of information and providing misinformation are widely used to prevent civil society organisations to promote informed public discussion of policy decisions, scrutinise their implementation and seek to correct wrongdoing.

The declining importance of ideology in politics and the acquisition and retention of power becoming the primary motivation for political parties has further eroded their interest in and capacity to implement much needed reforms. Those who hold office in the state and central committees of their parties and those elected to Parliament and state legislatures are the most influential. Regular and open elections to higher level party offices are rare. These and candidacy for elective offices are decided by the leader or higher level party organs on considerations of caste, family background, electoral record, personal loyalty, capacity to fight elections and mobilise resources for the party. Political and administrative experience at the district level used to be an important consideration in appointments to these positions but now seems to be becoming much less important. One gets the impression that selections are more biased in favour of those who come from established political families, those who have ample resources, and are 'strong men'. This limits the opportunities for local party leaders to move to the higher tiers which tend to be controlled by a more restricted group. The upper tier group has got used to exercising considerable influence in administration and developmental activity at the local level and takes advantage of the opportunity it offers for securing power, patronage and personal gain.

Impact of New Economic Policy

The apparent success of the new economic policy in increasing the rate of GDP growth during the last decade and a half seems to have persuaded a significant section of the political class in governments that free trade in goods and services and free flow of capital will generate rapid growth, reduce poverty faster and also help the fiscal situation by faster increase in revenues. This has made them less concerned about the need and urgency for internal reforms. Practically no government in power is willing to take the drastic measures needed to contain the fiscal deficit and improve the efficacy of public enterprises and services. Practically all of them are favourably inclined, even if in varying degrees, to seek foreign funding, including direct investment, in infrastructure. More and more of them are also willing to consider privatisation of existing enterprises and facilities in the public sector and leaving their expansion and improvement to the private sector. This complacency is misplaced for several reasons.

The euphoria about accelerated overall growth ignores the fact that most of it has occurred in organised sectors of industry, trade and services even as growth in agriculture and related activities, which remain the main source of livelihood of the large majority of the population, has been much lower and has tapered off. Agricultural growth has to be stepped up to and maintained at around 4 per cent per annum (compared to the long term average of around 2.6% and less than 2% during the last decade) if the dreams of 8 and 10 per cent annual GDP growth are to be realised. The key to it lies in better management of land and water, revamping the research system to generate varieties, and technology to make better use of inputs, especially for rainfed areas. This is not merely a matter of increased investments in the aggregate but requires redefining priorities, ensuring more effective implementation and management of watershed programmes, irrigation facilities and research. All these call for major restructuring of existing institutions that deal with these tasks.

Secondly, shortages and poor quality of infrastructure facilities and services are a severe constraint on the growth of the rest of the economy. Their privatisation remains politically controversial. Even its ardent supporters recognise that the public sector will have to continue to bear the major responsibility for these activities. The lack of internally generated resources to fund expansion and improvement is basically due to inefficient management compounded by perverse government policies and sheer failure of governance. These can be overcome by institutional reform to eliminate governmental interference in the management of these undertakings and leave them free to manage themselves efficiently and determine their pricing policy to earn a reasonable rate on investment subject only to review by an independent regulatory authority.

The unwillingness to grasp this nettle has led the political class to bank on foreign direct investment (FDI). The optimism about massive FDI flows into infrastructure is quite misplaced. No foreign investor will risk his funds unless the government is prepared to guarantee a reasonable return on investment. This means giving them freedom in technology choice and pricing backed by strong governance to enable them to collect dues fully and promptly. The dangers of the former course have been dramatised by Enron. The alternative would be to agree to purchase their output at prices that give a guaranteed return with the responsibility for determining and collecting user charges remaining with them. Judging by the way public sector utilities now function, the latter course would only lead to larger deficits and add to the burden on the general budget.

The third problem is that recent growth has been highly uneven between sectors, across regions, between rural and urban areas. Much of this growth has been in the organised, modern sectors of industry and services. Agricultural output has always grown much slower than in non-agricultural activities, but this differential has increased sharply because of a deceleration in agricultural growth to near stagnation in the last few years. Value added per worker in agriculture has also been much lower than in non-agricultural sectors. With non-agricultural employment not increasing fast enough to reduce dependence on agriculture for livelihood, the trend of widening disparities in output per worker between the two sectors has been greatly accentuated. This and the fact that the impact of government programmes for rural development and poverty alleviation have fallen far below promises and expectations have aggravated the sense of neglect and deprivation among the rural population.

Within the non-agricultural sector, the rapid growth in 'modern' organised sectors (including especially the IT-BPO boom) and the growing lucrative job opportunities in the developed countries for Indian professionals have mostly benefited urban educated classes and professionals. A growing number of young people in families of public sector employees and workers in the organised private sectors also aspire to take advantage of these opportunities. And their families are willing to invest heavily in education

—much of it in the private sector—to equip them for this purpose. Wage and salary differentials between the organised and the informal sectors and even within the organised sector have palpably widened. A large segment of population in the urban informal sector not only feels left out but also has little or no chance of accessing opportunities it would like to.

The upwardly mobile middle classes, and those aspiring to get on the bandwagon, are strong supporters of the new economic policy. These new elite and influential opinion makers in the media and the bureaucracy have become so preoccupied with making it in globalising India that they have little interest or involvement in addressing larger issues. So have significant sections of the intelligentsia. Some of them see no virtues in the public sector, consider it impossible to make it function better and even question the justification for wasting huge amounts on employment guarantee, poverty alleviation and helping the underprivileged.

The outcome of the 2004 elections is widely interpreted as a reflection of the growing feeling of neglect and anger among the rural population and the urban poor. The Common Minimum Programme of the UPA government acknowledges this explicitly and commits itself to correct the imbalance by giving special attention to addressing their concerns. This has been followed by the announcement of a series of programmes—the NREGP, Bharat Nirman, Rural Health Mission, making education a fundamental right—backed by huge resource allocations. Strong pressures from a section of the United Progressive Alliance (UPA) have led to substantial increase in the allocation of funds for these initiatives. But funds and programme guidelines are not enough to make any significant impact unless the many serious deficiencies in implementation are addressed. The architects of these programmes are aware of the need for major institutional reform to address these deficiencies but do not take them up, perhaps because they are too weak to generate strong enough political pressures for such reform.

The Way Ahead

The deficiencies in governance and in the functioning of public systems and enterprises are due largely, though not wholly, to the attitudes and behaviour of the political class. The vested interests of the political class in the existing regime are far too entrenched and strong for it to take the initiative to introduce needed reforms. Growing pressure from the public and by watchdog institutions has forced it to pass legislation meant to restrict its capacity to manipulate the system with impunity and widen the domain from which the political class is drawn. The 73rd and 74th amendments to the Constitution, laws to curb corruption, hold public hearings on major projects and enable citizens to access information relating to the functioning of government and changes in electoral law are notable cases in point. But since the political class controls the legislative process, these laws provide far too many loopholes to be effective. In other cases—notably the 73rd and 74th amendments—implementation has been effectively stalled. There are other areas—especially electoral reform to check malpractices, prevent persons with criminal records from contesting and reduce the role of money power in contesting elections—where much remains to be done. Stronger pressure is needed to ensure effective implementation of existing laws and legislative measures as well as strengthen the independence and integrity of watchdog institutions.

These pressures are getting wider and stronger: the grassroots clamour for devolution of authority with resources for local development to the elected *panchayats* is growing. The increasing tension between local and upper tiers of politics is to be welcomed because it generates pressures for empowering elected *panchayats*. The Judiciary, the Vigilance Commission and the Election Commission are also getting more actively engaged in pushing for stricter codes and their enforcement in their respective domains. The media too help generate pressure by exposures of corruption and misuse of power by politicians and the bureaucracy, and by highlighting the ineffectiveness of watchdog institutions. The intelligentsia and civil society organisations need to take advantage of these trends to mobilise public opinion to reinforce and strengthen pressures for reform.

10 Decentralisation and Community Action

Introduction

The present appears to be an appropriate context for a discussion of the evolution and practice of decentralisation. The appropriateness is as much due to the continuing importance of decentralisation as the uneven success it has had across the country. Further, new and to some extent unexpected problems confront us in this behalf. This paper focuses on the concept and practice of decentralised people's planning and its future role in India's development. What I wish to do is: (1) briefly review the chequered history of democratic decentralisation and the factors that impede the process; (2) emphasise the importance of collective and cooperative actions to deal with a wide range of social and economic activities at the local level; and (3) the necessity to give greater attention to strengthening existing and creating new community level institutions for managing these activities.

I should enter a couple of caveats at the outset. Much of what I have to say is neither new nor original. It is not based on any research of my own but on knowledge and impressions gained from reading research papers, talking to persons with first-hand knowledge of the field, and interactions with NGOs and elected *panchayat* leaders.

Decentralisation is a deeply political issue and therefore I will be stressing the political aspects which are common to the process in all parts of the country.

I will not be discussing specifically any one state although there are some outstanding practitioners of decentralisation such as Kerala and to some extent Karnataka. I confess that I am an admirer of the sustained efforts of the left front governments in Kerala and the People's Science Movement to promote it against great odds.

Chequered History

The rationale for decentralisation is both ideological and functional. Its ideological roots can be traced to Gandhiji's concept of *'gram swaraj'* and self-governing and self-reliant villages as the basis on which the country's democratic super structure should be built. The Constitution makers however chose in favour of a modern Anglo-American system of governance. The Constitution envisaged a federal system and did not mention villages much less give them a place in the country's governance structure. After a good deal of effort, *panchayats* found a place in Part IV under the Directive Principles of State Policy in Article 40.

Experience with the Community Development Programme of the fifties showed that centralised programmes, however well conceived, did not produce desired results in terms of development at the grassroots when implemented through the bureaucracy. It highlighted the importance of people's involvement and participation in local development. This realisation led to the appointment of the Balwant Rai Mehta Committee which came out strongly in favour of entrusting the responsibility for planning and implementation of local level development programmes to democratically elected village and block level bodies and a largely ex officio one at the district level.

The recommendations of this committee were implemented with varying degrees of zeal across the country, but by the late 1970s, signs of stagnation were visible. Due to this fatigue as well as to other significant political changes at the macro level (including the Emergency and its after effects), there developed a feeling that the question of decentralisation required a fresh look. And this resulted in the constitution of the Ashok Mehta Committee which gave its report in 1978. This committee went further than the predecessor Balwant Rai Mehta Committee and explicitly envisaged a political role for local level institutions. Its recommendations found zealous adherents in some states that were already committed to devolution such as West Bengal and later Karnataka. But the pitch was becoming more decentralisation friendly.

There was much debate and controversy over the structure of Panchayat Raj (PR), the powers and functions of their different tiers as well as their relations *inter se* and with the state government. The state governments and the bureaucracy were far from enthusiastic about handing over resources and authority to PR bodies to choose and implement programmes in their domains. Local MLAs and MPs were strongly opposed because they felt that it would reduce their political power and influence. The opposition from the upper tier political class across practically all parties and the bureaucracy became stronger as the scale of rural development and poverty alleviation programmes increased. The impasse was sought to be resolved by inducting them formally into the process of advising or deciding on local development schemes and restricting the executive and financial powers of elected local bodies.

The attitude of states to PR remained indifferent. Many did not even bother to hold regular elections. A few did take bold initiatives to revive democratically elected Panchayati Raj Institutions (PRIs) and to enable and empower them. Karnataka under Ramakrishna Hegde's first ministry, in fact, enacted legislation that sought to give PRIs unprecedented autonomy and resources. Kerala in the seventies passed a law that was even more radical in seeking to broaden the role of local bodies to cover law and order and justice. But no attempt was made to implement the Kerala law; while in Karnataka it was soon amended under pressure to restore the status quo.

Meanwhile as the poverty alleviation programmes sponsored and funded by the Centre grew apace, concerns about diversion of funds, the poor quality of their implementation, and massive leakages and corruption also increased. Rajiv Gandhi's famous public statement that only 15 per cent of the expenditures serve the intended purposes and reach the target beneficiaries articulated this concern. Then followed his attempt to transfer central funds to and deal directly with district officials and *panchayats* rather than through the state governments. It had to be abandoned in the face of the entirely well founded furore that the move would subvert the federal structure. It is a reasonable, and plausible, conjecture that this triggered the idea of changes in law that would give PRIs as well as urban local bodies a formal status in the governance structure of the country with mandatory provisions for regular elections, specifying local development functions to be entrusted to them along with authority and resources. This was the purpose of the 73rd and 74th amendments to the Constitution.

The amendments were passed by Parliament unanimously without much substantive discussion and secured the approval of the majority of state legislatures. This is rather surprising because there was no sign of MPs and MLAs, the upper tier political class in general or the bureaucracy being persuaded or willing to shed their control over local level development programmes. Their approval was obtained by leaving several important details regarding the role of PRIs in planning and implementation of local development to be decided by the states. This left enough room for them to maintain the status quo.

In the event, while all states have followed the letter of the constitutional amendment, MLAs, MPs, influential local political figures along with the bureaucracy continue to play the major role in decisions on where and which schemes are to be implemented and who gets the loans/ grants and contracts. In addition, MPs and MLAs also voted themselves large grants from the exchequer for sponsoring and funding development projects in their constituencies.

The implementation of the spirit of the constitutional amendment has been very uneven and half-hearted: some states are more proactive than others; the large majority of them are lukewarm. In the event, they have not made much of an impact on the way local level social and economic development schemes at the grassroots are planned and implemented.

State governments, upper tiers of the political class and the bureaucracy continue to stall transfer of resources, authority and responsibility for local development to PRIs. Central grants meant for rural development and poverty alleviation programmes are diverted for other purposes; the transfer of funds to the accounts of PRIs is held up or delayed. PRIs are only nominally involved in planning and implementing local development and poverty alleviation programmes. Local MLAs and MPs continue to have a significant, if not dominant, say in these matters by virtue of their membership of advisory committees. Executive authority for final approval, financial sanctions and release of funds remains with the officials of the state government.

Instances abound of projects on which allocations are spent, allotted funds are certified to have been utilised and works are reported to be completed but with little or no trace of the work on the ground. A high proportion of the loans and grants ostensibly meant for the poor never reach the poor. There is a conspicuous lack of interest or concern for observing guidelines regarding maintenance of accounts, register of projects completed and under construction and registers of beneficiaries, regular independent audit, and making information available to all members of the *gram sabha*. Nor does the Centre insist on states following the guidelines or devise its own mechanisms to check the veracity of reports sent by states and for monitoring ground level reality. All this leaves much scope and opportunity for cynical misuse of public resources for corruption and political patronage.

There is widespread scepticism, not only among politicians and the bureaucracy but also in influential segments of intellectuals, about the efficacy of democratic decentralisation based on the alleged widespread corruption in PRIs; their lack of experience and professional competence necessary to plan and implement schemes efficiently; and the continued dominance of large land owners and upper castes in local power structures.

Corruption

The apprehension about corruption in *panchayats*, the noise that is made about it by governments, their bureaucracy and the media, and the tendency of the state governments to wield the big stick to check it, are vastly out of proportion to its incidence and magnitude compared to what happens in the rest of publicly funded development programmes.

Corruption is indeed widespread. It is common knowledge that a large part of funds allocated to local development schemes is being hived off to sustain widely diffused and institutionalised patronage networks through which the parties in power share the 'spoils of power' with their functionaries and cadres down the line. Empowering PRIs in the spirit of the 73rd amendment would cut deeply into these opportunities. Apprehensions on this account and fears that empowering elected local bodies will lead to wider and more intense competition for access to higher tiers of politics, explain the strong opposition to decentralisation from incumbent and aspirant members of legislatures and Parliament who are entrenched in the upper tiers of the political class.

Under this system, the *panchayat* members are not the main culprits. PRIs have little or no role in planning and implementation of rural development (RD) and poverty alleviation (PA) programmes. But they can and do get easily co-opted as partners into the larger network for distribution of the gravy. Their role and take however is, at present, miniscule compared to that of local MLAs and MPs, contractors chosen by them and the local functionaries of various government departments. This is not to say the elected members of PRIs are incorruptible. But by making their activities more visible to the people of each community and open to scrutiny and questioning, incumbents in office, who have to seek re-election, are likely to be far more restrained.

Capacity of PRIs

An obvious constraint on PRIs' ability to play an effective role in local development is funding. At present they do not mobilise tax or non-tax revenues of their own on any significant scale. They depend mostly on transfers from state government out of its revenues according to the recommendations of the state finance commissions (SFCs) and from the centre for centrally funded RD and PA schemes. But these funds are routed through the state governments which do not always hand them over fully and promptly to PRIs. Their freedom to determine the use of these transfers is also severely constrained in several ways:

- PRIs are expected to meet the cost of their staff, most of whom are employees of the state government which also fixes their emoluments. There are differences with respect to this among the states but on the whole *panchayats* everywhere face some form of constraint on their autonomy. Possibly this is most visibly seen in relation to expenditure.
- Central grants are tied to a variety of programmes. Switching of funds between different schemes is not allowed. The components of each programme and allocations of funds among them are spelt out in detailed and rigid guidelines.
- Central grants are meant for plan schemes without any provision for continuing maintenance and operation.
- In any case PRIs' authority to sanction schemes and expenditures is severely limited.

Relaxing these constraints is of paramount importance for realising the potential of decentralised development. Kerala government's initiative of transferring 30 per cent of plan funds and 20 per cent of its revenues to PRIs as block grants must be commended as a big step in this direction. One would like to see more states taking similar initiatives and leave enough freedom and flexibility for PRIs to decide the use of resources according to local needs, possibilities and priorities.

It should be noted however that the scope for flexibility in the use of state government revenue grants by PRIs is extremely limited as most of it reportedly goes to pay salaries and benefits of their staff on secondment from the state. There is much to be said, both in the interests of economy and ensuring greater control over staff, to allow PRIs greater freedom to appoint their personnel and determine emoluments. As a major source of funds for local development, the Centre can make a significant difference by reducing the number of central schemes by grouping and eventually merging them into a few functionally homogenous categories, and by giving PRIs the flexibility, subject to broad guidelines, to decide their utilisation.

PRIs cannot discharge their responsibilities if they depend, as they currently do, mostly on transfers from the states and central governments. At present, since they have hardly any role in deciding the utilisation of these funds, PRIs are under no pressure, nor do they have any incentive, to raise their own resources. But there are indications that they do mobilise local resources when they have an active role in local level planning by way of, for example, voluntary labour contributions, higher collections from auction of community resources (such as fishing rights of tanks, trees, tank bed silt), construction and renting out commercial buildings. In principle, PRIs can also borrow from financial institutions to finance infrastructure schemes provided that they are viable and the PRIs show the capacity to manage them well and have the capacity to repay.

Institutions

Larger and more flexible funding is a necessary but not sufficient condition unless accompanied by more effective and efficient use of funds. There is much scope for improvement in these aspects even under the present regime by addressing well known structural defects in the existing programmes by:

- rationalising RD and PA programmes to eliminate overlapping/ duplication and bring about convergence;
- involving PRI representatives and knowledgeable local people to assess and prioritise local felt needs;
- taking advantage of their first-hand knowledge of conditions specific to each community;
- devoting more resources for preparatory surveys and technical design for resource development schemes;
- eliminating the contractor system and encouraging communities to take the responsibility for constructing works; and
- making adequate provisions for proper maintenance and management of completed works.

The more difficult task is to build the institutional capacity at the district and sub-district levels for planning, implementation and continuing management of development activities.

Initiatives for improving public health, education, water supply and sanitation services and for raising the production potential of the communities' land and water resources have almost exclusively come from the government. Local bodies and village communities have for long got used to, and conditioned to expect, that the government will decide, implement, finance and manage all local development works.

They tend to rely on local leaders with access to the wider political and bureaucratic network to lobby for schemes and handouts, often for the benefit of particular groups rather the community as a whole.

Villages do have traditional institutions for management of village temples, tanks and community festivals and for regulating access to and use of common lands. Well intentioned interventions like taking over the responsibility to restore derelict and damaged traditional local irrigation works and maintain them in good repair weakened pre-existing institutional mechanisms for community management. Attempts have also been made to foster institutions for new forms of collective action—of which cooperative credit societies are an outstanding example. But these are not conspicuous for their success which only underscores the weak tradition of community based institutions for collective action. More recent state initiatives to create institutions for participatory management of social services and common production resources have also failed to build vibrant local institutions capable of handling these tasks.

The space for their development has been severely constrained, in fact choked, by the government taking over these functions and managing them through a centralised bureaucracy. At present these tasks are almost entirely in the hands of staff belonging to various departments of state governments which control their appointments, emoluments, postings and promotions. They work by general government rules and departmental instructions. PRIs have no control over any of these aspects, nor do they have any power to discipline them. Since they belong to and are answerable to different line departments, it is extremely difficult to check avoidable duplication and achieve convergence of related activities.

The logical and ideal solution for this hiatus would be to give *panchayats* the freedom to appoint their own staff, determine their emoluments, spell out their duties and enforce discipline. But this is not possible because of strong resistance to any such move on the part of unions of government employees. But this option should be made available at least in respect of appointments of new personnel. At a minimum, it is necessary to entrust the responsibility for supervising the work (attendance at work, discharge of their assigned duties and responsiveness to the community's needs) to citizen committees under the PRIs and making their assessment a mandatory input in evaluating the performance of functionaries.

While the current situation is far from satisfactory, we need to take note of significant changes that are taking place in the attitudes of village communities and elected functionaries to PRIs and their functioning:

- the spread of education and the democratic electoral process has led to the emergence of leaders interested in development and keen to play a more active role;
- increasing awareness among elected representatives in PRIs about the possibilities opened by the Constitutional amendment;
- growing frustration among PRIs over the severe constraints—in terms of both authority and control over resources—that prevent them from playing an effective role in local development and articulating

demands for relaxing these constraints and giving them far more freedom and flexibility in matters of local development; and

- growing articulation of people's resentment at the way projects are decided and the inefficiencies and corruption in their implementation.

There is, at the same time, considerable evidence from different states that, even within the severely constrained space they now have, village communities are becoming increasingly conscious of the enormous waste and leakage under the existing system. Several are willing to take the responsibility for implementing government projects, contribute a part of the cost and complete the works faster, better and at lower cost.

The role that NGOs have played and are playing in the sphere of rural development is particularly important. At present numerous NGOs work with communities directly or in collaboration with financial institutions (notably the rural infrastructure development fund (RIDF) projects of the National Bank for Agriculture and Rural Development (NABARD)) to mobilise them for different kinds of development activity, identifying projects suitable to local needs, providing technical support and expert advice, and interceding with officials to relax conventional rules and procedures to allow communities greater role in implementing schemes. They help communities to create/improve institutions for collective action in such activities as watershed development.

There are numerous instances of infrastructure projects being done with NGO help in consultation with communities and with their active participation, including contributions of labour and cash to cover a substantial portion of the costs. The record of works implemented in this fashion is found to be markedly better in terms of time taken relative to estimated costs and quality. There is also some evidence that though this model focuses on particular types of projects, they have significant spillover effects in stimulating community interest over a much wider range of activities.

Other welcome developments include criteria based devolution of state government revenues to PRIs by state finance commissions; efforts of the Planning Commission to evolve explicit criteria for determining entitlements for plan grants for centrally sponsored RD and PA programmes to different states and tiers of PRIs; and, thanks to concerted mass campaigns by civil society institutions—the passage of the Right to Information Act, and commissioning of independent social audits of major employment and rural development schemes.

Public awareness is also growing about the failure of the state itself to ensure that the facilities it helps create are managed by its functionaries efficiently. Mechanisms to ensure efficient management of these facilities, observance of regulations by users and checking their unauthorised use are inoperative and violated with impunity on a massive scale. These governance failures, which arise in large measure from the conflation of administrative, regulatory conflict resolution functions with the political executive, have reached such serious proportions that governments are beginning to recognise the need for institutional reform.

Attempts, though patchy, limited and half-hearted, are being made to separate executive from regulatory functions, promote participatory management of key rural programmes including notably public irrigation systems, watershed development and forest management.

All this gives sufficient basis for optimism that decentralisation of authority and resources for development, with a clearly defined limit of resource transfers from the state and leaving PRIs free to decide the content of their programmes without interference from bureaucracy or local political leaders will force the communities to address local developmental issues and sort out the problems involved. NGOs will then have scope for helping the process of mobilisation and providing information, expertise and advice to the community. An expanded RIDF model of financing with NGO collaboration and strict monitoring of projects in all phases can then be used to greater effect in improving project performance. This process will of course have to be consciously encouraged by the governments.

Strategy for Reform

The key issue is how to bring this about in the face of the strong and determined resistance of the upper strata of the political class and the bureaucracy. Efforts to explain and persuade them about the need for these reforms must of course be sustained and intensified. But there should be no illusion that this will bring about a change in their hearts. It is necessary to combine exhortation with inducements. The experience of the ongoing reform of the rural credit cooperatives suggests a promising strategy.

The Experience of Cooperatives

There are strong parallels between the evolution of cooperative credit and democratic decentralisation. Cooperatives are an early example of state initiative to promote new forms of collective institutions. Nearly a century back, colonial government officials came to the conclusion that the best way to free agriculturists from the clutches of usurious money lenders was to get them together as self-governing organisations to promote thrift and mutual help among members. But they also felt that strong guidance and supervision by the government was essential to ensure their healthy functioning.

The movement grew fitfully in the first half of the century but did not make a significant dent on the problem it was expected to solve. It neither succeeded in promoting thrift nor in prudent management of (mostly borrowed) funds. The government's response was to increase direct government intervention in the running of societies.

Despite this experience, governments post-Independence period adopted a proactive policy of encouraging and supporting a rapid expansion in cooperatives especially credit co-ops in rural areas. This policy found strong support from independent scholars and experts, and was accepted both by the central government (which provided the finances) and the state governments (which defined and administered the legal framework).

The number of societies, their geographical spread and membership grew to unprecedented and impressive levels. So did the volume of credit disbursed. But this was made possible not on the basis of members' thrift but by huge infusion of public funds directly and through the financial institutions at concessional rates of interest.

Sanctions for prudent management, weak to begin with, were further weakened everywhere by state government interference in the working of societies through executive orders on lending policies and interest rates and by appointing department officials to manage them. Elections were not held or were rigged. Supervision, to the extent it existed, was impotent to check mismanagement. The societies came to be treated and used by the political class as a powerful and lucrative instrument for dispensing patronage and garnering electoral support (by controlling the distribution of loans, getting government to go easy on recovery and/or granting outright waivers). Despite all this, the scale of lending (almost entirely financed by public funds) continued to increase under government fiat despite mounting losses and overdues bringing the movement to the point of collapse.

The growing hiatus between the government's declared objective of rapidly increasing the supply of institutional credit to rural areas on the one hand and the deteriorating financial health of the co-ops and the declining share in total credit flow on the other, led the Government of India to appoint several committees to suggest ways of revitalising the system.

Most recommended liberal assistance by Centre to clear accumulated losses and increase the capital to a prudentially adequate level combined with major legal and institutional reforms to free cooperatives from government interference and make them function efficiently. But states were more interested in central financial assistance and showed little concern for institutional reform. Nor did the centre. The latest in this series of committees, which I had the privilege of chairing, emphasised that financial assistance without institutional reform would be futile. Therefore, it recommended that liberal central assistance to clean up past sins must be made strictly conditional on implementation of legal and institutional changes to ensure transparent and democratic governance, with well defined internal and external mechanisms to ensure proper management and accountability, with government's role confined to legislating the framework in which the societies will function. Apart from general oversight, it suggested that the responsibility for regulation should be internalised and taken out of government.

Phased release of central assistance linked to fulfilment of specific undertakings on reform measures was designed to give a strong inducement for states to implement legal and institutional reforms. The package has been accepted by the centre and the states after a series of high level political consultations. As many as 10 states have formally agreed to implement them with the help of the centre on condition that specified conditions of reform will be met.

This gives basis for optimism that a similar approach to create strong inducements to loosen the political opposition to decentralisation can open up spaces for a more vibrant role for democratic and decentralised local development. The key is to reduce the scope and opportunities for abuse of funds and corruption in local development programmes to an extent that politicians in legislatures and parliament, and those aspiring to these positions, will not find it worthwhile to interfere in local development schemes.

This can be done by a bold initiative from the central government —which is the main source of public funding for local development—to restructure its programmes to achieve the following:

- minimising the subsidy/loan component of local development programmes;
- replacing the contractor system by encouraging communities to take the responsibility for construction works;
- ensuring, with severe penalties for non-compliance, that records, accounts and progress reports are maintained according to prescribed format;
- ensuring, again subject to severe penalties for non-compliance, regular annual audit of accounts of all PRIs to be placed before the *gram sabha*;
- institutionalising a system of periodic and independent professional social audit of the performance and outcomes of the local development schemes; and
- making it mandatory to place it in the public domain and have it discussed in the state legislatures.

These measures, combined with empowering PRIs with the resources and the authority to choose, implement and manage local RD and PA works without external interference, will enable PRIs to play a larger, more effective role. They will not make angels of PRIs but by making their activities more visible to the people of each community and open to scrutiny and questioning, incumbents in office, who have to seek re-election, are likely to be far more restrained about misuse and far more concerned about real performance.

Democracy and Equity

However, we have to recognise that there exists a sizeable segment of opinion, especially among progressive parties and influential segments of the intellectual community, which holds that truly democratic functioning of elected *panchayats* is not feasible in a highly unequal society stratified economically and by community and caste. There is an apprehension that the well-to-do and/or numerically dominant castes will manage to get elected and exercise power for their benefit rather than for the benefit of the poor and socially disadvantaged segments (women, scheduled castes). These apprehensions are exaggerated.

In the first place, experience has belied the expectation that elected state and central governments managing a benign state will not be embroiled in local factions and quarrels and therefore better placed to serve the interests of the poor. Those elected to run the state and central governments have no doubt been long on this rhetoric but grievously short in safeguarding, much less promoting, welfare of the poor.

Moreover, stratified economic and social structures everywhere make for unequal distribution of power and influence. Our experience of electoral democracy at the state and the central levels during the last five decades has however shown that it can challenge and change entrenched power structures. There is no reason to suppose that this is not possible at the lower levels of governance right down to villages. Properly implemented in the spirit of the 73rd amendment, decentralisation will provide space and opportunity for the diverse interests of different constituents (caste, class, gender) in a community to be articulated and contested publicly.

One cannot expect PRIs to correct the deeper social and economic roots of inequality and privilege. But they can help to ensure that programmes meant for the poor and disadvantaged are better managed and the benefits reach the groups for whom they are intended. The growing political awareness and assertiveness of the OBCs, Dalits and other underprivileged is not confined to state level politics. It is also happening at lower levels and can in due course alter local power structures to be more sensitive to the interests of the underprivileged.

All this will not change local power structures everywhere or soon. But it will change power configurations in at least a sizeable proportion of communities in ways that stimulate and enable them to address local problems more effectively and use available resources more efficiently and with less corruption than under the present dispensation. Devices such as reservations for women and Scheduled Castes will help underprivileged groups to have a stronger voice in the development and use of community facilities and resources. This is the best that we can expect: short of the ideal but far better than the present concentration of power in state and central politicians and the bureaucracy.

We should also guard against taking a purely instrumentalist view of PRIs. The fact that regular elections are mandatory has brought about significant changes in attitudes and perceptions to issues of development and governance. The poor and the disadvantaged are able to articulate their interests and claims on the resources available to the community. It has bought about changes in the local leadership. They are increasingly resentful of the severely restricted role in local development and clamour for more resources and authority. As these trends intensify, tension between them and the upper tier of the political class, state and central level politicians, will also grow. The intensification of this tension is to be welcomed as a creative force for change not only by increasing internal pressures for better implementation of development schemes but also for widening the pool of people experienced in the practice of democratic politics and administration available for the upper tiers of the system, thus widening and deepening democracy.

The conflict between PRI leaders and the higher level politicians/ bureaucracy is as yet incipient but growing in strength; more visible and articulate in some states/regions than others. The dialectics of this conflict has the potential to become one of the most important sources of change in the configurations of politics and power. It is therefore important to look more closely at the process of change: whether, in what ways and where PRIs are leading to significant changes in the kind of people who are emerging as local leaders, their attitudes to and interest in development, the perception of different segments of the community, the kind of works they take up, the process by which they are decided and the efficiency with which they are implemented and managed. There is much to learn about the dynamics of the process from such an approach and this learning will help forge more effective ways to further the process. The emphasis, let me repeat, should be not on the ideal but on the movement towards the desired ideal, and quickening its pace.

Conclusion

The complexity and difficulty of the needed reforms cannot be underrated. But it should not be made an alibi for letting the present regime continue. That high rhetoric about eradicating poverty, and the huge amounts of public funds being spent for that purpose, have not made a significant impact on the conditions of the rural population and the underprivileged is now widely recognised. There is growing grassroots resentment at the enormous waste and corruption in the way these resources are spent. The resentment is being further fuelled by the feeling that far too little of the benefits of the much vaunted acceleration of GDP growth rates due to globalisation has percolated to rural areas. In fact, there is compelling evidence that in every respect—incomes, employment, educational and health services and amenities—rural-urban as well as rich-poor disparities are widening. The underprivileged are becoming more and more assertive in articulating their discontent in a variety of ways. Failure to address this by continuing business as usual can only aggravate the tensions with potentially explosive social and political consequences. I hope that this will not be dismissed as unwarranted pessimism and that all of us, and especially the political class, will recognise the urgent need for reform and work seriously to bring it about.

V

Data Base: Availability and Application

11 State of the Indian Statistical System

The current debate on the impact of economic reforms on poverty and inequality centres around widely divergent estimates of poverty incidence derived from different sources of data. While the debate is heavily coloured by ideological predilections for and against the reforms, it also raises questions about the quality and reliability of the data and assumptions underlying estimates of growth of income and consumption, their distribution between regions and classes, and price indices. Similar concerns have also been voiced in respect of a wide range of other socio-economic data put out by different organisations, governmental and non-governmental. The public, indeed even professionals, are understandably befuddled. That specialists are unable to sort out the issues, adds to the confusion and erodes confidence in statistics and the statistical system. The purpose of this paper is to give an overview of the organisation of the statistical system, the way data are collected, their deficiencies and needed remedies.

The country's statistical system, as we see it today, was built almost entirely since Independence. In 1947 only a few departments in the Central government and the revenue departments of the provinces collected data mostly through, and as a by-product of administration. The range of data was also very limited. The foundations of the present system were laid and nurtured by Prof Mahalanobis. As honorary statistical adviser to the government, he played a key role in creating the Central Statistical Organisation (CSO) and in the creation of professional statistical units in various central ministries and the state governments, as well as in several quasi-government organisations.

Perhaps his most important, and lasting, contributions are the popularisation of sample survey techniques to collect socioeconomic data and the creation of the National Sample Survey Organisation (NSSO) as a professional agency separate from and independent of executive agencies of the government. Apart from the government, over the years, numerous non-government institutions (mainly research organisations and universities) have also been collecting data on various socioeconomic aspects.

An Overview of the Statistical System

In judging the working of the statistical system, we need to distinguish broadly between three different means by which socioeconomic data are gathered: Censuses; information gathered by and through executive agencies of government; and sample surveys conducted by governmental and quasi-governmental agencies. All three are important in the Indian context. It must of course be noted that considerable amounts of data are collected by individuals, research institutions and non-governmental organisations (NGOs). The subsequent discussion is however, confined to data generated in the government and the public sector.

Censuses

Censuses involve complete enumeration of all constituent units of the 'population' for which information is sought. The advantage of censuses is that they give information for every constituent unit of the 'population' which is both necessary (as with population censuses) and also useful. But they are also costly, and call for massive and difficult operations in terms of the number of personnel to be trained, deployed and supervised. In this respect the Indian population census have earned a well-deserved reputation both for the efficiency of organisation and management as well as for the amount of data that it makes available in the public domain. The data are used for a large variety of purposes such as, to mention but a few, a detailed picture of the size and characteristics of settlements and their population down to the village level, delimitation of electoral constituencies and preparation of electoral rolls and for tacking changes in demographic characteristics, urbanisation, and pattern of economic activity, as well as for regional planning, at a highly disaggregated level.

The censuses of agriculture and livestock, by comparison, are not as successful. Censuses based on complete enumeration are also conducted (some of them at quinquennial intervals) in several other areas notably agriculture, livestock, minor irrigation, establishments and of families below the poverty line. The design, organisation and conduct of each of these surveys however leave much to be desired. They are costly: the outlays in conducting them run into several hundred crores. Despite substantial financial and professional support from the central government, the state governments, which are responsible for collection and dissemination, have not taken these tasks seriously.

There are questions about the completeness of coverage, quality of field staff collecting the data and their supervision, comparability of concepts and categories over time. Published tabulations are very meagre, uneven and often inordinately delayed. Primary data for past censuses are not archived. Though data for more recent censuses are supposed to be digitised, the archive is hardly used even by concerned departments. They are not accessible to departments and agencies within government; access to interested researchers and NGOs is severely restricted.

All this raises serious questions about the justification for spending enormous amounts of effort and resources on them. There is a strong case for reducing the frequency of these censuses, and supplementing them with well designed sample surveys to generate comparable and validated information on specific aspects at more frequent intervals.

Executive Agencies

The second major mechanism for data collection is through administrative departments of the government. Statistics of land use, cropping and irrigation have for long been compiled by records maintained by village revenue officials. During British times, since tax on land was the main source of government revenue, the government attached great importance to maintaining accurate records of all land holdings. Till 40 years back most states also relied on collation reports of village revenue officials to estimate crop yields. The situation has changed dramatically since.

Land revenue now constitutes a negligible proportion of government revenues; some have altogether abolished it. Consequently, the importance attached to maintenance of land records by village officials and to their supervision has declined. At the same time, village officials are now expected to perform a large number of functions leaving them less time to devote to maintenance of land records. Some states have abolished the system of appointing local people as village revenue officers, replacing them with a statewide cadre of transferable functionaries. All this has led to a considerable disruption of the system for compilation of land use and crop wise recording of data and deterioration in their reliability.

The introduction of sample surveys under the NSSO for estimating land use and area under different crops and sample crop cutting surveys for estimating yields was meant to provide an independent source of data at lower cost. Based on rigorous statistical design and procedures (including verification), they were meant to give state level estimates with a low margin of error. But land use and crop area surveys were given up in the 1960s. But crop-cutting surveys have been continued and their coverage progressively expanded. They are now the basis on which yields of all major crops are estimated. The procedures are supposed to be implemented under the supervision of the state statistical agencies. But the responsibility for the fieldwork has been distributed between different departments (Statistical Bureaus, Departments of Agriculture, Revenue, etc.). This has made it difficult to ensure that fieldwork conforms to the prescribed procedures and standards. Nor has the provision for independent checking of fieldwork by the State Statistical Bureaus (SSB) and the NSSO been as strict and effective as it should be.

Statistics in respect of several minor crops (of which fruits and vegetables are perhaps the most important) still depend largely on village records (in respect of area) and impressionistic estimates (for yields). The area under these crops being very small, the village *patawaris'* recording was not reliable even in the best of times. The situation is now much worse. Yield estimates remain notional. Differences between estimates provided by different sources are very large. It is widely believed that these crops have been growing rapidly and so also their importance in total agricultural output. This was the basis for the recent major upward revisions of their estimated output in national income estimates. But in the absence of a systematic and objective survey of these crops—for which appropriate methodologies have been evolved but have not been implemented—the revisions are arbitrary. The cumulative effect of all this has been to erode the confidence in the reliability of agricultural statistics both in terms of levels and composition at a point in time and, perhaps even more, in respect of changes over time.

Statistics relating to industries, energy, transport and foreign trade are also compiled largely by concerned departments directly (as in the case of foreign trade) or on the basis of periodic reports sent by individual enterprises/organisations in these sectors. Coverage is incomplete and variable; all units do not send in regular reports; and the reliability of their reports is not checked.

Thus in the case of industrial production, the coverage is limited to organised sector. Before liberalisation and decontrol, though reporting was voluntary, the fact that industrial establishments had to get licences and permits from the central government gave a strong in-built incentive for them to send the data. Even then a sizeable proportion did not report at all or, more commonly, sent delayed reports. Adjustments for these were made in the published statistics of industrial production but without clearly spelling out the magnitude or the basis for making them. These problems have been aggravated after deregulation of the industrial sector inasmuch as there is neither a legal obligation nor any incentive for enterprises to report production regularly. How much and in what aspects are not known to the public and, by all accounts, even to the government.

The Annual Survey of Industries, based on annual returns which establishments registered under the Factories Act are required to submit, also suffer from several limitations. Though reporting is compulsory, the lack of updated lists of factories in operation and the fact that a sizeable number of units fail to register, raises doubts whether it covers all the units in that domain. Non-response and incomplete and inaccurate response are also significant. Inordinate delays—sometimes several years—in processing and publication of data limit their usefulness.

The position in respect of non-factory industry is worse. Registered small industrial units are encouraged to report production data to the small industries directorate. There have also been occasional censuses and sample surveys of this segment. But the domain being ill-defined and there being no complete and updated list of establishments to provide a proper sampling frame, the usefulness of the data in improving the quality of estimates for even the modern small industry sector is quite limited. For national income purposes, the CSO relies on ingenious but indirect ways to estimate output of different segments of non-factory industry.

Much the same is true of other sectors including especially trade, road transport and services. Attempts by the NSSO and the CSO to fill the gaps in data for these and other unorganised sectors have faced serious difficulties in getting the required information: partly because these establishments typically do not maintain records and partly due to their reluctance to reveal information.

A universal problem with data compiled through administrative agencies is biased reporting. Government departments/organisations themselves are prone to doctor their reports whenever budget allocations, staff sanctions and performance assessment depend on the information given in their reports: window dressing of budgets, and exaggeration of the impact of drought and natural calamities being all too familiar examples of a pervasive phenomenon. For much the same reasons and also because the information can influence government policy (e.g., on tariffs, pricing, taxes/subsidies), there are incentives for biased reporting by private enterprises as well. Since there is in general no mechanism for independent verification and checking of the veracity of the reports, it is difficult to be confident about the accuracy of the data. The one significant exception is the population census: not only is it conducted by a specialised agency, but the reliability of the count is also verified by post-enumeration check for a small sample of households.

The constitution of advisory committees with non-official experts on particular subjects (e.g., national income, cost of living, cost of cultivation surveys) is meant to ensure that proper concepts, methodology and procedures are followed and that revisions are made after due deliberation. But these advisory groups are not in place in all cases and are not uniformly active.

The advisory committee for the decennial census of population and the National Income Advisory Committee of the CSO are among the significant exceptions. They meet regularly and all revisions in methodology have been made with their approval and explained clearly to users. By and large, however, the above arrangement has not been effective in ensuring objectivity and integrity of the system. Nor can the CSO and the SSB themselves do much in this respect because they are neither empowered nor equipped to do any independent verification. An autonomous, professional agency for direct collection of data and their validation is clearly both desirable and necessary.

Sample Surveys

The adoption of sample surveys through the NSSO, state statistical agencies and NGOs is a means of obtaining key data by getting relevant information directly from a representative sample of the enterprises/households/institutions through an independent professional agency. The NSSO at the Centre and the state level statistical bureaus are the main agencies for the purpose. But sample surveys have been widely used for getting data on a variety of subjects by other organisations, both in the public and in the private sectors.

Making the NSSO an autonomous organisation under a respected academic as chairperson and a board comprising official and non-official experts was a major step to build an independent statistical system free from government interference. While this purpose has been largely achieved and zealously maintained in the case of NSSO, the effort at making SSBs to serve as independent, professional agencies has not been successful.

The aspects on which data is to be collected, the kind of data to be collected and the manner of collection are discussed and decided by this executive in consultation with user agencies mostly governmental. But the responsibility for design, concepts and methodology, for organising and supervising the conduct of fieldwork, and processing the data are left entirely to the professionals. A system was also introduced whereby the data were collected separately for a central sample (by field staff of the NSSO) and for a state sample canvassed by staff of the SSBs based on a common sampling design, questionnaires and fieldwork procedures decided by the NSSO governing council.

These sample surveys, which have now been conducted every year for nearly 50 years, cover a very wide range of socioeconomic aspects. Some of the inquiries, especially land and assets holdings of households, private consumption, social consumption and employment have been repeated periodically with a conscious effort at ensuring comparability of data over time. The results—which have been published regularly and are accessible to the public—have been invaluable for tracking, analysing and interpreting various important socioeconomic features of India (some of which are not covered at all or only partially by the official sources), the contrasts between regions and between rural and urban areas, and how they have been changing.

Critique

The quality and reliability of the National Sample Survey (NSS) data have been under constant debate, both within the NSSO and outside. Though there have been significant improvements in the surveys, concerns about their reliability and the relative merits of NSS and other sources remain. These concerns—evident in the current debate on trends in poverty incidence—arise from: (a) differences between the NSS estimates and those obtained from other sources, namely, data compiled by government agencies and surveys conducted by other organisations; (b) the quality of field work and the accuracy of information provided by respondents (c) the effect of changes in scope sampling and questionnaire design and field procedures.

That data obtained by different agencies differ is not surprising. They are to be expected because the scope, source, content and methodology used by them are seldom identical. Much effort has gone into critical examination of the differences in estimates from different sources and reconciling them. This is particularly noticeable in respect of private consumption expenditures from which poverty estimates are derived. These exercises are valuable but only up to a point. A satisfactory reconciliation is not possible because—as the poverty debate illustrates—it is difficult to adjust fully for differences in scope and concepts; because estimates from different sources are all subject to unknown margins of error; and typically, for most sources, comparability over time is affected by changing design, concepts, etc.

No matter how well surveys are designed, the quality and veracity of information depends very much on how questions are framed; how informants understand the questions; and whether they are willing and able to give accurate information. These sources of error, which affect all systems of getting data, are difficult to eliminate and difficult to measure. While sample surveys have the merit of being economical and are not subject to biases of the kind affecting data collected by executive agencies, they are not free from errors arising from deficiencies in the conduct of fieldwork and inability or unwillingness of informants to give correct information.

NSS field investigators are given special training and detailed instructions in every survey before fieldwork begins. Nevertheless, the scale of the surveys requires a large number of investigators dispersed widely all over the country. Though there are well defined, explicit procedures for supervision and checking of their work, it is difficult to ensure that they are enforced uniformly and strictly everywhere. That the field work depends wholly on a permanent cadre of government staff with limited opportunities for career advancement and that too unrelated to performance compounds the difficulty.

There is also evidence of systematic differences in the quality of fieldwork between the central and state level organisations. Though both are expected to adopt identical procedures, estimates from state samples are known to differ significantly and systematically from those obtained from central samples. While the reasons for these differences have not been properly investigated and corrected, there is good reason to believe that state bureaus are not as strict in supervision and checking as the central organisations. In fact, most state bureaus publish only a fraction of the planned tabulations and even these are not easily accessible. Most of the detailed discussions based on NSS data rely on estimates from the central sample.

A legitimate criticism of the NSS is that it has not paid enough attention and resources to refining and improving survey methodology in the light of experience. In the initial stages, there was a great deal of emphasis on this aspect, thanks to Prof Mahalanobis and the fact that the Indian Statistical Institute (ISI) was intimately involved in NSSO. Over the years, several improvements have been made, but methodological research on questionnaire design; relative merits of single and multipurpose inquiries; the characteristics of respondents and their ability to give needed data; reference periods; fieldwork procedures; and related aspects has been neither sustained nor adequate. This requires close collaboration and interaction with academic institutions like ISI which has greatly weakened during the last three decades.

A more general criticism—which applies not only to the NSS but to the statistical system as a whole—is that information is collected without adequate attention to the purposes they are meant to serve and the cost involved; that only a fraction of the information collected is utilised; and that it takes an inordinately long time to publish it.

There is considerable force in the criticism about conducting too many census type enquiries and detailed/disaggregated surveys whose data are not utilised, nor perhaps necessary. In some cases, user agencies seek information at a level of detail and disaggregation (there are instances where they want data at the block or even village level) unmindful of the costs and in the event, do not put them to any use. .

For example, it is not clear what purpose is served by conducting quinquennial economic censuses and censuses of agricultural holdings and National Council of Educational Research and Training (NCERT's) education surveys at enormous cost in terms of money and diversion of staff from their regular duties. The Economic Census is meant to give a complete list of establishments engaged in non-agricultural activity to serve as a frame for sample surveys. Summary tabulations based on the census are published, but the detailed lists of establishments, which in principle should be available by village and town, are rarely maintained in a compiled form. They are not always available when needed; nor are they accessible to the public.

If the purpose is to provide a sampling frame, it is adequate to do a census of commercial and industrial establishments once in two decades. Provided the lists are properly maintained, the frame can be updated in selected localities before selecting the ultimate sampling units. In the case of other censuses—including landholdings, minor irrigation, livestock and education—mobilising the necessary personnel and getting them to do a proper job of enumeration has proved difficult. Quality suffers because of lack of supervision—sometimes no supervision at all! being based on village revenue records whose veracity in reflecting actual current position is open to serious question.

As for delays in processing and publication, one reason is the inadequacy of resources allocated for this purpose relative to what is spent on collection. This is especially the case at the state level where even the basic tabulation programme approved by the NSS governing council is not completed. Very little of it is available in accessible publications.

This would not be a matter of concern if the concerned agencies or researchers are enabled to do more detailed tabulations and analysis depending on specific issues they want to examine. But this requires the preservation of the primary data and making them accessible to users. Before computerisation, the information from individual sample units of NSS used to be stored in punch cards: there is a huge godown in Kolkata where they are kept but have become unusable over the years.

Computerisation has overcome this problem but only to some extent. Since the early 1990s, NSS has been preserving primary data in tapes. Accessibility to outside users, especially indigenous researchers, has also improved considerably because the CSO and the NSS supply the data on CD-ROMs for a reasonable charge. But in the case of agricultural, livestock and establishment censuses, the primary data are not maintained in a properly compiled and retrievable form. It is reported that the agricultural and minor irrigation census data have been computerised, but many people, including both officials and non-officials, who have tried to get hold of these data sets have drawn a blank. What then is the use of such data?

Most, if not all, of the above mentioned concerns have been articulated and debated by several committees, seminars and conferences organised by professional associations and some by government. To cite a few: the Indian Econometric Society conducted five seminars on various aspects of database of the Indian economy during the 1970s and 1980s. The papers and proceedings of all of them are published. During the 1990s, questions relating to data were again comprehensively reviewed in a seminar organised under the auspices of the Indian Council of Social Science Research (ICSSR) and another by the CSO. These discussions focused on gaps and deficiencies in respect of practically every important aspect of the economy and came up with concrete suggestions to remedy them. That these have not been acted upon is, in large measure, a reflection of apathy among administrators and policy makers.

There is among them an ill-informed scepticism, if not hostility, to data and empirical analysis. Policy makers and high level officials have shown little interest in ensuring that they get reliable and timely data.

Certainly they have not exerted themselves much to create institutional mechanisms for independent checking and verification of information they get from within their own departments. As already noted, there are in-built incentives for biased reporting within the government, by the government to the public and also by households and enterprises. Control over information and the ability to manipulate it are often, all too often used by government, as indeed by private interests to influence public opinion and policy decisions in particular directions. There are instances of officials who insist on reporting data collected by following proper procedures having been punished because the figures were not in the state's interest. And when independent sources give estimates which are inconvenient to one or other interest, the tendency is to dismiss such data rather than commission a serious examination of the reasons for the differences among estimates. More generally, the tradition of promoting policy discussions and arriving at decisions on sound data-based analysis and of making the data and the analysis available in the public domain remains very weak. Secretiveness and selective and motivated release of information being the norm, it is not surprising that there is so little interest in measures to ensure the integrity of the data system. Academia too has contributed to this situation by not exploiting the potential of published data, examining them critically and using them for rigorous analysis. Inadequacy of data and difficulty of access tend to be overused alibis.

Some Remedies

Focusing on the deficiencies in the statistical system is not meant, in the least, to undervalue its strengths and achievements. We have in place a nationwide professional network which collects and disseminates an exceptionally large and rich amount of information on the most important aspects of the economy and society. Much of this information is available in the public domain. The open and free debates on the relevance and quality of data and the fact that improvements have been made in response, are signs of health. But, clearly there are important gaps and weaknesses which need to be addressed to ensure the independence and integrity of the system; improve the quality and reliability of data; and easier, fuller accessibility to the public.

This is not the place to offer a blueprint for reform of the statistical system. This task is being addressed by a Commission (chaired by Dr Rangarajan) specially appointed for the purpose. Substantive questions relating to quality, reliability and other substantive issues have been widely discussed and need not be repeated here. Ensuring the independence and integrity of the public statistical system is however an important issue and one which has not received the attention it deserves.

1. In the first place, the format, content and procedures of data collection by executive agencies need to be reviewed. In several key areas—especially agricultural and industrial production—the existing reporting systems are unable to ensure correct, complete and timely reporting; they suffer from biases and are not immune to manipulation. Changes in the law making it obligatory on the part of both public and private entities to provide data to the authorities, with effective sanctions against non-compliance are necessary. More systematic and extensive use of sample survey techniques rather than reporting through executive departments is desirable. Where reporting is done by and through departments, a system for sample verification of the veracity of the returns would help. In order to ensure that these tasks are carried out objectively and professionally, they need to be entrusted to an agency independent of the executive departments.

2. Census type enquiries, other than the population census, should be fewer and far less frequent than is currently the case. The possibility of entrusting the conduct of such censuses to the central statistical authority deserves serious consideration. While enumerators may be drawn, as at present, from revenue officials, teachers and other departmental functionaries, alternative arrangements like hiring personnel for doing this work with proper training and stronger supervisory arrangements should be explored.

3. Sample surveys should be the main instrument for getting data on most aspects of economy and society. They arc a more economical way of getting data of greater detail and refinement than through censuses and are amenable to greater control over quality. While the scope, content and periodicity of these surveys must be guided by the requirements of policymakers, concepts, sample size, questionnaire

design and field investigation must be decided with due concern for the costs involved, relative to the degree of disaggregation and precision.

4. National level surveys on selected major themes, which need to be done periodically, should be entrusted to the NSSO and designed to provide state level estimates at a small margin of sampling error. Except for periodic censuses, the national statistical system should not be required to produce estimates below the state level.

5. In order to insulate the statistical system from influence and manipulation by executive agencies of government, the tasks of design, collection and verification of data, and their compilation and publication should be entrusted to autonomous, professionally competent organisations outside and independent of executive departments of the government. The CSO and the NSSO are natural candidates for this purpose. But they will need considerable strengthening and reorientation. In particular, even as their own professional staff concentrate on design, questionnaire design, training and strict supervision of fieldwork, they should be encouraged to explore the possibilities of collecting data from primary units of inquiry (i.e. households and enterprises) through universities, research institutions and, on occasion, NGOs. The experience of the National Family Health Survey (NFHS) and the Cost of Cultivation Surveys shows that this is a feasible option provided the operation is planned and implemented carefully.

6. The CSO and the NSSO should be separate organisations: it is undesirable to have a single super authority or department for all statistics. Each should have its own governing council (comprising representatives of key ministries and non-official economists and statisticians of eminence) with expert committees to advise on substantive and technical issues relating to specific subjects. They should preferably report to the Prime Minister directly or through the Planning Commission.

7. Given the vastness of the country and the fact that state governments also need reliable data relating to their domains, active cooperation and participation of the states is essential for a satisfactory national

statistical system. This is essential for the conduct of census type inquiries. NSS can, as they are at present, be designed to provide state level estimates within acceptable margins of sampling error. But the states should be left to get disaggregated region level estimates by pooling central and state samples.

8. For this purpose they have to canvass data for a larger sample and pool their data with that from the national sample. The existing practice whereby the states follow the designs, schedules, subjects of inquiry and instructions to investigators decided by the NSSO is adequate and should be continued. The collection and maintenance of local level data must however be entrusted to the local bodies, which are better placed to collect local information according to their needs. The state and central organisations must of course help by training and technical guidance.

9. The real problem however is to make state governments aware of the importance of reliable data for policy formulation and informed public discussion of the issues involved, accord their statistical agencies and sample survey units a higher and autonomous status, increase their professional calibre and allocate adequate funds. The suggestions regarding functions and organisation at the national level outlined above are equally applicable to states.

10. Statistical agencies at all levels must be brought under the purview of the Right to Information Act with the obligation to make the data they collect, and the manner in which they are collected, freely accessible to interested public and supply such data—including primary data, with suitable safeguards to protect individual privacy—at reasonable cost.

11. The agencies should be encouraged, in fact required, to have much closer interaction, interchange and collaboration between their staff and universities/research organisations. Besides involving the latter in detailed analysis of primary data and, increasingly, in collecting primary data on behalf of and under the schemes devised by official statistical agencies, they should be actively encouraged and supported to do research on survey design and methodology and to analyse the data collected by them.

Postscript

Since this paper was written, the Rangarajan Committee, set up by the central government, prepared a comprehensive review of data on all important aspects of the economy and society being collected by the government and its agencies. The report has identified the deficiencies in the scope, content and reliability of these data, in the mechanisms for collection and validation and suggested a number of measures to remedy them. Following this report an autonomous National Statistics Commission comprising experts, knowledgeable and experienced statisticians and economists is constituted to help in implementing the recommendations. At the initiative of the Commission, special committees, with representatives of official agencies collecting and collating data, as well as official and non-official users, have been appointed to work out detailed action programmes to strengthen and rationalise the institutional arrangements to ensure timely and reliable data in specific areas. Several—notably the ones concerned with agriculture, industrial statistics and evolving a legal framework empowering official agencies to collect data—have already completed the work. The implementation of their recommendations is in process. The process has underscored serious weaknesses arising from the current fragmentation of responsibility of data between numerous departments and agencies within the central and state governments—the fact that statistical agencies, especially in the states, do not have an independent status, authority and adequate qualified professional and supporting field staff. The weak tradition of data based analysis for public policy and objective evaluation of programmes and policies, compounded by indifference bordering on hostility to these, continue to be a major handicap.

12 Role and Relevance of Social Science Research

Role of Social Science Research

The function of 'research' is to broaden and deepen knowledge through systematic investigation to discover new information or reach a new understanding of various phenomena. This is as true for social sciences as the natural and physical sciences. Intellectual curiosity to explore the unexplored, and explain the unexplained by improving on extant theoretical and analytical frameworks or creating radically new ones are basic driving forces of research. Research of this genre that questions received wisdom and seems to expand and deepen the boundaries of knowledge is conventionally the domain of universities and academic institutions.

Not all 'research' is a quest for knowledge for its own sake. In the case of social sciences, research is stimulated by controversial and hotly debated issues of public policy on contemporary socioeconomic issues, as well as by dissatisfaction with the existing social order and its functioning and the desire to transform it into something more efficient, more just, more humane or more sustainable.

At a practical level, research contributes to better understanding of the nature of specific socioeconomic problems, critical exploration of alternative ways of addressing them and assessing how attempted solutions in fact work. Its functional role in enabling public policymakers as well as managers of government, public and private institutions and enterprises to deal with practical problems in an informed way and after due deliberation is also an important driving force. This role is of crucial importance in a democracy.

Social science research has special features arising from the multi-faceted nature of society and societal processes—the fact that several disciplines, which differ in their focus, perspectives, analytical frameworks and techniques, are involved; that ethical issues of good and bad, just and unjust have a salience in dealing with social issues to a far greater and more pervasive extent; and that history plays a far more important role in social processes than in natural and physical phenomena. Because of these, a unified framework of theory that encompasses different aspects and facets of society and their complex interactions is inherently difficult. More so because of wide differences in focus and methodological perspectives of the researchers from different disciplines. It is therefore hardly surprising that there are widely divergent views on the role and relevance of social research, the relation between theoretical and applied research, techniques of empirical observation, the role of quantitative analysis, and the possibilities of interdisciplinary research.

The choice of specific issues for research and approaches to their study is influenced not only by the academic background and interests of researchers, but by the nature of the institution where they work, its ethos and orientation, the scale and source of funding. Over the years there has been a palpable decline in intellectual curiosity among researchers to pursue sustained studies in areas of their choice and interest. Part, but by no means the only reason, is that sponsored research has become the dominant source of funding and shapes the scope and priorities of research. Much of social science research in India, sponsored by public sector as well as non-governmental and private organisations, is focused strongly on applied empirical studies of specific issues of socioeconomic development to help devise practical strategies, programmes and policies to tackle and also to critique them. Besides providing an opportunity to get to know programmes and policies in the concrete, and the ground realities of the way they operate, these studies also raise interesting new research issues of broader significance. This potential, regrettably, is not exploited adequately.

There is a misplaced notion that academic research tends to focus on abstract concepts and theoretical frameworks and interpret societal problems at a far too general level to be of value for tackling practical issues. In point of fact, ideas generated in 'academic' debates have a profound influence in shaping views on the appropriate strategies, programmes and policies for tackling current problems at different levels. Several important broader issues of development strategy and policy have been and continue to be under intense and lively debate among scholars. Academic debates and critiques have influenced several of the major changes in strategies relating to such diverse areas as employment and poverty alleviation, agricultural and rural development, fiscal policy, industrialisation, economic liberalisation, and decentralisation of governance and development. Perceptions and understanding on many of these aspects have changed in the light of studies of emerging experience.

Conceptual frameworks, as well as the analytical and empirical techniques emerging from academic research are widely used in 'policy' formulation on current issues. At the same time, research on contemporary problems often challenges extant concepts and highlights their inadequacies and thereby provides a strong stimulus to search for improvements in theoretical and analytical techniques. It is important to recognise and appreciate this complementary and symbiotic relation between the two.

The impact of research on policy works partly by influencing perceptions and attitudes of stakeholders, policymakers and managers and by providing information and analysis relevant to address specific problems. But decisions are not always or entirely based on logic and reasoned analysis. In many cases, suggested reforms to address specific problems are rejected or ignored by policymakers. Their attitudes and reactions are strongly influenced by political assessment of the extent of support and opposition from various interest groups, the possibility of arriving at a widely acceptable compromise, and keeping in view the likely impact of decisions in terms of electoral support. Politics apart, there are also serious issues concerning the scope and methods of inquiry used by researchers, the nature of data used and the way they are analysed, and the reliability and validity of the inferences drawn from them. Some of these issues relating to applied empirical research will now be addressed.

Quality and Reliability of Data

Researchers, policymakers and public discourse make extensive use of quantitative data and statistics for tracking and interpreting socioeconomic trends, as well as for design of policies and programmes and evaluating their impact. As a long standing believer and practitioner of applied empirical research, let me start by commenting on the widespread scepticism of statistical data, their use and abuse, their reliability for understanding social reality and as a basis for policy.

An enormous amount of resources is spent on collecting data on a wide variety of subjects by government statistical organisations, administrative departments, academic researchers, NGOs, and private consultancies. A great deal of effort goes into designing and organising data collection. Information is collected in some cases through complete enumeration and more generally through sample surveys based on structured questionnaires to elicit quantitative information through interviews of a large number of respondents using a large number of investigators. Economists and statisticians play an important, and some would say a dominant, role in the process.

Surveys differ hugely in scope, scale and design as well as in the organisation of fieldwork and therefore in the quality and reliability of data they generate. Specialised statistical organisations of the government (notably the Registrar-General and the National Sample Survey Organisation (NSSO)) take great care in design, collection and validation of data. Such changes as they make in these respects from time to time are published. Their published tabulations are detailed and extensive. Moreover, researchers can access the primary data.

However, much of the data collected by numerous other censuses and surveys conducted by or through administrative departments and under publicly funded projects are processed, if at all, only partially, and only processed data are available in the public domain. Data collected under projects funded by non-government agencies, and the analysis based on them, are mostly not published.

There is considerable scepticism of the way data are collected, and about their quality and reliability. In part, this reflects doubts about the ability of sample surveys to provide reliable and accurate estimates of socioeconomic characteristics. However, even when surveys are well designed, there are concerns about the quality of investigators as well as the organisation and supervision of fieldwork, the veracity of information provided by informants and the rigour with which post-enumeration checks are carried out.

These concerns are all the greater in the case of data collected by, or reported to, administrative departments and state level agencies. The incidence of incomplete coverage, non-reporting and inaccurate reporting is greater and the indifference to taking corrective action is far more serious. An added reason for concern is that the statistical agencies of administrative departments do not have the professional status and autonomy to publish the data fully and without making any arbitrary adjustments. Large unreconciled differences in estimates of the same characteristic made by different agencies reinforce doubts about the credibility of data.

A deeper objection to structured surveys relates to the efficacy of seeking information using standardised concepts and categories, unmindful of wide differences in language, socioeconomic status and education. Critics are sceptical of the extent to which informants understand the import of questions and also their ability and willingness to provide reliable responses, especially when information sought is very detailed and relates to sensitive matters and, therefore, about the accuracy of estimates based on them. In addition there are logistical problems of organising and supervising data collection through a large number of fieldworkers and in ensuring that instructions are followed strictly by all fieldworkers. There are also growing indications of respondent fatigue and bias.

Even the most carefully conducted surveys cannot avoid these problems. Supervision and post-survey verification of responses on a sample basis are used both by censuses and sample surveys to ensure that enumeration errors are within acceptable margins. But the information they collect and the estimates based on them necessarily have errors arising from non-response, inaccurate response or biased response.

Errors in data are by no means unique to social sciences. They are present in natural and physical sciences. Wholly objective and accurate observations are impossible. But given the fuzziness of concepts and measures, data on social characteristics and attitudes are likely to have much larger margins of error. Estimates of absolute magnitudes obtained from surveys, no matter how well designed, must therefore be used with great caution. The need for caution is much greater when the scope, concepts and design of different surveys, and of the same survey over time, are not comparable.

All estimates are subject to unknown margins of response and estimation errors because of inherent difficulties of getting direct estimates of several characteristics. For example, in several cases (sectoral outputs,

GDP, investments and consumption) estimates are based on secondary data and assumptions rather than reliable and complete data on actual realisations. Estimates of income and consumption, poverty incidence, female work participation, savings and investment made by different sources, using different definitions vary, often by a wide margin. Estimates of some characteristics (notably poverty incidence, nutritional status) are based on normative rather than objective standards of what is considered acceptable/necessary.

Micro surveys and case studies used in combination with large scale surveys would provide deeper and more generalisable insights if they are planned well and conducted in multiple locations. They need not be selected on rigorous sampling. Purposive selection based on typological classification would be adequate and in any case is more practical. It is important to ensure that all components have a common focus in terms of issues to be studied. Repeating such studies in the same locations periodically will be an effective way of studying dynamic processes.

There are some promising efforts in this direction—for example, in research on demography, education, health, land improvement and irrigation, and performance of employment guarantee programmes, but these are exceptions. Such an approach requires a degree of careful planning and sustained, collaborative effort among researchers for which the current institutional environment and funding prospects are far from favourable.

That quantitative socioeconomic data collected through large scale surveys are incomplete and noisier to a greater extent than in physical sciences, does not render the data useless. Since controlled experiments are impossible in social sciences, survey data provide the best available and most valuable basis for empirical research on the nature of variations across different segments of the survey universe and to explore the factors underlying these differences. Explorations of systematic patterns of variation, exceptions to the pattern and differing patterns open up exciting possibilities of research. It requires great care, circumspection and also ingenuity to extract insights from imperfect and noisy data. But neither academic nor non-academic researchers are sufficiently sensitive to the weaknesses of data and the need to use them after careful scrutiny of their scope, relevance and reliability for the purposes of study. There is an increasing tendency among researchers to select such data as are available in readily accessible publications or websites that seem relevant to their particular topic and proceed to put them through mechanical applications of statistical packages.

Need for Broader Perspectives

Much of applied empirical research tends to be policy-centric. Besides tracking and analysing emerging trends in various aspects of economy and society, the emphasis is on contributing to, or critiquing, strategy and policies, both overall and in relation to different regions and sectors, for determining the viability of specific project proposals and for evaluating the implementation and impact of programmes and projects. This policy-centricism narrows the scope of analysis to techno-economic and managerial dimensions without considering the wider ramifications of particular programmes and policies, their impact on other programmes and policies and the larger context in which they operate.

Being part of, and embedded in, the larger society, the economy cannot be understood without taking into account its interface and interactions with social, cultural and political aspects—all of which are changing over time. The premises and presumptions of conventional economic theory about consumer sovereignty, competition and free markets have no doubt undergone significant changes with the growing recognition of the role of government, of social structure and norms, as well as the organisation and functioning of institutions, which have been the domain of other social science disciplines. This has helped widen the perspectives of economists and facilitated interactions with other disciplines to some extent. It has also had an impact on survey design and methods. Besides widening the scope of surveys, to use different techniques to elicit information of a qualitative nature has also become more widespread.

But scepticism persists. Anthropologists, in particular, believe that societal processes are far too complex and multidimensional to be explored through large scalc surveys with preconceived concepts and categories. They emphasise the need for deep, open-ended and detailed exploration of structures, relationships and processes through participant observation of select communities and social groups. Such an intensive effort is however necessarily limited in scale and in practice, as also in scope. While they do offer insights that conventional surveys cannot, the immense diversity among social groups and communities makes generalisations of the larger picture nearly impossible.

One need not accept the methodological perspective of anthropologists to recognise that micro studies focused on specific aspects make it possible to explore them in far greater detail, get a more fine-grained picture and deeper insights than can be obtained from large scale surveys. The two approaches should, however, be viewed as complementary rather than as mutually exclusive alternatives. It would also require imaginative use of different survey techniques—structured surveys, rapid assessments, focus group interviews and opinion surveys—both on large samples and for micro studies.

Inadequate Analysis

Economists' use of quantitative data and quantitative techniques of analysis is open to criticism for being excessively policy-centric, descriptive rather than analytical, and paying inadequate attention to non-economic aspects of socioeconomic change. Attempts to explore the factors responsible for the variations in socioeconomic characteristics and processes generally do not go beyond highlighting differences in associated characteristics. Techniques of multivariate analysis (logit, probit and more conventional regression techniques) are increasingly used to assess the relative strength of 'plausible' quantifiable factors in accounting for variations in characteristics and in the rate and direction of their change. The coefficients give an idea of the net strength of the association of independent on dependent variables, some of which have a direct impact while others affect outcomes indirectly. In the absence of a clear understanding of the manner in which each variable affects a particular characteristic and of the interrelations and interactions among them, it is difficult to interpret the substantive significance of the statistical coefficients. Since details of methodology, data used and analytical arguments are not always transparent, the interpretations and insights they have to offer on underlying causative factors are limited and incomplete.

There is also the deeper problem that these analyses do not capture the role of physical environment, social structure, cultural values, political processes and other non-economic factors in determining the nature, pace and impact of socioeconomic change. But all these aspects are inter-related and interact in complex ways which cannot be unravelled if, as is the current practice, different disciplines tend to focus research on aspects of development programmes and policies which they consider important.

On Interdisciplinary Research

Bringing different disciplines into closer and more meaningful interaction to promote multidisciplinary research is a daunting task. We do not have, and are unlikely to have, a unified theory of development. A more practical approach would be to constitute multi-disciplinary research teams, and have each of them explore, from their respective perspectives, the factors/forces that shape the performance of a particular programme, or of differential performance of different programmes of a given genre. This can provide an opportunity for better appreciation of the relevance of different perspectives, a basis for more meaningful interactions across disciplines leading to richer insights, and hopefully stimulating more such collaborative research.

An alternative approach is to internalise an interdisciplinary approach in one's own research. Initially, in my research, I focused on exploring regional variations in agricultural performance, rural employment and poverty incidence, and on their associated characteristics that seem from extant knowledge to be important. In the process I was sensitised to inadequacies in available data (in terms of concepts, detail and reliability of different data sets and wide differences in all these respects and in estimates from different sources) and in the current conceptual frameworks and techniques used for analysis. Relatively simple regression analysis seemed to provide plausible explanations in some cases. But where (as in agriculture) the determinants of output and its changes are complex and interdependent, both the specification of the 'independent' variables and interpretation of results proved problematic. Simpler techniques—cross tabulations with appropriate partitioning of data—seemed to be more meaningful. Much of my recent work on agricultural growth uses this approach.

Some Illustrative Examples

This experience led me to a closer study of concepts, design, and mechanisms of collecting the data, as well as the kinds of errors and biases that the process involves. It also led me to take an active part in ongoing efforts to improve the database. While recognising the need for caution in interpreting results of analysis based on imperfect and noisy data, I found that a closer look at the patterns could suggest interesting new issues for research: the relation between irrigation, fertilisers and agrarian structure and agricultural growth; the role of animals in the agricultural economy; determinants of intensity of labour use in agriculture and diversification into non-farm activities; the puzzling differences between Indian and Chinese agriculture in labour intensity, use of animals and wage labour; and the apparent anomaly of Kerala having a relatively high level of health indicators despite levels of food intake below those recommended by nutritionists.

Questioning extant frameworks and explanations opened up further issues for inquiry and underscored the importance of extra economic factors—ecology, technology, economic environment, institutions and politics—in shaping economic outcomes. This meant tackling the problems of interdisciplinary research. Much of my recent work is an attempt to meet this challenge, partly by internalising basic scientific knowledge of the role of environment and different elements of technology in shaping agriculture and animal husbandry practices. This led to a study of spatial variations in crop yields and their relation to differences in rainfall, irrigation and fertiliser use, and of the impact of ecology on the size and composition (by species and use) of animals and in turn on intensity of human labour use relative to animals and machines. The developments in institutional economics provided the framework for understanding the role of markets, public and private organisations, and collective/community institutions in agriculture, and especially in irrigation and land improvement. It has led to a number of detailed studies of the institutional arrangements and their functioning in different types of irrigation systems under different agro-climatic conditions. These have proved to be very exciting both in terms of understanding the important role of such studies in diverse locations and, more importantly, in terms of the insights they offer. Many of these insights are tentative and would need far more detailed, sustained and refined work in many more locations.

In the sixties there was a controversy over the desirability of allowing cow slaughter, despite opposition on religious grounds, for more efficient use of cattle. Both propositions were questioned on the ground that actual age and sex composition of cattle was more or less similar in different parts of South Asia with very different religious compositions and that it is shaped by rational considerations given the imperative need for bullocks as a source of draught power for agriculture, and the use of cows primarily for breeding bullocks. More detailed analysis of regional variations in density and composition of cattle showed that use of bullocks was nearly universal and that they are a function of rainfall, population density and inequality in land distribution. It further turned out that, over the years, as the average size of land holdings declined and small sized holdings proliferated in absolute terms and as a proportion of total holdings, the advent of mechanical equipment for land preparation, harvesting, transport and lifting water, combined with rising cost of labour led to rapid reduction in the bullock population in most parts of India.

By contrast, in China, and East Asia generally, traditionally animals were rarely used for operations and these were conducted mostly by human labour using the hoe and other implements. Investigating the reasons for it led to an exploration of the role of climatic differences (temperature, rainfall and its seasonal distribution) in explaining the contrast. In most parts of India, the preparation of land for timely sowing on the onset of the monsoon after a long hot summer was not possible without animal power. But lower temperatures, ample and seasonally well distributed rainfall permitted hoe cultivation over most of China. The differences in these respects also seem to have been a significant factor in shaping the characteristics of irrigation systems and the evolution of institutional arrangements in the two countries. The necessity of having bullocks and the inability of the landless and land-poor to afford their own bullocks resulted in lower incidence of tenancy and high incidence of wage labour in India. By contrast, conditions in China facilitated tenancy as the means to meet the mismatch between distribution of land ownership and labour power. Differences in social composition—caste based stratification in India and a greater social homogeneity in China—also seem to have made an impact on the politics of land reform.

In my more recent work on agricultural growth, dissatisfaction with viewing agricultural growth as a function of investment, an undifferentiated concept of technology, and prices taken individually, led me to take a closer look at different components of agricultural technology and their role in raising production, and to explore the individual and collective impact of changes in environment, growth promoting technology, economic environment (defined by markets and government policy) and the functioning of institutions (comprising agrarian structure, institutions for managing common pool resources and those that generate technology and provide support services).

In respect of irrigation, this approach is the basis for the design of structured surveys of a number of irrigation systems to understand the organisation of management, its interface with users, the rules for distribution of water, the extent to which they are observed, and the impact on actual use and productivity of water among different segments of users in different types of systems under different conditions.

Going beyond the conventional frameworks of inquiry is challenging. It requires the researcher to learn from different disciplines about the role of environment, technology, economics and institutions and their interactions. The range of information needed is far more diverse. Their analysis uses methods from different disciplines and tends to be eclectic. The results of examples cited are highly tentative and open to contestation. But it does open up exciting new possibilities of comprehending the complex and ramified ways in which natural environment, technology, incentives and socioeconomic institutions influence and shape agrarian structure and change.

Current State of Social Science Research

In India, research is done by numerous organisations including universities, government and non-government research institutions, international ones, well organised professional consultancy organisations, and freelance consulting firms and individuals. The scale and scope of social science research of all types have expanded greatly.

A recent survey identified over 400 institutions—190 universities, 67 government institutes and over 160 non-government institutions (including 27 of the Indian Council of Social Science Research (ICSSR) family)—currently engaged in social science research with full or partial public funding on a continuing basis. The majority of universities and a sizeable number of publicly funded non-government institutions (mainly in the

ICSSR family) cover different disciplines and are meant to be free to pursue their own research agenda. The rest are institutions specialising in different disciplines and research on particular aspects of society.

The conditions and performance of this class of institutions, which are expected or claim to be centres of independent, rigorous research on social problems give cause for concern. The nature of their malaise has been widely discussed. Public funding of research in this class of non-governmental institutions, has not kept pace with rising costs of even maintaining their core activities, let alone expand and improve them. Over time, most of them have been forced to depend increasingly on projects sponsored by government agencies, private trusts, foreign organisations and the private sector. This has led to the focus of research being determined by the issues of interest to the sponsors rather than sustained work on a clearly defined agenda. Inadequacy and uncertainty of funding for centres that enables them to pursue independent research is an important, though not the only, reason for their increasing dependence on sponsored projects.

They face great difficulties in getting and retaining professionally trained and motivated researchers for reasons beyond their control. Major changes in the pattern of job opportunities for professionals have eroded the attractions of social sciences for able and motivated students for even undergraduate, not to mention postgraduate degrees. Even better known universities face declining interest of students in postgraduate degrees in social sciences. This trend is even more striking at the PhD level as the better performing postgraduates prefer to go abroad or get attractive jobs in the burgeoning sectors of the new economy. The cumulative impact is felt in the difficulty of getting good faculty in both universities and research institutions. The spirit of inquiry spurred by intellectual curiosity, which drives good research is on the wane even as many exciting and puzzling issues are being thrown up by the ongoing turbulent process of social, economic and political change.

The adverse impact of these factors on the quality and motivation of research personnel has been aggravated by internal weaknesses in governance, the adoption of personnel policies that give little room for objective assessment of performance, and incentives based on such assessments. The professional quality of research in academic institutions, their contribution to widening and deepening knowledge, providing rigorous analyses of trends and underlying factors, and shaping public policy are far from impressive. There are of course significant but regrettably few exceptions.

Even as publicly funded research institutions have suffered, there has been a mushrooming of NGOs, consultancy firms and individuals in the social science research business. It is impossible to know even the number of freelance consultants and consultancy firms in this field. A recent (incomplete) compilation by the National Social Science Documentation Centre (NASSDOC) lists some 800 or so organisations reported to be engaged in research. Information on the areas and topics of research is not available in most cases; and in others it is quite sketchy. Closer scrutiny suggests that a large number of them are not engaged in any serious research.

Civil society organisations seek to critique the basis of public policies and their implementation and play an advocacy role to make them more responsive to people's needs and more accountable. NGOs are directly involved in development projects of different sorts at the community level in an effort to improve the efficacy of government schemes and also try out innovative approaches to promote participatory development. These roles require them to assay relevant information and knowledge and to learn from their field experience. Several of the larger NGOs have research wings for both purposes. These efforts, commendable as they are, are subject to inherent limitations arising from lack of conceptual and analytical clarity, a propensity to generalise from the particular, and the difficulty of ensuring detachment and objectivity inherent in self-evaluations. The possibility of learning from their collective experience is impeded because of their marked reluctance to engage in open, introspective interaction among themselves and with others.

Business enterprises (both public and private) and their associations have in-house research units and also sponsor studies to review the current state of information and knowledge on status and prospects for specific sectors and industries and studies relevant for formulation and appraisal of specific projects and policy decisions. International aid agencies—both public and private—have emerged as important sponsors and financiers of such 'research'. Their agenda is entirely client driven and policy-centric. The basis of and procedures for sponsoring 'research' has led to rapid commercialisation of research and the mushroom growth of private consultancy organisations. Most are individuals and small firms; corporate consultancy firms (both domestic and foreign) have become increasingly prominent players. The data they collect and reports they prepare are meant exclusively for their sponsors. Sponsors (including public agencies) use them usually in a selective way and the results are not made public. The material is extensively used in discussions on public policy but not available for independent critical scrutiny. The knowledge they generate is not accessible to the wider public, and tends to be used in selective ways to serve particular interests and lobbies for particular viewpoints rather than contributing to better understanding or informed public debate.

The growing importance of sponsored projects has intensified and fragmented the policy-centric focus of research. It has also led to a proliferation of studies of particular schemes viewed in a narrow perspective. The opacity of the process and the fact that the results of most of these studies are not available for scrutiny has greatly reduced their social value for improving our knowledge and the quality of public policy. There are however some significant exceptions: notable recent examples include the evaluations of Integrated Rural Development Programme (IRDP), and National Rural Employment Guarantee Programme (NREGP) (all of which were funded by the government and public sources but entrusted to a network of independent research institutions, taking care to ensure that they followed a common methodology). Their professional credibility and the fact that their methodology, data and results were published, stimulated extensive discussion in the public domain and have led to significant modification of these programmes.

Revitalising Social Research

These deficiencies have been highlighted in the report of the Fourth Review Committee of the ICSSR. Recognising that intellectual curiosity cannot be kindled by exhortation or fiat, it argued for creating an environment that is conducive to and encourages research, which widens and deepens our knowledge and makes it available for contestation in the public domain. It emphasised the importance of larger public funding contributed by agencies involved in development through an institutional mechanism which is autonomous, professional, credible in terms of objectivity and transparency in the manner in which agenda is decided, proposals and performance are evaluated. It visualised a restructured ICSSR to play this role. Instead of the present practice of the ICSSR providing open-ended commitments to support core activities of select institutions, the Committee suggested that access to funding for programmes and projects should be widened and renewal of research programme grants linked to the performance in terms of peer evaluated output quality.

While giving ample freedom to researchers to decide their research agenda, the priority should be to provide liberal institutional grants for sustained medium-term programmes for studies on selected broad themes. A conscious effort should be made to encourage collaborative multi-centric, multidisciplinary research on select topics and themes, especially for in-depth micro level studies, and impact evaluations repeated periodically in the same locations. Also underscored was the importance of making all data collected by public agencies or with public funding to be placed in the public domain through digitised data banks.

The Report was placed in the public domain and also sent to the government in March 2007, but it has not attracted much attention or discussion in the media or in the social science community. There has been no reaction from the government. Several respected social scientists supported the main recommendations for restructuring ICSSR into an autonomous, professionally credible institution but raised doubts about the proposal to establish an Indian Academy of Social Sciences in its place. The central issue of alternative practical ways to establish an autonomous institution which will promote and sustain high professional standards and transparent functioning was however not discussed. I can only hope and plead that the larger social scientist community will evince interest in discussing the issues seriously, mobilise support for much needed reforms and pressure the government to take appropriate action.

13 Econometric Analyses of Agricultural Growth

Reflections of a Non-Econometrician

Most economic and social phenomena are shaped by multiple factors and our ability to disentangle and assess the effects of different factors has been greatly enhanced by the development and progressive improvement in econometric and statistical techniques. These techniques—ranging from regression analysis to general equilibrium models—are widely used for quantitative analysis of various aspects of structure and change in agriculture. There is extensive literature of this genre seeking to estimate trends and fluctuations in area, production and yields; the sources of spatial and temporal variations in output and productivity; supply responses to price changes; contribution of technological change to output growth and even returns to research; and optimum allocation of resources.

The literature generated in the process is impressive in volume and the range of subjects covered; but its contribution to understanding of the way the sector is structured and the rate and pattern of its change is considerably less so. The aim of this paper is two fold: (a) Focus on the limitations of widely used techniques to assess the rate and volatility of output growth and in output; and factors contributing to it; and (b) indicate, with concrete applications to Indian data, how some of these limitations can be mitigated.

Growth and Fluctuations

Statistical trend fitting is commonly used to measure, at the national and state levels, trend growth rates of area, production of yields for all crops taken together and individually. They are also used, though less commonly, to assess whether the trend is steady, accelerating or decelerating; and examine the extent of variability around the trend. Whether faster growth resulting from new technology is associated with greater variability is another question that has attracted attention.

Of the many different functional forms available, researchers use one or more of the following: the linear (constant absolute change per unit of time), log linear (constant rate of change with respect to time) and quadratic (variable rate of changes) forms are the most widely used. A few have tried other forms (like the Gompertz and kinked exponential functions) that can capture more complex patterns of variations in trend. Of all these, the log linear is the most widely used. For the most part, analysts tend to use the log linear. This is arbitrary inasmuch as it ignores the diversity in the time pattern of change across regions and crops. And in doing so can lead to misleading conclusions.

Even when different forms are estimated, it is rare to find researchers choosing the best fitting form based on explicit criteria. One can take the position that fitting a particular function is meant to test a maintained hypothesis regarding: the time pattern of change in output (or yield or area) and use the tests of statistical significance of the coefficients as corroborating or rejecting the hypothesis. But this raises the question as to the basis for a particular 'maintained' hypothesis. There is, in any case, no basis to postulate that all crops and regions confirm to the constant growth rate pattern. On the contrary, even a cursory examination of available information would show that growth trajectories are varied. The task of analysis is to find out the nature and extent of these differences. The mere fact that judged by the usual statistical tests, the results do not reject the hypothesis of constant growth rate cannot get around this difficulty.

Under these circumstances it would be more appropriate to fit a number of different functional forms and choose the best fitting function —i.e., the one that provides the best summary description of the series— leaving the explanation of differences in patterns for separate analysis. It is also appropriate to measure the extent of instability with respect to the best fitting trend line.

State-wise time series of gross cropped area from 1960-61 are available in publications of the Ministry of Agriculture. The Central Statistical Organisation (CSO) has published estimates of gross value of crop production at constant prices for all states from 1960-61 to the mid-nineties. Combining the two gives a series for gross output per hectare of gross cropped area. We fitted the following three alternative functions to each of these series, covering the period 1970-71 to 1991-92:

$$Y = a+bt$$

$$\text{Log } Y = a+bt$$

$$\text{Log } Y = a+bt+ct^2$$

Table 13.1 presents the best fitting function (based on R^2 and significance of coefficients), to each of the above variables and for each of the major states. It is clear that no single function fits all of them.

- In the case of area none of the forms give a significant fit in 2 states. Among the rest, the best fit is given by the linear form in 6 states; the constant growth rate function in one (all showing growth); and semi log quadratic in four (all showing a decelerating trend in growth).
- In the case of output all series show trend increases: the linear form fits the series best in 4; the constant growth function in 8; and the variable growth form in 2—the coefficients indicating decelerating growth.
- Yield per hectare shows a significant linear trend in 5 states, a constant rate of growth in 3, an accelerating growth in 5; and a decelerating growth in 1.
- It is also apparent that in several cases, the proportion of variation 'explained' by the best fitting function is lower in the case of area compared to output or yields per hectare. In some the proportion of variance in yields 'explained' is relatively low (less than 65%).

Clearly the above approach makes a significant difference to our understanding of the nature and extent of differences in agricultural growth across states compared to the picture obtained from fitting only a single function (such as constant growth rate) to all variables and states. It would also make a difference to estimates of the extent of instability measured by deviations from the trend and factors underlying it.

It is worth noting that systematic variation in growth rate is built into the above equations: the linear form implying a progressive fall (or rise) in the growth rate and the semi-log quadratic form implying a constant

Table 13.1

Characteristics of Best Filling Trend Lines to State Time Series of Area, Output and Yield, 1970-1990

State	Gross cropped area				Gross value of output				Output per ha.			
	F	b	c	R^{-2}	F	b	c	R^{-2}	F	b	c	R^{-2}
Andhra Pradesh	None				2	***		0.84	3	**	**	0.93
Bihar	2	Neg*	NS	0.07	1	Pos***		0.74	1	**		0.82
Gujarat	3	Pos		0.03	1	Pos***		0.40	1	Pos***		0.46
Haryana	2	Pos***		0.61	2	Pos***		0.94	1	Pos***		0.95
Karnataka	1	Pos***		0.57	2	Pos***		0.88	3	Pos***	Pos*	0.89
Kerala	3	Pos***	Neg***	0.79	3	Pos***	Neg***	0.67	1	Pos***		0.50
Maharashtra	1	Pos***		0.43	1	Pos***		0.70	1	Pos***		0.70
Madhya Pradesh	3	Pos***	Neg***	0.91	1	Pos***		0.72	3	Pos***	Pos***	0.61
Orissa	1	Pos***		0.75	2	Pos***		0.85	3	Pos***	Neg**	0.62
Punjab	3	Pos***	Neg***	0.99	3	Pos***	Neg***	0.99	3	Pos***	Pos***	0.97
Rajasthan	1	Pos***		0.47	2	Pos***		0.78	2	Pos***		0.76
Tamil Nadu	1	Pos***		0.23	2	Pos***		0.69	2	Pos***		0.90
Uttar Pradesh	1	Pos***		0.93	2	Pos***		0.92	2	Pos***		0.89
West Bengal	3	Pos***	Neg***	0.93	2	Pos***		0.88				

Notes: * significant at 10% level; ** significant at 5% level; ***significant at 1% level. F stands for functional form; 1 is the linear form; 2 is log linear form; 3 is the log quadratic form.

increase (or decrease) in the growth rate. Testing for 'breaks' in trend involves somewhat more complex procedures. This is meaningful to assess whether identifiable, dated events such as introduction of major innovations like high yielding variety (HYV), or abrupt major changes in demand conditions, institutions or policies have in fact made a significant difference to the growth trajectory. But it does not make much sense to look for breaks in arbitrarily chosen periods. Indeed, given the rather uneven volatility of weather conditions across years, such tests may lead to quite wrong and misleading conclusions.

Time series of overall land use, irrigation and cropped area as well as crop wise estimates of area, production and yields for practically all crops at the district level are available in publications of the Ministry of Food and Agriculture. These have been used to study regional and even district level, differences in growth and fluctuations of some specific crops. However, time series estimates of output and productivity covering all crops at the district level remain to be compiled. What we have—thanks to work of Bhalla *et al.* (1979; 1989; 2001) in the Centre for Study of Regional Development in Jawaharlal Nehru University—are estimates of three-year averages of cropped area, irrigated area and total output values covering major crops in the early sixties, early seventies, early eighties and early nineties.

Their latest publication gives estimates for 35 crops at constant prices for all 4 triennia. At the national levels these account for most of the total output; the coverage does however vary between states and more so between districts. Though not as satisfactory as a full time series for studying growth and instability, they are the basis currently available for the purpose. That a great deal can be learnt from this data set about regional differences in growth rates, changing regional patterns of growth, inter-district variability of land productivity, disparities in the output per worker and several other interesting features is evident from the studies of Bhalla and his colleagues.

Table 13.2 extracted from the latest publication, brings out the enormous inter-district variations in agricultural performance. The proportion of districts reporting fall in output or slow growth (<2.5% per annum) have progressively declined in successive decades. An increasing proportion of districts have recorded output increases of better than 3.5 per cent per annum during this period. The study highlights the strong positive association between the level of productivity and the extent of irrigation development, fertiliser use and (in the eighties and nineties) with tractorisation—a progressive reduction in the degree of inequality across districts in respect of average crop yield levels, especially since the early 1970s, and a progressive increase in inter district disparities in output per worker. They also attempted to explain factors underlying spatial variations in productivity at different points of time using multiple regressions. For reasons to be discussed later, this exercise is subject to several limitations.

Tables 13.2 and 13.3 reconstructed from the data provided in the study, brings out some striking differences in growth performance (in terms of output per hectare of cropped area) across districts classified by level of rainfall and the ratio of irrigated to total crop area.

Overall, the proportion of districts reporting a decline in yields has come down drastically from 25 per cent in the sixties to less than 6 per cent in the eighties. A large, and increasing, majority has recorded increases in yields. Also the proportion reporting increases (>25 per cent) has also increased sharply from around 18 per cent in the sixties to nearly 60 per cent in the eighties. Correspondingly, those reporting increases of less than 10 per cent, which comprised about a fifth of all districts, fell to less than 10 per cent in eighties. (Table 13.2)

Table 13.2

Distribution of Districts by Average Annual Growth Rate of Crop Output

Growth Rate	*1962-1965 to 1970-1973*	*1970-1973 to 1980-1983*	*1980-1983 to 1990-1993*
>5	37	47	61
3.5 – 5	40	48	77
2.5 – 3.5	31	42	54
1.5 – 2.5	51	45	42
0 – 1.5	60	51	29
Negative	62	48	127
All	281	281	281

Note: Estimated from district-wise studies of Bhalla *et al.* (1979; 1989; 2001).

In a large majority of the districts, the rates of yield change vary from decade to decade. The majority (60%) of districts recorded growth of output in all three periods and 30 per cent experienced increasing rates of yield improvement in successive decades. Only six per cent of the districts, however, recorded 'high' (more than 25%) increase in yields in all three periods. On the other extreme, about six per cent of the districts report a progressive decline in growth rate. (Table 13.3)

Table 13.3

Distribution of Districts by Rainfall-Irrigation Zones and Percentage Change in Crop Yields during Different Periods

Zones	*N*	*Sixties*			*Seventies*			*Eighties*		
		Neg	*<10%*	*>25%*	*Neg*	*<10%*	*>25%*	*Neg*	*<10%*	*>25%*
LL	38	13	5	16	5	4	22	8	2	21
LH	30	2	5	16	4	3	12	1	1	24
ML	49	18	7	11	6	6	21	1	6	30
MH	43	5	11	10	2	24	24	0	1	34
HL	64	16	20	5	18	14	16	3	10	39
HH	33	6	9	6	11	5	10	2	3	21
All	257	64	57	64	42	46	105	15	23	179

Note: LL – Low rainfall low irrigation; LH – Low rainfall high irrigation
ML – Medium rainfall, low irrigation; MH – Medium rainfall, high irrigation
HL – High rainfall, low irrigation; HH – High rainfall, high irrigation
N – Number of districts; Neg – Decline
Estimated from district-wise studies of Bhalla *et al.* (1979; 1989; 2001).

The proportion of districts reporting growth and those reporting consistently high growth (25% over the decade) in all 3 periods is least in districts with low rainfall and low irrigation. Among the low irrigation districts, this proportion is larger among those with medium and higher rainfall.

In all rainfall zones, a larger proportion of districts with better than average irrigation development report sustained growth, and sustained high growth in all three periods.

A sizeable number of districts in all rainfall-irrigation categories report increasing growth rates during successive decades. This proportion is again markedly higher among districts with better developed irrigation.

Comparisons based on three-year averages are of course better than single year data for assessing trends. But in a sector so sensitive to weather conditions, and given that a run of good and bad years is not uncommon, conclusions regarding growth and instability must be interpreted with caution. Moreover, one should bear in mind that district estimates of crop yields are not based on crop cutting experiments and have a large element of 'judgment' and impression. More importantly, the proportion of total crop area covered by the crops included in Bhalla *et al. op.cit.*, estimates vary considerably across districts at a given point of time and in given districts over time. Inferring overall growth of total output and productivity involves a strong assumption that the productivity of crops not covered by the estimates is the same as the average for those included in the estimate. This could introduce significant, but non-uniform biases in the estimates of growth. State level estimates, while more complete, are not free of problems of reliability and comparability, but coverage is less of a problem.

Sources of Growth

Attempts to understand the sources of output change fall into two categories: (1) decomposition schemes; and (2) input output analysis. The former seek to measure the relative contribution of different component elements to changes in total output. Several such schemes have been proposed and applied: the relatively simple additive scheme proposed and estimated by Minhas and Vaidyanathan (1965) to measure the relative contributions of changes in area, crop pattern, and 'pure' yield to output changes was subsequently extended to assess the effect of changing spatial distribution of area and yield changes of various crops. (Dharm Narain, 1977; Vidya Sagar, 1980). Minhas also proposed a more elaborate multiplicative scheme. All these focussed on accounting for changes between two points of time rather than series data. They were done mostly during the sixties and seventies. But hardly any has been reported since, perhaps because of a growing fascination of researchers with econometric estimation of 'production functions'.

Decomposition of overall growth by component elements obviously is not adequate to unravel the determinants of the growth process. But it is an essential first step inasmuch as the factors influencing or shaping changes in different constituent elements are not the same. It also helps to avoid misapplication of the concept of production function to analyse output growth.

'Production function' defines the relation between output and inputs. Conventionally, economic theory has been viewed, usually measured by value added, as a function of primary factors namely, labour and capital.

(In the case of agriculture, land would be an additional primary factor.) Alternative functional forms capture differences in respect of returns to scale and the degree of substitutability between inputs. Refinements take into account the fact that output is a function not only of the quantity of the input, but also of changes in the productivity per unit of inputs due to changes in the quality of particular inputs and, more importantly, changes in productivity per unit of all factors (due to economies of scale, technological changes, learning, etc.). Much of the work on production functions for industry, and for the economy as a whole, is based on this understanding. Though there are problems about data and interpretation, the results of this class of production functions have provided useful insights.

Applying this framework to agriculture is beset with serious problems of data, specification and interpretation of results. A major constraint is lack of data on primary factors. This information is available for land in terms of area under cultivation, but this does not take into account variations in agro-climatic conditions. Estimates of the number of workers in agriculture are available from decennial censuses of population and of labour time spent on agriculture from sample surveys of employment and unemployment and farm management for different points of time. There are hardly any reliable time series estimates of total capital stock in agriculture even at the national level, not to speak of states and regions. Because of this, estimation of production functions with primary factors as inputs is not feasible and seldom attempted.

Faced with these difficulties, researchers tend to use a motley collection of inputs: some like proportion of area irrigated; current inputs of human, animal and/or machine labour (as sort of proxies for primary factors); non-primary inputs such as improved seeds, fertilisers, manures, and pesticides; and rural infrastructure in varied combinations.

Unlike the conventional production function, these specifications and the different functional forms used in estimation—linear, log linear, Cobb Douglas, constant elasticity of substitution (CES), Tornquist—betray a lack of a clearly defined and coherent concept of the production process and input-output relations.

A review of the agricultural production function estimates—and there are a large number of them—shows that the estimated coefficients for inputs are sensitive to how many and what inputs are included in the estimating function; coefficients are often not significant, their values unstable and on occasion even have the wrong signs! Faced with the pervasive problem of multicollinearity, analysts tend to drop variables with non-significant coefficients and report results for variants that give statistically significant and 'plausible' values. For all these reasons, it is difficult to make coherent sense of the estimated regressions, either as tests of hypotheses regarding: the factors determining output, the form of the relation between inputs and output, or for judging the impact of specific inputs on productivity and measuring trends in total factor productivity.

Part of the problem arises from the confounding of the conventional, primary factors centred around concept of the production process and one, which views it as a biochemical process. The two are of course interrelated and these interrelations need to be explored. But this is best done as a separate exercise. Confounding the two do not add much to our understanding of the factors underlying spatial or temporal variations in productivity.

For a meaningful analysis of input-output relations in agriculture, it is essential to keep these two separate and recognise that total output is the product of area and yield per unit area, each being determined by different sets of factors. Biochemical processes and inputs affect yields per unit of cropped area rather than cultivated or cropped areas. Climate, soil moisture and plant nutrients play a crucial role in the biological process of crop growth. The quantum and seasonal distribution of soil moisture depends partly on rainfall and partly on the extent and quality of irrigation. Given climate, larger and more assured supply of water provided by irrigation enhances the production potential of land by enabling more intensive use of land, shifts to higher value crops and increasing the quantum of nutrients, which the crop can absorb and the efficiency with which they will be converted into usable biomass. In other words, irrigation will cause the nutrient response curve to shift upward and outward.

Other biochemical inputs like seed varieties and plant protection inputs determine the position of the yield response curve for water and nutrients. An improvement in seed variety will shift the potential yield response curve for nutrients under given soil moisture conditions. The actual response curve will depend on how effectively weeds, pests and diseases are controlled. The more effective the control of these elements, the higher will be the response curve. Improvements in the quality of water management, and in the quality of agronomic management (as a result of extension and learning from experience), will also contribute to an upward shift in response curves of yields with respect to water and nutrients.

Biochemical inputs and primary factors are of course interrelated: Investments in land improvement, irrigation, research and infrastructure have an important bearing on the scope and incentives for use of biochemical inputs. The nature and intensity of application of the latter, the input of human labour, animal power and mechanical power, as well as the level and composition of agricultural investment are all interrelated. But their respective roles and the manner in which they affect output are different and therefore should be kept distinct. The interrelations among the two sets of factors are obviously important but they need to be addressed separately.

An additional compounding factor is wrong choice of the functional form. Several functional forms are used by researchers in this area: linear, log linear, log inverse, Cobb Douglas, Tornquist, etc. The linear form implies that the output increment per unit of each incremental input is constant and quite independent of its level and the levels of others. The log linear form implies that the elasticity of output response to each input is constant, again independent of its quantum and quantum of others. The Cobb Douglas form on the other hand assumes that the inputs are substitutable over the entire range of application and that the elasticity of substitution is unity. None of these take account of interactions between primary and biochemical inputs and between biochemical inputs.

Apart from interactions between primary and biochemical factors, interactions between different biochemical inputs are pervasive in agriculture and affect both the levels of use of different inputs and their yield impact. For instance, the level of fertiliser inputs and their yield response is very much a function of the soil moisture regime, the genetic potential of the seed varieties used and, to some degree, the level of inputs for control of weed, pests and diseases. The incidence of pests and diseases (and the cost of controlling them) is a function, among other things, of climate, crop and soil moisture conditions, and genetic characteristics of seeds. They vary from crop to crop. The relations are also marked by complex; complex complementarities, substitutability and synergies. None of the functional forms used for estimating agricultural production allow for them.

As for infrastructure, there are difficulties of defining and quantifying its content. More importantly, unlike water or fertilisers, it is not a direct input for crop production. Its impact on production, operating as it does via costs of assembling inputs, marketing output and accessibility to technological know-how, is indirect. Whether or to which extent, the extent and quality of infrastructure affects input use and productivity is certainly an important issue for study, but one whose inclusion as an input in an all-embracing production function is quite inappropriate.

Though conceptually clearer and more meaningful, specification and estimation of the biochemical production function present several difficulties; in part they arise from lack of necessary data. Data on rainfall and area irrigated by different sources are available but their coverage, reliability and comparability leave much to be desired. Moreover, the effect of irrigation on yields depends not only on the area irrigated but even more importantly on the quantum or seasonal distribution of irrigation water supplies. Hardly any data on these aspects is even compiled. Again, while estimates of the three main plant nutrients (namely, N, P205, and K20) in the form of chemical fertilisers are available down to the district level, there are no estimates of organic manures. Data regarding other input elements and their management are again inadequate or not available and in some cases difficult to quantify.

For these reasons, a satisfactory specification and estimation of a production function based wholly on the biochemical view of crop growth and incorporating all the important elements of these inputs seems unfeasible. A more tractable approach would be to focus on soil moisture and nutrients as the key determinants of yields on the reasonable presumption that they condition and mediate the impact of all other biochemical factors.

(It should be noted that 'other factors' include both those that increase productivity, given soil moisture and nutrient levels, and those that dampen or reduce it. The latter include, besides diminishing returns to increased nutrient application, land degradation (due to erosion, overuse and misuse of water, and deterioration in water quality), substitution of fertilisers for manures, unbalanced composition of nutrients, micro nutrient deficiencies, and the like.

On this understanding the 'production function' for crop yields can be written as

Yield = f (soil moisture, nutrients, other factors)

Even this cannot be cast into a meaningful and estimatable functional form. Part of the difficulty is that soil moisture is derived from rainfall and irrigation. The impact of irrigation on productivity of land is not independent of rainfall and more generally climate: irrigation is apt to make less of a difference to crop intensity and yields in regions with relatively high, assured and seasonally well distributed rainfall than in areas with low, seasonally concentrated rainfall. Also both the levels of fertilisers (as well elements subsumed under 'other factors') and their impact on yields are affected by the water supply and quality of water management.

In an attempt to get around the difficulty, Vaidyanathan, 1977 and Sarma and Roy, 1979 estimated the relative contributions of these elements (except rainfall) to changes in food grains production between different points of time. (The effect of changes in the distribution of area under different grains has been netted out.) For this purpose, prior information of the difference between irrigated and rainfed yields of food grains before the advent of fertilisers and yardsticks of yield response of fertilisers from field trials were used. The residual, which captures the effect of interactions between water and fertilisers and that of other factors, turned out to be increasingly negative. On this basis it was inferred that the productivity of nutrients has been less than attainable levels, and declining.

Attempts at econometric estimation based on this approach using the full time series data (Vaidyanathan and Mukherjee, 1987) have not been satisfactory either. Part of the reason is that these exercises focussed only on food grains and had to make arbitrary assumptions regarding the proportion of total fertiliser consumption allocated to food grains. Multicollinearity between irrigation and fertiliser use, and both with reference to time makes it difficult to interpret the coefficients. Combining irrigation and fertilisers into a composite input index using irrigation and fertiliser yardsticks does not get rid of the problem. Even so, the exercise suggested that, while we are unlikely to get far in estimating a detailed biochemical production functions for crop yields, this approach could help disentangle the relative contribution of changes in irrigation and fertiliser inputs and in productivity of these inputs.

We therefore tried to pursue this line of attack a little further with some modifications: first, the focus was shifted from quantity of food grain yields to total crop yields (valued at constant prices). Second, it was decided to assess how much of spatial and temporal variations in crop yields could be explained by rainfall, irrigation and fertilisers on the assumption that their effects are linear and additive. The difference between expected yields (given rainfall, irrigation and fertilisers and if their yield impact is linear and additive) and actual yields being taken as a measure of the contribution of interactions between these factors and the effect of 'other factors' on overall yields. Third, the scope of the exercise was widened to cover disaggregated analysis of district level data for different points of time classified according to level of rainfall and irrigation development as well as by agro-climatic religions; and to time series data for the period 1970-1990 for 13 major states. In the latter case, these residuals were examined for systematic patterns over time.

Results of the regressions for rainfall irrigation zones based on pooled data for three triennia (1962-1965, 1970-1973 and 1980-1983) are presented in Table 13.4. Given data inadequacies and collinearity problems, individual coefficients are not easy to interpret. I only want to draw attention to the fact that these three input factors account for a substantial proportion of inter-district variation in crop yields in all zones.

Table 13.4

Distribution of Districts by Rainfall Zones and Trend in Yield Growth Rates during the Sixties, Seventies and Eighties

Zones	*N*	*Growth in All 3 Periods*	*>25% in All 3 Periods*	*Falling Growth Rates*	*Rising Growth Rates*
LL	38	15	4	6	8
LH	30	23	7	3	7
ML	49	25	2	0	15
MH	43	36	6	2	15
HL	64	30	0	3	19
HH	33	19	1	1	13
All	257	148	16	15	77

Note: As in Table 13.3

The proportion 'explained'—ranging from 41 to 81 per cent—however varies across zones. In the low rainfall zone, they account for a larger proportion of yield variation in high irrigation tracts than across districts with less than average irrigation; in medium rainfall zones the proportion of 'explained' variance is roughly the same in both irrigation categories; while in high rainfall zones, these factors account for a substantially larger proportion of yield variation in tracts with the low irrigation than in those with relatively high levels of irrigation—position being reversed in medium and high rainfall zones.

We have also estimated this relationship for each of the three triennia separately. (Results not reported here). They show that the proportion of variance explained as well as the coefficients for the three factors differ significantly from period to period. R^2 increases progressively between these three points of time in four zones and is consistently above 80 per cent in one. The coefficients are not statistically in all years and zones. And except in the case of fertilisers, they show no clear trends. The fertiliser coefficients show a progressive fall over the period.

Grouping districts by rainfall and irrigation is one way disaggregating. Another would be to group them on the basis of agro-climatically homogeneous regions. Table 13.5 presents the estimated regressions based on pooled data for three points in time for 14 major agro-climatic regions. Again ignoring the significance and values of individual coefficients, it is apparent that the proportion of yield variation accounted by these three factors differs widely across regions, ranging from less than 5 per cent in some to about 75 per cent.

Table 13.5

Linear Multiple Regression of Crop Output Per Hectare on Rainfall, Irrigation and Fertilisers for Different Rainfall-Irrigation Zones based on Pooled District Level Data for 1962-1965, 1970-1973 and 1980-1983

Zones	*N*	*R^2*	*Coefficients for*			
			Intercept	*Rainfall*	*Irrigation*	*Fertilisers*
LL	96	0.62	-398.2	4.6	8.9***	75.3***
LH	75	0.81	195.8	2.9***	44.7***	39.6***
ML	135	0.41	1751***	1.0*	42.0***	27.2***
MH	123	0.42	5297***	-1.9**	24.2**	36.8***
HL	166	0.63	6282*	2.0***	1.8	77.5
HH	95	0.46	-213	2.6***	38.3***	37.0***

Note: As in Table 13.3.

There is clearly much room for refinement in both the specification of these variables and their measurement, and to examine whether the deviations in actual yields from predicted yields have any significant patterns of relationship to 'other factors' such as synergy between irrigation and fertiliser response, rainfall levels and seasonal patterns, nutrient composition, spread of HYV, etc.

Table 13.6 summarises the results based on time series data for 14 major states. Given their large size diversity in rainfall characteristics, it does not seem possible, at any rate with the data currently available, to work out a meaningful and representative rainfall index for states. Therefore, estimation is limited to irrigation ratio and fertiliser use. Together they account for between 40-50 per cent of the variation in crop yields in Gujarat and Haryana; the proportion exceeds 80 per cent in 8 states and 90 per cent in 5.

Table 13.6

Linear Multiple Regression of Crop Output Per Hectare on Irrigation and Fertilisers by Major States, 1970-1990

State	*R^2*	*Coefficients for*		
		Constant	*Irrigation ratio*	*Fertilisers/ha*
Andhra Pradesh	0.87	964	41.9	12.7***
Bihar	0.78	2669	-15.9	22.7***
Gujarat	0.19	1112	70	-2.3
Haryana	0.96	2141	8.8	24.3***
Karnataka	0.73	1650	38	6.5
Kerala	0.43	4572	31.7**	10.7***
Maharashtra	0.66	703	98*	12.1***
Madhya Pradesh	0.73	1260	-4.8	23.2***
Orissa	0.38	1985	-11	41.6***
Punjab	0.93	-2171	64.4***	6.7***
Rajasthan	.82	1267	-27.5**	65.2***
Tamil Nadu	.81	2844	-8.5	15.6***
Uttar Pradesh	.82	2344	-1.5	18.3***
West Bengal	.63	1200	-167.2	7.6

Source: As in Table 13.2.

The ratios of actual yields in each state to those that might be expected if the impact of irrigation and yields were linear and additive were estimated.

This shows significant differences in pattern across states. The year-to-year fluctuations in the ratio is more pronounced in some states (Gujarat, Rajasthan, Orissa and Madhya Pradesh) than others (for example Karnataka, Kerala); in some states (noticeably in Haryana and Karnataka) actual yields are less than predicted yields; there are indications that in some cases the residuals may have a 'trend'. The behaviour of this ratio and its underlying factors deserve closer analysis.

Perhaps the most striking feature is the absence of a strong rising trend in the ratio in any state. The expectation that productivity of irrigation and fertilisers would increase due to the synergy between irrigation and fertilisers, improvement in the quality of irrigation due to the growing importance of ground water, spread of improved varieties and farmers' learning from experience is thus belied. Perhaps these effects are offset by diminishing returns to fertiliser use, micronutrient deficiencies, soil degradation due to overuse and misuse of water and chemicals, and other factors. More details and incisive investigation will be needed to sort out these factors.

Clearly, both in terms of approach and, more so in terms of results, what I have presented is far from conclusive or definitive. Insofar as this is due to inadequate data, it gives pointers to the improvements needed and key gaps to be filled. One cannot do much about errors and biases in the data. They are unavoidable. Considerable insights can be gained from incomplete and noisy data so long as the noise can be reasonably assumed to vary randomly across space and time. There is however much scope for refinements in data and better measures of soil moisture and nutrients—also for extending and deepening the analysis to the district/agro-climatic region level. Analysis of residuals and the factors explaining their behaviour presents a major challenge.

I will not be surprised if the above approach does not enthuse strict adherents to econometric method (which I am not). I would nevertheless hope that you will give serious consideration to the criticisms of mindless application of this method to evaluating trends, and estimating ill-specified 'production functions' for agriculture. Possibly there are econometrically tractable ways of handling the complex interactions between inputs. Finding them would certainly be welcome. Meanwhile, I would appeal to you to examine dispassionately the logic of my approach and assess its capacity to give us a better understanding of the technical factors underlying agricultural growth and the role of economic and institutional forces in determining how much and how prudently different inputs are used.

References

Bhalla, G.S. and Y.K. Alagh (1979). *Performance of Indian Agriculture: A District-wise Study*. New Delhi: Sterling.

Bhalla, G.S. and D.K. Tyagi (1989). *Performance of Indian Agriculture: A District-wise Study*. New Delhi : Institute of Studies in industrial Development.

Bhalla, G.S. and Gurmail Singh (2001). *Indian Agriculture: Four Decades of Development.* New Delhi: Sage.

Minhas B.S. and A. Vaidyanathan (1965). "Growth of Crop Output in India 1953-54 to 1958-61", *Journal of the Indian Society of Agricultural Statistics* 17(2).

Narain, Dharam(1977). "Growth of Productivity in Indian Agriculture", *Indian Journal of Agricultural Economics* 32(1).

Sagar, Vidya (1995). "Fertiliser Use Efficiency in Indian Agriculture", *Economic and Political Weekly* 26(52).

Sarma, J.S. and S. Roy (1979). *Analysis of Indian Foodgrain Production and Consumption.* Washington DC: International Food Policy Research Institute.

Vaidyanathan, A. (1977). "Performance and Prospects of Crop Production in India", *Economic and Political Weekly,* Special Number, August.

Vaidyanathan, A. and Chandan Mukherjee (1987). "State-wise Analysis of Agricultural Growth", in Prem Narain *et al.* (eds.), *Recent Advances in Agricultural Statistics.* Wiley Eastern.

14 Socioeconomic Characteristics of Villages in North Arcot

An Exploratory Study

The Registrar General of India (RGI) has been publishing, after each census since 1961, village and town directories for each district. The directories contain information on several important socioeconomic characteristics of every village.[1] Since they also indicate changes in village boundaries, it is possible to match the village lists across different census years. This opens up a rich vista of opportunity for mapping the variations in village characteristics as well as changes therein, examining whether there are any systematic patterns in the variations and exploring the factors responsible for them.

Such an exercise is clearly relevant for planning. It will help locate deficiencies in terms of the production base and essential amenities. This knowledge is valuable for determining the development priorities of individual villages. It could also help ensure that the content and priorities of local development plans are geared to meeting specific deficiencies in each village and block.

Such information, when made widely and freely available to participants in panchayati raj institutions (PRIs), the bureaucracy and the public, will also generate greater awareness of the nature and magnitude of deficiencies. The problem of chronically laggard villages will be brought into sharper public focus. More informed deliberation of priorities and a

1. The information relates to total area; cultivated and irrigated areas; irrigation sources; population by sex, overall and separately for scheduled castes (SCs) and tribes (STs); overall literacy by sex; the distribution of total male and female workers by major sectors; types of school and public health care facilities available in the village (or the distance to the nearest point at which they are available); whether served by other facilities like *pucca* road, railway, telephone, post office, etc.; distance from the nearest town; and fairs and festivals.

certain amount of healthy political competition among the panchayati raj bodies in fulfilling the basic needs of the people, which this knowledge is sure to generate, will help make decentralised local planning more effective. Moreover, by stimulating scholars to examine the reasons underlying the variations, and persistent patterns in them, they will improve understanding of development processes at the ground level and, in due course, help ameliorate the design and implementation of policy.

The purpose of this paper is to illustrate some of the kinds of mapping and analyses of variations in socioeconomic characteristics across villages, which can be done with the directory data. It reports the results of an exploratory exercise for two census years (1971 and 1981) in one district of Tamil Nadu, namely North Arcot.[2]

Starting with a brief account of the average characteristics of the North Arcot village in relation to the state average, we look at the variations in the mean value of select characteristics[3] of villages classified into groups according to: (i) the size of its population; (ii) the overall level of economic development as reflected in the relative prosperity of agricultural classes and the degree of diversification of its employment; (iii) the level of female literacy; (iv) sex ratio (SR); (v) employment diversification and (vi) caste-class differentiation. The basis of the grouping is the value of each of the above in 1981. The mean value of various characteristics of villages in each group is computed for 1971 and 1981. The existence of any systematic pattern(s) of variation in various characteristics across village groups is examined. Also multiple regressions are estimated to assess the extent to which variations in literacy, SR and non-agricultural employment could be explained in terms of certain plausible hypotheses of determinants.

Villages of North Arcot: An Overall Profile

In 1981, there were 1,831 villages in the district with 1,835 inhabitants on the average. About 10 per cent of the villages are very small with less

2. A similar analysis of villages in South Arcot district is nearing completion.

3. We focus on the following: village size; sex ratio; the proportion of SCs and STs in the population; literacy rates of males and females; work participation rates of males and females; distance from nearest town; the extent of cultivated area per male agricultural worker; the ratio of irrigated to cultivated area; the ratio of male workers engaged in non-agricultural activities relative to agriculture; and caste-class differentiation.

than 500 inhabitants; a third of the villages have fewer than 1,000 people and another third have between 1,000 and 2,000 inhabitants. Relatively large villages—i.e., those with more than 4,000 people, which is roughly twice the average size of a village in the district—constitute less than 10 per cent of the total.

The proportion of scheduled castes (SCs) and scheduled tribes (STs) in the district is somewhat more than in the state as a whole. While cultivated area per male agricultural worker (0.79 ha) is below the state average, a larger proportion of it (45% compared to the state average of 43%) is irrigated. The rural population of North Arcot is more literate than in the average Tamil Nadu village. But non-agricultural employment in relation to total workforce is somewhat less than the state average; so is the rural SR (Table 14.1).

Table 14.1

Average Characteristics of Villages in Tamil Nadu and North Arcot District in 1981

	POPLN	*RSEX*	*RSCST*	*MLIT*	*FLIT*	*RCAMAW*	*RIACA*	*RMNAW*
Tamil Nadu	2050	987	23.1	51.2	25.8	0.87	0.43	0.34
North Arcot	1835	980	25.1	49.4	22.3	0.79	0.45	0.32

Note:
POPLN	Population
RSEX	Sex ratio
RSCST	Ratio of SC and ST population
MLIT	Male literacy
TLIT	Total literacy
FLIT	Female literacy
RCAMAW	Ratio of cultivated area to male agricultural workers
RIACA	Ratio of irrigated area to cultivated area
RMNAW	Ratio of male non-agricultural workers to male agricultural workers
RMALMAW	Ratio of male agricultural labour to male agricultural workers
NT	Distance from nearest town in kms.
DIFF. INDEX workers	Ratio of SC and ST population by ratio of male agricultural labour to male main
WPM	Ratio of male main workers to total male population
WPF	Ratio of female main workers to total female population

There have been considerable changes in these characteristics over time (see Table 14.2). Between 1971 and 1981 the mean size of North Arcot villages has increased by 15 per cent. The SR and the proportion of SC and ST have also risen slightly. The literacy rate of males has risen from 43.1 per cent to 49.4 per cent, and of females from 15.9 per cent to 22.4 per cent. The cultivated area per male agricultural worker has declined, but there has been a significant rise in the ratio of irrigated to cultivated area and in the proportion of male workers engaged in non-agricultural activities.

Table 14.2

Mean Values of Selected Characteristics and their Variability in North Arcot District, 1971 and 1981

	POPLN	*RSEX*	*RSCST*	*MLIT*	*FLIT*	*RCAMAW*	*RIACA*	*RMNAW*	*NT*
1971									
Mean	1597.00	972.2	23.5	43.1	15.9	0.92	0.33	0.26	12.1
CV(%)	85.01	6.9	91.2	34.1	54.2	102.00	65.70	204.00	65.3
1981									
Mean	1834.00	979.6	25.1	49.4	22.4	0.79	0.45	0.32	13.3
CV(%)	84.90	6.5	105.0	28.2	46.4	210.00	51.10	263.00	61.6

Note: As in Table 14.1.

Inter-village variability (measured by the coefficient of variation [CV] around the weighted mean) of literacy and irrigation has declined appreciably during the seventies. But the dispersion in the ratio SC and ST, cultivated land per agricultural workers, as well as the degrees of diversification in employment show significant increases.

Variations by Village Size

Several characteristics are seen to vary systematically with village size (Table 14.3). In general, the larger the village, the lower tends to be the SR, the smaller the proportion of SCs and STs in its population and the closer it is to urban centres. Larger villages also have higher literacy rates of both males and females and a higher proportion of workers engaged in non-agricultural activities. They tend to have a smaller amount of cultivated area per male agricultural worker and agricultural wage labour of a more heterogeneous caste composition. The proportion of irrigated to cultivated area does not show any systematic variation with reference to village size. In most cases the above patterns are also observed in 1971, the significant exceptions being the SR and the irrigation ratio. Both these increase with village size.

Table 14.3

Weighted Mean Value of Selected Characteristics of Villages Grouped according to Size of Population in 1981

North Arcot, 1971-1981

Population, 1981	*POPLN*			*RMNAW*			*RSEX*			*RSCST*		
	1971	*1981*	*% Change*	*1971*	*1981*	*% Change*	*1971*	*1981*	*% Change*	*1971*	*1981*	*% Change*
< 500	297	302	1.8	0.14	0.17	23.4	952.5	966.1	1.4	29.2	29.9	2.4
500-1000	663	737	11.1	0.16	0.18	13.3	969.9	989.2	2.0	27.3	29.4	7.5
1000-2000	1244	1427	14.7	0.20	0.22	8.4	970.3	982.2	1.2	25.8	27.7	7.3
2000-4000	2412	2791	15.7	0.27	0.34	25.9	973.5	981.3	0.8	23.0	24.3	5.7
4000-5000	3898	4427	13.6	0.28	0.37	32.1	974.3	975.1	0.1	20.4	21.7	6.3
> 5000	5778	6800	17.7	0.47	0.56	19.3	975.1	970.7	-0.4	19.6	21.5	9.5

Population, 1981	TLIT			MLIT			FLIT			RCAMAW		
	1971	*1981*	*% Change*	*1971*	*1981*	*% Change*	*1971*	*1981*	*% Change*	*1971*	*1981*	*% Change*
< 500	27.8	31.4	12.8	41.0	42.7	4.3	14.0	18.2	29.9	1.48	1.45	-2.1
500-1000	29.3	34.1	16.1	43.2	47.7	10.3	15.0	20.3	35.0	1.12	0.92	-17.7
1000-2000	28.7	34.8	21.3	42.4	48.7	14.9	14.5	20.6	41.7	0.97	0.82	-15.4
2000-4000	29.8	35.9	20.6	43.3	49.2	13.7	15.8	22.3	41.1	0.90	0.78	-13.3
4000-5000	28.7	35.3	22.9	41.3	48.5	17.3	15.7	21.7	38.1	0.75	0.72	-3.8
> 5000	32.3	40.3	24.7	44.8	52.8	18.0	19.5	27.3	40.1	0.75	0.68	-8.9

Population, 1981	RIACA			WPM			WPF			NT		
	1971	*1981*	*% Change*	*1971*	*1981*	*% Change*	*1971*	*1981*	*% Change*	*1971*	*1981*	*% Change*
< 500	0.28	0.44	53.2	0.60	0.61	1.8	0.16	0.29	78.8	14.7	16.4	11.6
500-1000	0.32	0.44	37.5	0.59	0.59	0.1	0.18	0.30	68.0	12.1	13.8	14.1
1000-2000	0.34	0.44	29.9	0.59	0.58	-0.8	0.18	0.28	57.1	12.3	12.8	4.4
2000-4000	0.35	0.45	29.3	0.57	0.57	-0.3	0.16	0.25	55.6	11.3	12.3	8.5
4000-5000	0.39	0.43	10.1	0.57	0.57	0.5	0.16	0.22	44.0	10.9	11.7	7.0
> 5000	0.40	0.47	17.1	0.55	0.55	-0.1	0.13	0.20	55.5	11.9	13.2	11.0

There is a systematic pattern in the rate, and even the direction, of changes between 1971 and 1981 in respect of some characteristics across different village size groups. The larger the village size, the larger the percentage increase in population and the larger the increase in overall and male literacy rates. But there is an inverse relationship between village size and the increase in irrigation ratio, the extent of decline in cultivated area per male agricultural worker and the increase in sex ratio. There is no clear pattern in respect of other features.

Level of Economic Development

The directory data gives us some idea of the differences in the level and pace of overall economic development across villages in the district. Estimates of output and income at the village level are not feasible with existing data. However, the availability of cultivated land, spread of irrigation and diversification of employment, taken together, provide an approximate basis to assess relative prosperity.

Since North Arcot is relatively monogenous in agro-climatic terms, the cultivated area per male agricultural worker and the extent of irrigation can be used to classify villages according to the relative prosperity of agricultural classes. Villages at different levels of agricultural prosperity can be further differentiated on the basis of the extent of diversification of employment into non-agricultural activity. Villages that combine high cultivated area per agricultural worker, high irrigation ratio and high ratio of non-agricultural to agricultural employment can be taken as being relatively the most developed in the district. By the same token, villages where all these indicators are low, comprise the least developed category. Table 14.4 presents an 18-fold classification of North Arcot villages on this basis and the mean value of selected characteristics of each group in 1971 and 1981. The following patterns emerge:

i) Both in 1971 and 1981, for any given combination of land per agricultural worker and irrigation development, villages with a higher degree of diversification tend to be larger in size, have more land per agricultural worker, have a higher SR and a higher literacy rate than those where the ratio of non-agricultural to agricultural employment is small.

ii) The smaller the extent of cultivated area per male agricultural worker, the larger tends to be the village. And for any given level of this ratio, better irrigated villages tends to be smaller in size, more literate and more diversified. These associations are considerably more pronounced in villages where the employment structure is more diversified.

iii) In villages at low levels of diversification, the extent of diversification does not seem to vary much across land per worker or irrigation categories. But in diversified villages, the ratio of non-agricultural to agricultural employment tends to increase as we move up the scale of land per worker and irrigation; this tendency being more pronounced in 1981 than in 1971.

iv) In general, the lower the land per agricultural worker, the lower tends to be the SR and the proportion of population belonging to SC/ST. This tendency is considerably more pronounced among villages that are not diversified.

v) Literacy is not systematically related to land per agricultural worker, but within each land per worker group, better irrigated villages have higher literacy. Whole overall literacy has risen in all categories; the differences associated with irrigation and diversification do not seem to have changed appreciably during this period.

vi) There are significant differences in the rate of change of population, cultivated area per worker, irrigation rates and diversification. Between 1971 and 1981, villages with low land-worker ratios show, on the average, slower increase in population, a larger decline in cultivated area per agricultural worker, a slower pace of diversification and a larger rise in the SR. Irrigation development does not seem to vary much across land per worker groups but, within each of these groups, villages that had better developed irrigation seem to have done considerably better than those with low irrigation development.

That the extent of variability across villages in the land/worker ratio and in the degree of diversification have increased considerably between 1971 and 1981 suggests that inter-village disparities have increased. Villages that were least developed in 1971 continued to be so in 1981: even as the most developed villages have substantially improved their position both in absolute and relative terms. The population of the least developed villages (LLL) rose at roughly the same rate as in the most developed ones (HHH), but the average land-worker ratio in the former group declined by nearly 40

Table 14.4

Weighted Mean of Selected Characteristics of Villages of North Arcot Grouped according to Prosperity of Agricultural Classes and Extent of Non-agricultural Employment

RCAMAW 1981	RIACA 1981	RMNAW 1981	SIZE	POPLN 1971	POPLN 1981	RMNAW 1981	RMNAW 1981	RSEX 1971	RSEX 1981	RSCT 1971	RSCT 1981	TLIT 1971	TLIT 1981	RCAMAW 1971	RCAMAW 1981	RIACA 1971	RIACA 1981
LOW	LOW	<.25	68	174.96	2041.29	0.13	0.06	963.12	971.93	22.58	24.89	25.12	30.13	0.72	0.44	0.30	0.24
(<.6)	(-.35)	>.25	37	2861.41	3392.16	0.41	0.60	975.81	973.55	14.06	15.81	31.30	39.34	0.67	0.46	0.28	0.25
	MIDDLE	<.25	103	1677.95	1916.43	0.14	0.12	956.54	965.07	23.61	25.38	24.51	30.31	0.71	0.49	0.37	0.46
	(35-.55)	>.25	43	2470.81	2880.60	0.45	0.56	980.19	973.87	22.86	24.12	33.89	40.65	0.58	0.47	0.39	0.45
	HIGH	<.25	129	1414.81	1600.89	0.16	0.14	969.40	976.39	24.41	27.46	27.69	34.03	0.63	0.43	0.48	0.73
	(.55+)	>.25	93	2619.17	3049.09	0.52	0.65	977.41	982.02	21.90	25.25	35.72	43.43	0.53	0.42	0.51	0.75
MIDDLE	LOW	<.25	129	1461.16	1642.65	0.15	0.13	964.14	982.43	24.01	26.10	25.82	30.61	0.95	0.75	0.31	0.26
(<.6)	(-.35)	>.25	47	2469.89	2816.23	0.32	0.49	965.01	973.36	18.05	18.37	31.41	37.82	0.86	0.76	0.31	0.25
	MIDDLE	<.25	131	1443.48	1646.86	0.14	0.15	973.99	973.95	21.90	22.70	25.95	31.24	0.92	0.76	0.36	0.44
	(35-.55)	>.25	77	2409.43	2776.65	0.46	0.66	974.84	977.14	22.40	23.63	33.72	40.95	0.77	0.73	0.41	0.45
	HIGH	<.25	120	1404.10	1634.17	0.14	0.13	966.71	983.15	24.57	25.18	26.39	32.33	0.90	0.75	0.47	0.75
	(.55+)	>.25	83	2099.73	2399.78	0.44	0.59	983.88	988.60	23.06	23.25	33.82	42.38	0.80	0.76	0.52	0.71
HIGH	LOW	<.25	201	1162.87	1317.13	0.13	0.13	969.90	978.65	26.59	29.59	24.38	30.11	1.40	1.26	0.24	0.23
(<.6)	(-.35)	>.25	97	1648.73	1903.05	0.41	0.66	973.65	976.93	25.07	25.91	31.79	39.82	1.32	1.31	0.28	0.25
	MIDDLE	<.25	126	1106.75	1223.76	0.13	0.14	972.38	996.89	22.95	25.87	26.40	32.57	1.23	1.15	0.34	0.44
	(35-.55)	>.25	90	1489.79	1706.73	0.42	0.69	988.57	996.85	22.36	22.99	34.78	40.70	1.27	1.24	0.35	0.45
	HIGH	<.25	71	1116.86	1297.70	0.17	0.14	980.30	984.43	23.61	24.26	28.25	35.13	1.38	1.18	0.44	0.74
	(.55+)	>.25	75	1365.72	1615.03	0.50	0.95	979.34	982.34	24.37	23.90	35.51	40.89	1.12	1.30	0.43	0.68

per cent, irrigation by about 20 per cent and the diversification index by over half. The HHH villages, on the other hand, recorded a sizeable increase in all these respects. More generally, the relative positions of villages classified by three development indicators in 1981 do not seem to have been very different in 1971. Consistently, villages with low level of diversification remain well below those that are more diversified and are much less dynamic. There is thus a clear and persistent dualism in development among North Arcot villages: villages that were relatively less developed to begin with have progressed much less than those that started off at a higher level.

Female Literacy

As everywhere else in the state and the country, females in rural North Arcot are less literate than males. There is also tremendous variability in this respect within the district. Some villages report zero literacy[4] among females, and a few report as much as 60 per cent in 1981. About one-eighth of the villages report less than 10 per cent female literacy, about 5 per cent report more than 40 per cent.

Table 14.5, which gives the mean value of selected characteristics of villages grouped according to the level of female literacy in 1981, shows some distinct patterns:

i) Higher level of female literacy is associated with larger village size, higher level of irrigation and a more diversified pattern of employment.

ii) Villages with very low literacy (<10 per cent) tend to have a relatively higher proportion of SCs, but above this level, higher literacy rate is associated with a larger share of SCs in the population.

iii) Villages with higher literacy have higher SRs (females per '000 males).

iv) Male and female rates are highly correlated and the disparity between the two narrows rapidly as we move from low to high literacy villages. However, the disparity is not eliminated, it remains substantial even in the most literate villages.

4. Figures refer to the overall literacy rate (i.e., proportion of total population classified as literate) in each category.

Table 14.5

Weighted Mean Value of Selected Characteristics of Villages Grouped According to Female Literacy Rate in 1981

North Arcot, 1971-1981

Female Literacy Rate 1981	POPLN			RMNAW			RSEX			RSCST		
	1971	1981	% Change	1971	1981	% Change	1971	1981	% Change	1971	1981	% Change
< 10	1013	1175	16.0	0.11	0.13	17.5	953.6	962.4	0.9	30.5	34.5	12.8
10 - 15	1426	1633	14.5	0.15	0.17	10.4	960.8	976.5	1.6	21.6	22.3	2.9
15 - 22	1598	1861	16.4	0.20	0.24	16.8	968.0	977.5	1.0	21.6	22.8	5.2
22 - 30	1773	2010	13.3	0.31	0.39	26.2	976.4	982.0	0.6	23.7	25.5	7.6
30 - 40	2007	2280	13.6	0.49	0.62	25.0	987.8	987.0	-0.1	23.9	25.1	4.9
> 40	1849	2167	17.2	0.67	0.87	29.7	989.4	995.8	0.6	24.8	28.1	13.2

Female Literacy Rate 1981	TLIT			MLIT			FLIT			RCAMAW		
	1971	1981	% Change	1971	1981	% Change	1971	1981	% Change	1971	1981	% Change
< 10	17.8	18.3	2.8	28.6	29.9	4.5	6.6	6.4	-3.3	1.03	0.91	-11.9
10 - 15	22.8	26.5	16.0	35.6	39.7	11.6	9.5	12.8	33.7	0.98	0.77	-21.6
15 - 22	26.7	32.6	21.9	40.0	46.5	16.2	13.0	18.4	41.3	0.94	0.79	-15.6
22 - 30	32.2	39.8	23.5	46.4	53.8	16.1	17.7	25.5	44.6	0.87	0.78	-10.0
30 - 40	38.8	47.8	23.3	53.2	61.2	15.1	24.2	34.3	41.7	0.84	0.76	-9.1
> 40	44.3	56.4	27.3	57.4	67.3	17.3	31.1	45.4	46.1	0.79	0.76	-3.8

Female Literacy Rate 1981	RIACA			WPM			WPF			NT		
	1971	1981	% Change	1971	1981	% Change	1971	1981	% Change	1971	1981	% Change
< 10	0.28	0.36	28.4	0.60	0.60	0.2	0.16	0.29	78.3	16.6	17.9	8.3
10 - 15	0.33	0.41	25.8	0.60	0.60	-0.2	0.16	0.31	89.8	12.8	14.5	12.8
15 - 22	0.35	0.44	25.1	0.59	0.58	-1.3	0.18	0.27	53.7	11.8	12.7	7.5
22 - 30	0.37	0.47	26.8	0.57	0.57	-0.0	0.17	0.24	39.7	11.2	12.1	8.1
30 - 40	0.39	0.53	36.4	0.54	0.54	0.1	0.14	0.20	47.2	10.5	11.2	6.7
> 40	0.43	0.57	34.9	0.51	0.52	2.0	0.12	0.19	56.9	9.1	10.3	13.0

v) Villages with higher female literacy, on the average, report lower work participation rates among both males and females, the difference being more pronounced in the case of females.[5]

vi) The above pattern is observed in 1971 as well except that, unlike in 1981, villages with low female literacy also tend to have a higher cultivated area per agricultural worker.

Between 1971 and 1981, villages with very low female literacy recorded a decline in mean female literacy. In all others, mean female literacy rose, the increase being somewhat faster in the groups with high literacy rates. The inter-village disparities in female literacy have decreased however. Villages with higher female literacy have experienced a faster spread of irrigation and a faster pace of diversification in rural employment. Villages at either extreme of the literacy spectrum seem to have a distinctly higher than average increase in population and share of SCs in the population.

There are thus discernible patterns of association between female literacy (and changes in female literacy) and various characteristics of the villages (and changes therein). It is significant, however, that in as many as 15 per cent of villages, female literacy has declined, the proportion being as high as 40 per cent in the least literate villages (i.e. those where literacy is < 15%). The reasons for the decline in these villages obviously deserve close scrutiny.

The nature of school facilities available within the village evidently affects literacy rates. Taking all villages together, those with no schools in 1971[6] had the lowest level of female literacy (15.5% in 1981), as well as male literacy (39.5%). Those with primary schools had a higher level of literacy (20% and 47.7% respectively) and those with middle and high schools even higher (25% and 52.5%). The inter-village variability in literacy is greatest in the no-school category. Villages with no schools tend to have

5. One can think of several plausible reasons: more literate villages are more prosperous; high literacy leads to change in job preferences; villages with high literacy have a larger proportion of younger people among whom school attendance and literacy rates are higher than among adults.

6. This is based on school facilities in 1971 on the premise that access to school facilities has a lagged effect on overall literacy rates. Their impact on the current enrolment rate would be more immediate. Nevertheless, perhaps one should look at the access to school facilities in both 1971 and 1981, recognising of course that availability of schools is a rather crude index of school facilities.

higher proportion of SCs in their population and larger cultivated area per male agricultural worker, but they tend to have fewer agricultural labourers relative to agricultural workers, fewer non-agricultural workers relative to agricultural workers, and a lower irrigation ratio (Table 14.6).

The foregoing are suggestive but do not give any idea of the relative importance of various factors affecting literacy. This requires a multivariate analysis guided by hypotheses on the determinants of literacy. It is expected that literacy will be an increasing function of the prosperity of agricultural classes (proxied by the cultivated area per male agricultural worker and the irrigation ratio) and the relative importance of non-agricultural activities (indicated by the ratio of male non-agricultural to male agricultural worker.[7]) It is expected to be a declining function of the extent of inequality among agricultural classes (proxied by the proportion of agricultural wage labourers among total agricultural workers) and the share of socially underprivileged segments (especially SG and STs). The availability and quality of school facilities is the other important factor affecting literacy.[8] To allow for this, villages have been classified into those with no school, those with only primary schools and those with primary and middle/high schools. For each category the following linear multiple regression was estimated.

$$\text{TLIT 81} = f\left(+\frac{\text{CA}}{\text{MAW}}81, \frac{\text{IA}}{\text{CA}}81, \text{RMNAW 81}, \frac{\text{MAL}}{\text{MAW}}81, \text{RSCST 81, C71}\right)$$

Where TLIT 81 = overall literacy, rate in 1981; the same function is estimated for male and female literacy (LM and LF)

$\frac{\text{CA}}{\text{MAW}}$ = cultivated area per male agricultural worker

$\frac{\text{IA}}{\text{CA}}$ = ratio of irrigated to cultivated area

7. Throughout the paper, given the well-known problems about the reliability of data on workforce and employment of females, the indices relating to land-worker ratios, rate of agricultural labourers to agricultural workers, and ratio of non-agricultural to agricultural employment are all computed in relation to male workers.

8. These hypotheses draw largely from the proceedings of a workshop of researchers on elementary education under a project sponsored by the United Nations Development Programme (UNDP).

$\frac{MAL}{MAW}$ = ratio of male agricultural labourers to male agricultural workers

C = whether or not the village is connected by *pucca* road or railway station

Table 14.6

Results of Multiple Regression of Male and Female Literacy Rate on Selected Variables in 1981 (North Arcot, 1971-1981)

	RCAMAW	*RIACA*	*RMALMAW*	*RSCST*	*RMNAW*	*C*	*No. of Villages*	R^2
Male literacy								
Villages with no school	0.62	24.09*	-4.42	-0.24*	-0.16	-2.62	186	0.43
Villages with primary school	0.71	11.78*	4.98*	-0.12*	2.84*	-0.35	1249	0.15
Villages with primary school Middle/higher secondary school	2.80**	3.97***	5.93***	-0.07**	5.16*	-0.19	393	0.11
Female literacy								
Villages with no school	0.89*	11.91*	3.61	-0.08*	-0.22**	-1.74	186	0.24
Villages with primary school	-0.44	9.44*	11.09*	-0.02**	2.72*	-0.21	1249	0.17
Villages with primary school Middle/higher secondary school	1.87***	7.00*	12.23*	0.06**	5.41*	0.10	393	0.22

Note: *** significant at 5-10 per cent
** significant at 1-5 per cent
* significant at 1 per cent or less

The results (see Table 14.6) suggest that, in general and as expected, literacy (overall and for each sex) is an increasing function of irrigation and occupational diversification of the labour force. But, contrary to expectation, except for the no-school category, the relative importance of wage labour in the agricultural work force is positively related to literacy. The higher the proportion of SCs, the smaller tends to be the literacy rate. The availability of a *pucca* road or railway station does not have any significant effect on literacy in any group.

In other words, literacy tends to be higher in villages where irrigation is better developed, employment is more diversified and the proportion of wage labour in agriculture is high. The higher the incidence of SCs, the lower the literacy rate.

The selected factors 'explain' a higher proportion of variation in literacy in the no-school category, compared to those with schools. The explanation of variations in female literacy in villages with only primary schools is less than those with schools of all three levels, the opposite being the case with male literacy. It is also noteworthy that the impact of RMNAW, irrigation and the ratio of agricultural labourers to agricultural workers (AL/AW) increases as we move from villages with no schools (PMHs). That the value (and sometimes even the sign) of the coefficients in the various village groups is variable suggests that the underlying relations are complex and perhaps non-linear. This may partly account for the low R^{-2}, but the latter may also be due to the crude and/or unreliable measures used for the explanatory variables and other important factors, which do not figure in the above hypotheses.

Sex Ratio

The significance of this characteristic needs little explanation in the context of the widespread concern about the low and progressively declining ratio of females to males in most parts of India. Tamil Nadu as a whole (and also North Arcot) has a relatively higher SR compared to other states. Also, unlike in the rest of the country, the SR in rural Tamil Nadu and North Arcot showed a marginal rise during the 1970s.

The variation within the district is surprisingly large: from less than 900 in about 6 per cent of the villages to Cover 1,000 in about 3 per cent of villages in 1981. There is also considerable variation in both the direction and magnitude of change between 1971 and 1981 (Table 14.7).

Table 14.7

Weighted Mean Value of Selected Characteristics of Villages Grouped according to Sex Ratio 1981 (North Arcot, 1971-1981)

Sex Ratio, 1981	POPLN 1971	POPLN 1981	POPLN % Change	RMNAW 1971	RMNAW 1981	RMNAW % Change	RSEX 1971	RSEX 1981	RSEX % Change	RSCST 1971	RSCST 1981	RSCST % Change
< 900	782	935	19.6	0.20	0.28	38.7	871.8	863.8	-0.9	24.4	38.6	58.1
900-950	1553	1823	17.3	0.24	0.29	17.8	930.2	931.9	0.2	25.8	25.8	-0.2
950-1000	1892	2165	14.4	0.28	0.34	20.3	973.9	975.0	0.1	22.6	24.0	5.9
1000-1050	1674	1813	8.3	0.26	0.33	23.1	1018.4	1019.2	0.1	21.7	24.7	13.4
1050-1100	1287	1329	3.2	0.29	0.27	-7.4	1067.6	1065.7	-0.2	24.5	26.5	7.9
>1100	662	838	26.7	0.30	0.32	7.8	1149.8	1144.0	-0.5	30.2	22.3	-26.2

Sex Ratio, 1981	TLIT 1971	TLIT 1981	TLIT % Change	MLIT 1971	MLIT 1981	MLIT % Change	FLIT 1971	FLIT 1981	FLIT % Change	RCAMAW 1971	RCAMAW 1981	RCAMAW % Change
< 900	27.6	33.3	20.6	40.0	45.0	12.4	13.3	19.8	48.0	1.02	0.99	-2.8
900-950	27.6	33.5	21.4	40.2	46.0	14.5	14.1	20.0	41.9	0.89	0.76	-14.8
950-1000	29.7	36.3	22.3	43.1	49.8	15.4	15.8	22.5	42.0	0.91	0.77	-15.7
1000-1050	31.5	37.4	18.7	45.9	51.5	12.0	17.4	23.7	36.0	0.94	0.80	-14.1
1050-1100	34.5	37.6	9.0	47.8	51.8	8.3	22.0	24.3	10.4	0.99	0.94	-5.4
>1100	35.3	40.0	13.4	51.2	53.5	4.5	21.5	28.2	31.5	1.19	1.11	-6.5

Sex Ratio, 1981	RIACA 1971	RIACA 1981	RIACA % Change	WPM 1971	WPM 1981	WPM % Change	WPF 1971	WPF 1981	WPF % Change	NT 1971	NT 1981	NT % Change
< 900	0.33	0.35	5.1	0.58	0.56	-4.2	0.14	0.25	85.4	13.5	15.6	15.5
900-950	0.33	0.43	30.5	0.58	0.58	-0.1	0.15	0.25	72.9	12.3	13.4	9.1
950-1000	0.35	0.45	27.4	0.57	0.57	0.2	0.17	0.25	50.3	12.1	13.1	8.2
1000-1050	0.36	0.48	31.1	0.57	0.57	-0.8	0.18	0.26	42.8	11.9	12.7	6.3
1050-1100	0.35	0.43	20.5	0.56	0.57	2.4	0.15	0.26	79.3	12.1	13.3	10.1
>1100	0.37	0.40	9.3	0.57	0.56	-2.2	0.14	0.27	100.6	12.5	14.5	15.7

The mean characteristics of villages classified according to the 1981 value of the SR show a systematic pattern of variation:

i) On the average, villages with very low and very high SRs tend to be relatively small. The mean size increases as we move from villages with <900 SR to those where it is 950-1000; thereafter the mean size of villagers falls as we move up the scale of SR.

ii) In 1981 villages with very low SRs tend to have a relatively high proportion of SCs. Among other groups, there seems to be no significant variation in this respect. The pattern is not as clear in 1971.

iii) In both years, villages with lower SRs tend to have higher literacy (male and female), the difference being more marked among females than males.

iv) The cultivated area per agricultural worker shows a 'V' shaped relation to SR in 1971 and 1981, while the extent of irrigation development and non-agricultural employment show an inverted 'V' shaped pattern in 1981 but not in 1971.

Differences in the SR could reflect gender discrimination and/or differential migration of males and females. The former is reflected in female infanticide and/or relatively high female mortality. We cannot infer anything about either of these aspects at the village level from census or any other extant source of data. However, it seems reasonable to assume that differences in migration are likely to be reflected in differences in the size of villages: larger villages being more diversified are likely to have attracted more male in-migrants.

There is also reason to suppose that differences in the rate of population growth reflect differences in migration. Inter-village differences in the natural increase in population seem likely to be smaller than differences in observed population growth. The incidence of female migration between villages, being largely on account of marriage, is also unlikely to vary systematically across villages within a district. Relatively fast growing villages are therefore likely to have experienced a relatively larger in-migration of males (which would depress the SR). On the other hand, villages where population is growing slowly are likely to have a high out-migration of males (which increases the female-to-male ratio). On this reasoning, the faster the increase in population, the greater the probability of the SR being low and of the SR decreasing.

Female literacy is widely believed to have a bearing on attitudes to gender discrimination. One expects that the higher the female literacy (and changes therein), the higher will be the SR (and the larger the increase/ slower the decline).

The following function was estimated in the linear form to assess the impact of the above factors on the SR:

SR 81 = f (POP 71, POP CHANGE 71-81, FLIT 71)

The estimates (Table 14.8) confirm that, other things given, higher female literacy is associated with higher sex ratio; that the larger the village size and the faster the increase in population between 1971 and 1981, the lower the sex ratio. The results also suggest that changes in SR between 1971 and 1981 are positively related to female literacy and negatively to the initial (i.e., 1971) size of population and the per cent rise in population during the 1970s. In other words, the SR in 1981 is strongly and positively associated with the 1971 SR. Even more striking is the fact that villages that had inherited low SRs are not only likely to continue to have low SRs, but are also more likely to experience a faster decline (or slower rise) of the SR.

In an attempt to capture the factors affecting male migration, a more elaborate specification of the relationship was attempted. Other things being given, male out-migration occurs either because less land is available per head of agricultural worker or because non-agricultural opportunities are fewer. The latter is likely to be related to the prosperity of the agricultural classes, the size of the village, distance from (and ease of access to) the nearest town. SCs and illiterates are less likely to benefit from migration opportunities. These considerations are reflected in the following formulation:

SR 81 = f (POP 71, CHG POP 71-81, CA/NAW, IA/CA,
MNAW/MAW, SC/POP, NT)

CA/NAW - cultivated area to non-agricultural worker

MNAW/MAW - male non-agricultural worker to male agricultural worker

SC/POP - number of scheduled castes to population

The regression results (Table 14.8) show that the extent of diversification of employment and the proportion of SC/ST are both inversely related to SR, and the prosperity of agricultural classes tend to be positively associated with SR. The association between SR on the one hand, and village size, change in village population and female literacy rate on the other are as indicated earlier. The strong relation between SR in 1971 and SR in 1981 stands confirmed. Any investigation of the behaviour of SR must focus on the reasons for villages having persistently low or high SRs. While this may be due in part to noise in the data, it also suggests the need to extend and refine the hypotheses.

Table 14.8

Results of Multiple Regression of Sex Ratio in 1981 and Changes in Sex Ratio during 1971-1981 on Selected Variables, North Arcot District

	No. of Villages	*POPLN. 71*	*PERCHA POP*	*FLIT 71*	*RSEX 71*	*RSCST 81*	*RCAM-AW81*	*RIA-CA81*	*RMN-AW81*	*R Square*
Sex ratio, 1981	1831	-3.10**	-0.07*	0.77***	0.41***					0.22
	1831	-0.002***	-0.096***	0.555***	0.376***	-0.670	9.372***	12.460**	-1.987***	0.22
Changes in sex ratio 1981	1831	-0.003	-0.07	0.77	-0.59					0.33

Note: * significant at 5-10 per cent.

** significant at 1-5 per cent.

*** significant at 1 per cent or less

Non-agricultural Employment

Our focus is on the ratio of male workers engaged in non-agricultural activities to males engaged in agriculture, i.e., cultivation and agricultural labour. There is a clear pattern in the variation of village characteristics relative to the MNAW/MAW in 1981 (Table 14.9). The higher this ratio, the larger the mean village size and higher the literacy. Cultivated area per agricultural worker shows a 'V' shaped relation, and the irrigation ratio an inverted 'V' shaped relation with MNAW/MAW. The incidence of SC and ST, the work participation rates and the distance from the nearest town are inversely related to the diversification of employment. These patterns except for village size and SC ratio are also noticed in 1971.

Table 14.9

Mean Value of Selected Characteristics of Villages Grouped according to Ratio of Male Non-agricultural Workers to Male Agricultural Workers in 1981

North Arcot, 1971-1981

MNAW/MAW 1981	POPLN 1971	POPLN 1981	POPLN % Change	RMNAW 1971	RMNAW 1981	RMNAW % Change	RSEX 1971	RSEX 1981	RSEX % Change	RSCST 1971	RSCST 1981	RSCST % Change
<0.2	1531	1479	-3.4	0.26	0.11	-58.9	972.2	976.3	0.4	22.9	27.4	19.3
0.2-0.5	1624	1940	19.5	0.25	0.32	24.6	973.0	986.1	1.3	23.4	24.1	3.0
0.5-0.9	1842	2559	38.9	0.25	0.66	168.0	974.6	981.6	0.7	26.2	23.2	-11.2
0.9-1.1	1574	2837	80.2	0.24	1.00	308.8	975.8	978.1	0.2	25.7	21.0	-18.3
1.1-2.0	1539	3251	111.3	0.26	1.42	436.1	958.7	976.3	1.8	23.7	21.4	-9.4
>2.0	2203	3175	44.1	0.44	3.14	609.5	970.1	967.7	-0.2	20.9	21.6	3.2

MNAW/MAW 1981	TLIT 1971	TLIT 1981	TLIT % Change	MLIT 1971	MLIT 1981	MLIT % Change	FLIT 1971	FLIT 1981	FLIT % Change	RCAMAW 1971	RCAMAW 1981	RCAMAW % Change
<0.2	29.9	30.6	2.3	43.4	43.6	0.6	16.0	17.1	7.1	0.93	0.79	-14.9
0.2-0.5	29.2	37.2	27.3	42.4	50.8	20.0	15.8	23.4	48.7	0.91	0.60	-12.6
0.5-0.9	28.9	42.2	45.9	42.2	55.9	32.5	15.3	28.2	84.3	0.92	0.71	-19.6
0.9-1.1	27.3	43.2	58.2	40.3	57.4	42.3	13.9	28.6	105.8	0.94	0.76	-19.7
1.1-2.0	31.9	45.6	43.1	45.6	59.1	29.5	16.9	31.8	87.9	0.87	0.88	1.0
>2.0	33.6	48.1	43.0	46.9	60.7	29.5	20.0	35.1	75.5	0.83	1.08	30.6

MNAW/MAW 1981	RIACA 1971	RIACA 1981	RIACA % Change	WPM 1971	WPM 1981	WPM % Change	WPF 1971	WPF 1981	WPF % Change	NT 1971	NT 1981	NT % Change
<0.2	0.34	0.43	24.5	0.57	0.59	2.9	0.17	0.29	73.8	13.8	15.2	10.7
0.2-0.5	0.37	0.46	23.5	0.58	0.57	-0.8	0.15	0.26	66.0	11.2	11.8	5.7
0.5-0.9	0.33	0.48	43.2	0.58	0.55	-4.3	0.17	0.21	24.2	9.5	9.8	3.3
0.9-1.1	0.36	0.53	47.8	0.58	0.55	-4.4	0.16	0.18	13.6	8.2	9.1	11.1
1.1-2.0	0.33	0.50	52.1	0.57	0.54	-5.5	0.15	0.18	23.9	8.0	8.1	2.2
>2.0	0.29	0.48	63.3	0.59	0.53	-8.6	0.16	0.14	-11.9	7.7	8.6	11.9

There is a strong positive association between ratio of MNAW to MAW in the base year and the rate of change in the ratio during 1971-1981. That is, villages that are already more diversified have experienced a faster pace of diversification. Total population as well as the irrigation ratio have recorded faster increases in villages with more diversified employment. Work participation shows a large rise (or smaller decline) in villages with low diversified employment. Literacy rate changes and changes in MNAW/MAW show an inverted 'V' shaped relation.

The extent of diversification in rural non-agricultural employment is postulated to be an increasing function of the prosperity of agricultural classes (proxied as before by CA/MAW and IA/CA), the inequality within agriculture (proxied by MAL/MAW), size of the village, literacy rates, and distance from the nearest town.

The results of multiple regression analysis (Table 14.10) largely confirm these expectations. In both years, NAW/MAW increases with ratio of cultivated area to agricultural worker (RCA/AW), the ratio of irrigated to cultivated area, village size and MAL/MAW. That is, the larger, agricultural classes in greater tend to have more diversified employment. In 1971, proximity to towns makes a significant difference to the extent of non-agricultural employment, and there is a strong positive association between literacy and non-agricultural employment. But in 1981, distance from town becomes significant and the impact of literacy on non-agricultural employment is significantly negative. It is noteworthy that the proportion of variance in MNAW/MAW 'explained' by the regression is remarkably high (close to 80%) in 1981 but only 15 per cent in 1971. Closer probing of these differences is obviously necessary.

Table 14.10

Results of Multiple Regression of Male Non-agricultural to Male Agricultural Employed on Selected Variables (North Arcot District, 1971 and 1981)

Year	*N*	*R Square*	*POPLN*	*TLIT*	*RCAMAW*	*RIACA*	*NT*	*RMALMAW*
1971	1718	0.158	0.00008***	0.012***	0.120***	0.317***	-0.006***	0.172***
1981	1720	0.800	0.00046***	-0.005	3.636***	2.066***	-0.06	1.764***

Note: * significant at 5-10 per cent.
** significant at 1-5 per cent.
*** significant at 1 per cent or less

Caste-Class Differentiation

The ratio of the proportion of SCs in the total population to male agricultural labourers to total male workers (MAL/TMW) is used as a measure of this feature.[9] On the reasonable assumption that, in general, SCs are predominantly agricultural labourers, this ratio can be interpreted as follows: if the ratio is <1, not all agricultural labourers are SCs. The lower the value of this ratio below unity, the greater the caste wise differentiation of the agricultural wage labour class. When it is = 1, there is a caste-class congruence; and when it is > 1, the SCs are economically differentiated, the extent of the differentiation rising as the value increases beyond unity (Table 14.11).

It would seem that villages where the agricultural labour class is heterogeneous are also economically diversified, tend to be relatively small in size, have relatively more land per agricultural worker and a relatively low AL/AW. The differentiation index is positively correlated to the percentage of SCs and access to communications. This pattern is seen in both years.

Relatively small, less easily accessible villages where SCs are dominant and AL/AW is low, tend to be the ones where SCs are economically diversified. They participate more widely in non-agricultural activities and probably own more land. At the other extreme, relatively small villages where SCs constitute a small minority, the AL class is differentiated even though AL/AW is high and non-farm employment is sizeable.

There has been relatively little change in the extent of class-caste differentiation except in the groups where the AL class is caste wise highly differentiated (index value <0.2). Here the differentiation has increased significantly. This is associated with a relatively stagnant population, a decline in the proportion of SCs in the population and little change in the ratio of NAW to AW. At the other extreme, in villages where SCs are highly differentiated in terms of occupation, the degree of differentiation has increased, as has the proportion of SCs in the population. They also report a marked increase in non-agricultural employment. Population increase is lower than average.

---

9. Since the tribal population in the district is very small, we focus only on SCs here.

Table 14.11

Weighted Mean Value of Selected Characteristics of Villages Grouped According to Degree of Caste-Class Differentiation (North Arcot, 1971-1981)

Caste Class Differentiation, 1981	POPLN			RMNAW			RSEX			RSCST		
	1971	1981	% Change	1971	1981	% Change	1971	1981	% Change	1971	1981	% Change
<0.2	1072	1070	-0.2	0.26	0.26	0.7	975.7	984.9	0.9	4.3	1.9	-55.5
0.2-0.5	1922	2224	15.7	0.23	0.27	19.7	977.8	979.3	0.2	12.9	11.1	-14.0
0.5-0.9	2067	2259	9.3	0.27	0.29	8.0	972.2	981.6	1.0	22.5	21.8	-2.8
0.9-1.1	1639	2032	24.0	0.32	0.36	12.7	972.5	979.5	0.7	27.3	30.5	11.4
1.1-2.0	1602	1889	17.9	0.29	0.37	30.8	973.0	977.8	0.5	30.8	32.8	6.5
>2.0	1137	1276	12.3	0.22	0.35	55.0	959.0	974.9	1.6	41.5	44.9	8.4

Caste Class Differentiation, 1981	TLIT			MLIT			FLIT			RCAMAW		
	1971	1981	% Change	1971	1981	% Change	1971	1981	% Change	1971	1981	% Change
<0.2	29.4	35.4	20.4	43.8	50.2	14.4	14.7	20.5	39.4	0.92	0.87	-5.4
0.2-0.5	28.8	34.5	19.8	42.1	48.2	14.5	15.3	20.3	35.0	0.88	0.71	-19.9
0.5-0.9	30.3	36.7	21.0	43.4	50.1	15.3	16.8	23.0	37.0	0.85	0.74	-12.7
0.9-1.1	31.6	37.6	19.1	45.4	50.7	11.5	17.3	24.3	40.2	0.97	0.73	-24.8
1.1-2.0	30.2	36.6	21.3	43.6	50.0	14.6	16.3	22.9	40.2	0.95	0.85	-10.6
>2.0	27.0	33.1	23.5	39.7	45.7	15.1	13.8	20.7	50.4	1.09	1.00	-8.4

Caste Class Differentiation, 1981	RIACA			WPM			WPF			DIFF. INDEX		
	1971	1981	% Change	1971	1981	% Change	1971	1981	% Change	1971	1981	% Change
<0.2	0.34	0.45	35.1	0.58	0.59	1.0	0.17	0.25	48.0	0.16	0.09	-47.73
0.2-0.5	0.38	0.46	20.2	0.58	0.58	-0.2	0.18	0.26	47.8	0.39	0.38	-4.07
0.5-0.9	0.36	0.46	27.3	0.57	0.57	1.2	0.17	0.27	60.8	0.71	0.70	-0.82
0.9-1.1	0.35	0.47	34.5	0.57	0.57	-0.9	0.16	0.25	57.4	0.99	0.99	-0.01
1.1-2.0	0.35	0.46	31.0	0.57	0.57	-1.5	0.16	0.25	57.2	1.37	1.40	2.46
>2.0	0.30	0.37	23.5	0.58	0.58	-1.6	0.14	0.22	61.9	3.60	3.67	1.80

Conclusion

The purpose of this exercise was to explore the potential of using village level data from the population censuses to understand the nature of variation in terms of select socioeconomic features (and changes therein) as well as in factors that account for these variations. The first cut results presented here confirm that the potential is indeed rich. The variations are large; there are distinct, but far from uniform or simple, patterns of association between different characteristics; and at least some of the variability is consistent with plausible *a priori* hypotheses regarding factors underlying them.

It might be asked whether the census data collected by teachers, village officials and others, with practically no professional training or interest, are reliable enough to support such analyses. The post-enumeration sample check, meant to verify the accuracy of the headcount, shows that the estimates of total population are indeed pretty accurate. The same cannot be said about the data relating to other characteristics of the population. Since these aspects do not form part of the post-enumeration check, it is difficult to assess their accuracy. One must therefore be cautious in using the data if the interest is to get accurate measures of the absolute value of particular characteristics, either for the population as a whole or for particular segments of it.

The fact that the data does not give reliable estimates of absolute values does not, however, vitiate their use for getting a picture of relative values of characteristics as between villages and population segments and for analysing the nature and sources of variations in them. Given the very large number of enumerators involved and the extensive arrangements for supervision of their work, it is reasonable to suppose that there is little systematic bias in the data. Such biases and errors as may exist can be reasonably assumed to be more or less in the nature of random noise.

The data can therefore be used with considerable confidence to assess the relative position of villages, regions and classes in terms of several significant socioeconomic characteristics, the relative time profiles of change in these characteristics and of associations among these. The factors accounting for those differences can also be examined up to an extent using multivariate analysis based on hypotheses derived from *a priori* reasoning. It is also possible by suitable stratification and partitioning to see whether the underlying relations are similar across strata/groups. In several cases, our results suggest complex patterns, which cannot be quite captured by linear multiple regression. Clearly, there is much room for ingenuity and imagination for wider and deeper statistical analysis of this data set.

Of course, this will not give definitive or complete explanations of variations. But it can provide valuable insights, help develop typologies based on variation in characteristics and their behaviour in time, and identify anomalous situations. Together, such typologies could be a valuable framework in which detailed surveys and micro-enquiries can be designed more efficiently and with a sharper focus. This will not only save effort and resources, but by locating microstudies in the diversity of contexts and experiences, conclusions can be drawn from such studies.

Perhaps even more importantly, the data enables us to identify the location and characteristics of specific villages, which are currently 'backward' and/or have been persistently lagging in terms of one or more development indicators. By focussing public attention on these villages, pressures can be generated for government agencies (including the Panchayati Raj bodies) to find out the reasons for the condition of these villages and implement remedial measure.

15 Crop-Weather Relationship

A Review

Economists' interest in the study of crop-weather relations is of relatively recent origin and reflects the growing realisation that the effect of weather needs to be taken out of the observed behaviour of crop yields before the contribution of technology and inputs can be properly evaluated. However, their work on the subject shows little awareness of the research already done by agricultural scientists and agro-meteorologists, or of the painstaking effort that went into the collection of the relevant basic data. The seminar on Data Base and Methodology for the Study of Growth Rates in Agriculture, organised by the Indian Society of Agricultural Economics, suggested that a brief critical review of the past scientific work on crop-weather relations should be prepared and published along with the papers discussed at the seminar. The present review was prepared in response to this suggestion. It is far from exhaustive: much of the work is reported in specialised journals, which are not easily accessible to readers outside the profession. Though limited to a few papers, it is believed that the review covers a wide enough cross section to give the main contours of past research in this field.

The subject of crop-weather relations has attracted attention of Indian scientists for several decades. While some work has been done by agricultural scientists (notable examples being Harold Mann, 1955; Kalamkar and Satakopan, 1940 and Kanitkar, 1960), the main centre of research on crop-weather relations during the past half-a-century has been the Indian Meteorological Department (IMD). To encourage a proper scientific study of the relation between weather and plants, a separate division of Agricultural Meteorology was started in 1932 and its pioneering work has been widely recognised. In its early years the division was mainly concerned with macroanalysis of distribution and variability of rainfall, and estimation of evaporation and crop-weather requirements, as well as with microstudies of climatic variables near the ground to improve the understanding of the environment affecting plant growth.[1] Indian Council of Agricultural Research (ICAR) launched an All-India Coordinated Crop-Weather Scheme (AICWS). Under this scheme specialised meteorological observatories were set up for 'systematic recording of crop-weather observations on paddy, wheat and jowar, at a network of selected experimental farms throughout the country.' These observatories were later extended to sugarcane and cotton as well. The object of the scheme was to 'formulate, in quantitative terms, the effect of different growth factors on the growth and yield of crops under observation...'[2]

The All-India Crop Weather Scheme

At its peak activity, there were 125 observatories under this scheme, of which 50 centres recorded detailed and systematic observations, on a uniform basis, regarding the growth and yield of selected crops as well as the meteorological factors experienced by the crops during their life cycle. It is useful to know the scope and design behind this endeavour.

"At each station, two varieties of the crop under observation are grown according to the following layout plan, with 6 plots under each variety.

$$V_1\ V_2\ V_2\ V_1\ V_1\ V_2$$

$$V_1\ V_2\ V_2\ V_1\ V_1\ V_2$$

V_1 = I Variety

V_2 = II Variety.

"The size of the plot is 1/40 acre. The sampling unit is 8 ft. length (ultimate units) in adjacent rows. Three such samples are selected by randomization from each half of the plot, giving 36 samples or 72 ultimate units, for each variety. The two end plants of each ultimate unit come under measurement.

> The height measurements are thus made on 144 plants in all, for each variety, selected by randomization. The height is measured from the ground up to the base (juncture) on the topmost fully opened leaf. The height values represent the average of the heights from the ground to juncture of the topmost fully opened leaf, based on the measurements made on 144 plants of each variety

1. Ramdas (1960).
2. Mallik (1958).

> selected by randomization, at a time when the height of the crop has reached the maximum. The yield values, however, are based on the yield of all the six plots of each variety, pooled together.[3]
>
> The data are tabulated on standard printed forms, according to standard weeks and periods of the 'Growers Year'. The advantage of using the 'Grower Year' is that each standard week of the year covers the same calendar dates every year and it is, therefore, convenient to obtain normals for each standard week, when data for a sufficient large number of years are accumulated. The tabulated data are promptly scrutinized at the office of the Director of Agricultural Meteorology and care is taken to ensure that the accumulating data remain free of any serious shortcomings.
>
> After scrutiny, both the meteorological and the crop data for each crop, for each year are represented pictorially in crop-weather diagrams... Such diagrams summarise a wealth of data depicting the life history of the crop from sowing to harvest, indicating the dates of commencement and completion of various growth phases such as germination, tillering, or branching, elongation, flowering and yield.[4]

One cannot but be impressed by the care and imagination, which evidently went into the design of the crop-weather observations. A large mass of information was collected from the 50 stations for periods ranging from 5 to 20 years. But, for reasons which are not very clear, the collation and publication of the data in the standardised format was rather fitful and incomplete. The crop-weather scheme in its original form was discontinued from the late sixties. The present position is explained by Sarker thus:

> In the last two decades, large changes have taken place in the country in agricultural production technology. Old crop varieties and the agricultural operations have also undergone substantial changes. To be in tune with and to cater to the need of these new developments, the precision crop-observations are being replaced by those requiring the recording of simple observations on the growth, development and yield of important crop varieties from all agro-meteorological stations, such that enough data becomes available for analysis is a short period of time... The information collected from the network of observations is also being mapped for issue as an agro-climatic atlas of India. The crop and meteorological data under the crop-weather scheme are being summary of the week by week progress of the crop growth and the weather conditions experienced by it.[5]

Precise information on the data collected under the new scheme, the format of presentation and the nature of the publication are not available.

3. Mallik (1958): 377.
4. Mallik (1958).
5. Sarker (1977).

Analytical Work on Crop-Weather Relations

The empirical work on crop-weather relations is largely on the AICWS data. Reviewing the status of this work, Sarker (1977) reported:

> Some tentative crop-weather relationships have been established with respect to the crops at different crop-weather stations by applying statistical methods. Response of a few crops in yield to distribution of rainfall during the life cycle of the crop has also been obtained. Similar studies in relation to other meteorological parameters like maximum temperature, sunshine and humidity are in progress.

Some of the early attempts at analysing AICWS data used relatively simple techniques to get an idea of yield-weather relations. For instance, Mallik[6] examined nine years' data for three crops at the Dharwad Research Station and found that in the two years when the wheat yields were very low due to a rust attack, the number of hours of bright sunshine days during November was abnormally low. From this he concluded that 'unseasonal rain and cloudy conditions created conditions favourable for several rust attacks.' On the other hand, in *jowar*, on the basis of a comparison of rainfall during the growing season in two years of very good harvest with that in two years of very poor harvests, he argued that '*jowar* crop at Dharwad is rather susceptible to excessive rain during the growing period.' Using a similar approach it was further suggested that the 'spell of cloudy and rainy weather extending over 3 consecutive weeks during the growing season of cotton appears to create conditions favourable for pests like shoot borer and red-cotton bug.'

In another paper Mallik (1958) attempted a more elaborate analysis of ten years' data relating to *jowar* from five stations. He postulated, partly for lack of any other basis, that optimum amount and distribution of rainfall during the growing period of *kharif jowar* is approximated by the amount of rainfall and its distribution (in each of 12 weeks prior to earemergence). He then estimated the correlation coefficients between: (a) height and yield; (b) the percentage of the deviation of actual weekly rainfall during the growing period in each year from the rainfall in corresponding weeks of the 'optimum' year (i.e., the year of the maximum yield in the sample) and the percentage deviation from the maximum height and (c) deviation in rainfall from the year of optimum yield and deviations from optimum yield using

6. Mallik (1958).

a similar procedure as in (b). He found the correlation coefficient of (a) to be significantly positive (0.59), and of (b) and (c) to be significantly negative (0.42 and 0.51 respectively). The correlation coefficient of yield and rainfall on height was also significantly negative (0.35). Apart from the fact that there is no explicit *a priori* basis for the relation sought to be estimated, the analysis, as the author recognises, is limited and tentative as it does not consider the effects of other meteorological variables or the effects of rainfall and other meteorological factors between earemergence and harvest, and because it is based on pooling of observations from different stations with varying agro-climatic conditions and possibly different varieties of each crop.

A subsequent paper[7] attempted a rather more elaborate analysis of data for cotton from some 12 stations. Here again, the stations were pooled into two groups (on the basis of rainfall in the reproductive period) to get a sufficient number of observations for studying correlations between: (a) different growth features and yield and (b) meteorological factors and some growth features. In both groups of districts, the selected growth features (germination rates, number and height of plants at first picking, number of branches, total number of flowers and of bolls at first picking) were found to explain more than 92 per cent of the yield variations. Of the meteorological variables, the correlation analysis found that for one group of stations: (i) greater rainfall during the four weeks preceding the branching period, as well as during the period, and more rainy days during branching increased the number of branches; (ii) greater rainfall and more rainy days during boll formation reduce the number of bolls available per picking and (iii) higher maximum temperatures during boll formation tend to increase the number of bolls for picking. In the second group of districts the relations are much less clear: greater sunshine during the four weeks prior to germination seems to increase the germination rate, while more sunshine during boll formation has a marked negative effect on the number of bolls picked.

This kind of analysis, which tries to scan the strength and pattern of relations between a variety of meteorological variables, which are expected on *a priori* grounds to affect yield is valuable, especially when there is not a well formulated hypothesis on the precise nature of the relationship. The problem posed by pooling of observations could be overcome, once sufficient number of observations are available for a particular variety and station.

7. Mallik *et al.* (1960)

But this approach was apparently not pursued very far. At any rate, the next major paper on the subject is already cast in the framework of regression analysis.

The simplest of these estimates a linear regression of yield on the values of selected meteorological variables during selected 'sensitive' periods.[8] The procedure seems to involve screening the relation between weekly rainfall and yield, and choosing those which gave statistically significant correlation coefficients. In order to arrive at the periods of rainfall critical to yield, a further selection is made from among these 'by an elimination process and from considerations of crop physiology.' The details of the procedure are unfortunately not reported in the paper. They are presumably reported in another study.[9] Incidentally, for the two stations for which this approach was tried, Sreenivasan reports a multiple correlation coefficient of 0.66-0.68.

In another paper, Sreenivasan and Banerjee (1973) present the results of a linear multiple regression of the yield of *rabi jowar* in Raichur on mean maximum temperature, mean minimum temperature, total rainfall and number of rainy days. The multiple correlation coefficient is around 0.54, but no further details (e.g., the statistical significance of the coefficient, or the basis for the model chosen) are available.

The paper then goes on to experiment with the 'multiple curvilinear regression' techniques evolved by Ezekiel and Fox (1965) on the same body of observations. The starting point is the linear multiple regression of the standard type,

$$Y = a_0 + a_1X_1 + a_2X_2 + \ldots\ldots\ldots\ldots\ldots + a_nX_n \qquad \ldots.(1)$$

While this is a useful first approximation, the relation between Y and each of the independent variables may have different, and not necessarily linear, forms. The true relationship, in other words, would be of the following form:

$$Y = a_0^1 + a_1^1 f_1(X_1) + a_2^1 f_2(X_2) + \ldots\ldots\ldots + a_n^1 f_n(X_n) \qquad \ldots(2)$$

where $f_1(X_1)$, etc., may have different forms, not necessarily linear. The nature and shape of $f_i(X_i)$ are got by a process of successive approximation

8. Sreenivasan (1973).

9. Sreenivasan (1970).

using free-hand curves. The multiple and partial correlation coefficients are then estimated by feeding the free-hand approximation of the curvilinear functions into equation (2).

The method is found to explain a much higher proportion of the observed variations in *jowar* yields in Raichur than the linear regression. But a high R^2 is not a sufficient basis for selecting one 'model' over another even when standardised and objective techniques of curve-fitting are available. Such techniques have not been developed for curvilinear regression. Ezekiel and Fox (1965: 240-41) stressing the limitations of this technique, said:

> The results of the corn yield analysis apply only to the same area from which the data were drawn and to the period they covered. Thus they provide no basis for estimating corn yield in other seasons, and their use in estimating yield in other periods—as in subsequent years—is attended by increasing risk due especially to the necessity of extrapolating the trend regression ...

In any event, unless the underlying model is firmly grounded on theoretically sound and consistent hypotheses derived from the relevant disciplines, its utility for understanding crop-weather relations remains doubtful, no matter how high the R^2.

Some attempts have also been made to apply what is called the 'regression integral technique' developed by Fisher (1924) for analysing crop-weather relations. An early and frequently cited example of this is the paper by Kalamkar and Satakopan (1940). There were also others, e.g., Nair and Bose (1945), Acharya *et al.* (1960), Gangopadhyay and Sarker (1963), Ramamurthy and Banerjee (1966) and Singh *et al.* (1970). But none of these was available for reference. The only two papers in this category, which the author could get are those of Sreenivasan (1973) and Shaha and Banerjee (1975) who applied the technique to analyse AICWS data for cotton in Madhya Pradesh (Indore and Khandwa) and Coimbatore respectively.

The technique is meant to 'take into account not only the total amount of rainfall during a certain period, but also the manner in which it is distributed over the period under consideration.' The basic relation between yield and meteorological factors are cast in the linear form thus:

$$Y = C + a_1 r_1 + a_2 r_2 + \dots\dots\dots\dots a_n r_n \qquad \dots (3)$$

Where Y stands for yield; r_1, r_2 ..... r_n the values of a meteorological factor r in n period, and the periods represent equal sub-divisions of the total period over which the effect of the meteorological factor is to be studied; and the partial regression coefficients a_1, a_2, etc., give the responses of r_1, r_2, etc., on yield. At the limit, when the duration of each time interval is very small, (3) becomes

$$Y = C + \int_0^T ar\,dt \qquad ....(4)$$

For each meteorological factor r, Meteorological Distribution Constants (MDCs) are 'estimated for each year by fitting an orthogonal polynominal of the 5th degree in tune to the values r_1, r_2 .... r_n.'

$$r = A_0P_0 + A_1P_1 + ... A_5P_5 \qquad ....(5)$$

Yield response to the MDCs (A_0, A_1 ...) assumed to take the following polynominal form:

$$a = B_0P_0 + B_1P_1 + ... B_5P_5 \qquad ....(6)$$

In order to estimate B_0, B_1, yield is regressed on A_0, A_1 ....;

$$Y = B_0A_0 + B_1A_1 + ... B_5A_5 \qquad ....(7)$$

Both the papers also examine the data to see whether there is any significant secular change in yield and/or the MDCs, and describe a procedure for eliminating such trends.

Sreenivasan's (1973) paper is concerned with estimating the relationship between the distribution of rainfall and cotton yields in Madhya Pradesh. The partial regression coefficients for the MDCs differ substantially in strength (though not in sign) between the two stations studied. The proportion of variance explained by this technique (0.53 to 0.63) is actually lower than that of the simple linear regression of yield on the values of selected meteorological variables in different stages of crop growth (0.66-0.67). Both techniques are reported to do equally well when judged by the closeness of the predicted to the actual yield levels.

Shaha and Banerjee (1975) examined the effect of rainfall, humidity, sunshine, maximum and minimum temperatures, each taken separately (and considering the values of each variable over the entire growing season) on cotton yields. Some of the main conclusions of their analysis are: while the significance of the effect of rainfall, sunshine and maximum temperature (on yield) could not be established clearly, there is indication that "more sunshine during the crop period and more rainfall up to the middle of

January were beneficial; more relative humidity during elongation and branching period is useful for crop"; and "minimum temperature plays the most important role in explaining about 72 per cent of the total variation in cotton yield" (p. 524).

It is obviously difficult to judge the effectiveness of the regression integral technique in relation to others on the basis of these two applications. Nevertheless, at the conceptual level, the major limitations of this method, at any rate as applied so far, is that it estimates the effect of each meteorological factor (and its time distribution) on yield separately but not in combination. This would require a more complicated model of the relation between yield, on the one hand, and different meteorological factors and their distributions taken in combination, on the other. The simplest would be an additive model, i.e., one which postulates the separate effects of each meteorological variable, like those of the values of any particular meteorological factor in different parts of the growing season, are independent of each other. This can of course be questioned. For instance, there is strong reason to believe that the adverse effect of moisture stress at different stages of crop growth tend to be cumulative rather than additive.[10] Thirdly, since the study is meant to examine the relationship between the two on the basis of data from experiments specifically designed to control for all influences on yield other than the meteorological factors, the rationale for the elimination of trends in meteorological variables and yields is not clear.

Forecasting Crop Yields on the Basis of Weather Parameters

In 1945, the Agro-Meteorology Division of the IMD started preparing monthly crop-outlook assessments based on the week-by-week progress of weather for the use of the Ministry of Food and Agriculture. More recently, efforts are being made to develop techniques for quantitative crop yield forecasts on the basis of 'long series of past crop yield data and meteorological parameters.' "Regression formula connecting crop yield and weather parameters in critical crop periods have been developed to forecast the yields of *Kharif* Rice in 22 meteorological sub-divisions and wheat in 9

10. Minhas *et al.* (1974).

sub-divisions."[11] We have reviewed two of these studies (Das and Vidhate, 1971; Das *et al.*, 1971) to illustrate the methodology.

The first paper relates to wheat in Uttar Pradesh taken as a whole. Data relating to average yield per acre and average rainfall, temperature (maximum, minimum and mean) and humidity during the growing season from 1921 to 1966 have been used in the analysis. The average yield is correlated with the above meteorological variables in different phases of the crop.

> To get the periods in which meteorological factors have a significant effect on yield, the linear correlation between yield and rainfall, temperature and humidity have been worked out for overlapping period of seven days to ninety days of the crop growing season...All the correlations have been examined and from them the periods in which a particular weather element is significantly correlated with yield are marked out. By using these factors, the multiple correlation with yield has been calculated. Some of the factors used are not significant at 5 per cent level. In order to find out the combination in which the parameters used are all significant at least 5 per cent level,...Multiple correlation coefficients of all combinations (are calculated) dropping gradually one or more variables till a combination is found out where all parameters used are significant.[12]

All values are averaged for the whole state and no distinction is made between irrigated and unirrigated areas. The increasing trend in yield observed since 1951, being assumed to be due to various development programmes, is sought to be taken into account by introducing 'a suitable time scale linear variable in the regression analysis.'

The regression which is eventually chosen on the above basis includes seven variables, which together explain about 73 per cent of the observed variance in yield in 1921-1965 and 70 per cent in 1951-1965. The signs of the coefficients for each variable are the same in both periods, though the magnitudes are different. Predicted yields in 1966-1970 are closer to the expected yields computed from the regression for the longer time series (the difference is within 4%) than from the regression for 1950-1965 (where the difference is around 10%).

The paper by Das *et al.* (1971), attempts a similar exercise for *kharif* paddy in three regions of Mysore based on yield data for periods ranging from 24 years in one region to 53 years in another. Again no distinction is

11. Sarker *op. cit*: 7.

12. Das and Vidhate, 1971: 3.

made between yield under irrigated and unirrigated conditions; and while the change in methods of yield estimation of the 1950s are noted, their implications for the comparability of the two series are not considered. As in the study of wheat in Uttar Pradesh, a time trend variable is introduced in the region to take out the effect of rising trend in yield after 1950, and the regression is estimated for the longer time series and the post-1950 period separately.

The following is a list of the explanatory variables found to have a significant effect on yield in each region.

Variable No.	*Central Mysore*	*Interior Mysore North*	*Interior Mysore South*
X_2	Restricted rainy days 1 July–15 September	Mean May temperature July/September	September rainfall
X_3	Occasion of droughts and floods in August/September	X_2^2	June rainfall
X_4	June rainfall	Occasion of drought and flood in August/ September	Occasion of drought in July/August
X_5	Mean maximum temperature July/August	July rain	Mean maximum temperature July/August
X_6	X_5^2	Square of July/August rainfall	X_5^2
X_7		Technological trend	

The mean maximum temperature in July/August or July/September and the incidence of drought and floods in August/September figure as significant variables in all regions. With one or two exceptions, the signs of the coefficients are all the same in both the periods, but, unlike in the longer series, a majority of the regression coefficients for the 1950-1964 period are statistically non-significant, even though the proportion of variance explained by the regions exceeds 90 per cent. Predicted outputs between 1965 and 1968 based on regression coefficients from the longer series are in general quite close to actual output in coastal Mysore; they do rather less well in the other two regions, especially Interior Mysore South. The predictive power of the regression based on the shorter series is uniformly much poorer, the expected values diverging from the actual by 10 per cent or more in 8 out of 12 cases.

That the models reported in both these papers do so well in predicting the time series of actual yields and also in forecasting the yields for at least a four-year period beyond the time span of the series is indeed remarkable. It would be interesting to know whether these types of 'models' do as well in other regions for which they have been tried, whether they predict as well the yield of more recent years and whether such work has been extended to other crops.

Be that as it may, this type of approach leaves one rather uneasy from a methodological view point, especially when one is trying to understand the nature of crop-weather relations. To take but one example. The failure to distinguish yields of irrigated from rainfed land is obviously hard to defend because the effect of meteorological factors, especially rainfall, is apt to be very different in the two cases. Taking values of meteorological factors as a simple average of the values observed at the meteorological stations is questionable in a state as large and as varied in climatic conditions as Uttar Pradesh. So is the highly empirical approach to screening the explanatory variables using R^2 and tests of significance of the coefficients as the basis for selecting the final regression. The introduction of a linear trend variable to eliminate technological trends for a part of the series is highly arbitrary. For instance, both the papers assume that the technological improvement and the consequent trend rise in yields is a post-1950 phenomenon. The graphs of the time series for Mysore raises strong doubts about this assumption. It would seem that yields have been on a rising trend from the early forties in Central Mysore and Interior Mysore South and from the mid-thirties in Interior Mysore North. And in Central Mysore, the rising trend after early forties was preceded by two decades or more of a secular decline in yields. That these aspects are not taken into consideration in the analysis makes these regression models of limited value as a basis for understanding crop-weather relation.

Conclusion

The above review is obviously far from complete in its coverage of the work done at the IMD and other scientific bodies on crop-weather relations. But in so far as the papers covered form a fairly representative cross-section of the work, we could, at some risk, attempt to summarise the state of knowledge they reflect: it is evident that the AICWS was a well-designed enquiry and that it did generate a mass of crop-weather information under controlled conditions for different parts of the country. Unfortunately, much of this data remains unpublished, and its quality and utility for analysis of weather-yield relations remain to be properly tested. The analytical work done on this body of data is far too inadequate a basis for evaluating the AICWS. This work opens up interesting possibilities, but they need to be tried out on many more stations and crops on the basis of much closer and conscious interaction with plant scientists to enable the formulation of meaningful hypotheses for testing. The forecasting models based on macro data, being highly empirical in their approach, are of doubtful value for understanding weather-yield relations, but seem to be quite good for statistical predictions of yield given the values of the meteorological variables. Here again it would be useful to examine: (a) the predictive power of these models in the case of other crops and regions for which they have been attempted, as well as (b) the closeness of actual yields to the advance yield forecast reportedly made by the IMD every year for the use of the Ministry of Agriculture.

References

Acharya, B.C., M.N. Alam, B.B. Sinha and K.L. Khanna (1960). *Indian Journal of Sugarcane Research and Development* 4(4).

Das, J.C. and S.G. Vidhate (1971). "Forecasting Wheat Yield with the Help of Weather Parameters–Part II–Uttar Pradesh", *Scientist Report* No.160. Indian Meteorological Department.

Ezekiel, M. and Karl A. Fox (1965). *Method of Correlation and Regression Analysis.* New York: John Wiley & Sons.

Fisher, R.A. (1924). "The Influence of Rainfall on the Yield of Wheat at Rothamstead", Philosophical Transactions of the Royal Society of London, Series B, No. 213.

Gangopadhyay, M. and R.P. Sarker (1963). Agricultural Meteorology, 1965 and "A Correlation Study on Crop-Weather Relationship—Sugarcane", *Indian Journal of Sugarcane Research and Development* 8(1), October-December.

J.C. Das, A.K. Mehra and M.L. Madnani (1971). "Forecasting the Yield of Principal Crops in India on the Basis of Weather", *Indian Journal of Meteorology and Geophysics* 22(1).

Kalamkar, R.J. and V. Satakopan (1940). "The Influence of Rainfall Distribution on the Cotton Yields at Government Experimental Farms at Akola and Jalgaon", *Indian Journal of Agricultural Sciences* 10.

Kanitkar, N.V. (1960). *Dry Farming in India*, New Delhi: Indian Council of Agricultural Research.

Mallik, A.K. (1958). "Effect of Weather on Crop Growth and Yield at Government Experimental Farm at Dharwar", *Journal of Biological Sciences* 1(1): 30.

———. (1958). "Height and Yield of Kharif Jowar in relation to Rainfall during Vegetative Growth", *Indian Journal of Meteorology and Geophysics* 9(4): 32-37.

Mallik, A.K., P. Jagannanthan, G. Rama Rao and J.R. Banerjee (1960). "Preliminary Studies on Crop-Weather Relations", *Indian Journal of Meteorology and Geophysics* 11(4).

Mann, Harold H. (1955). *Rainfall and Famine—A Study of Rainfall in the Bombay Deccan, 1865-1938*. Bombay: Indian Society of Agricultural Economics.

Minhas, B.S., K.S. Parikh and T.N. Srinivasan (1974). "Towards the Structure of a Production Function for Wheat Yields with Dated Input of Irrigation Ratio", *Water Resources Research* 10(3).

Nair, K.R. and P. Bose (1945). "Influence of Humidity and Temperature on the Yields of Cotton", *Sankhya* 7(2), November.

Ramamurthy, K.S. and J.R. Banerjee (1966). "On the Influence of Weather on Wheat Yields at Dharwar", *Indian Journal of Meteorology and Geophysics* 17(4), October.

Ramdas, L.A. (1960). *Crops and Weather in India*, ICAR Monograph, New Delhi.

Sarker, R.P. (1977). "Meteorology at the Service of Agriculture" (*mimeo*.), p.2.

Shaha, S.K. and J.R. Banerjee (1975). "Influence of Rainfall, Humidity, Sunshine, Maximum and Minimum Temperatures on the Yield of Cotton at Coimbatore", *Indian Journal of Meteorology, Hydrology and Geophysics* 26(4).

Singh, Chokhey, A. Seshagiri and Y.S. Kapse (1970). "Yield of Cotton in relation to Rainfall in Madhya Pradesh", *Indian Journal of Agricultural Sciences* 40(1), January.

Sreenivasan (1973). *Indian Journal of Agricultural Sciences*, September, *op. cit.*

Sreenivasan, P.S. (1970). "Studies in Agricultural Meteorology of Some Field Crops". Unpublished PhD. Thesis submitted to the Mahatma Phule Krishi Vidyapeeth, Rahuri.

———. (1973). "Influence of Rainfall on the Yield of Cotton in Madhya Pradesh", *Indian Journal of Agricultural Sciences* 43(9), September.

Sreenivasan, P.S. and J.R. Banerjee (1973). "Studies on the Forecasting of Yield by Convilinear Technique", *Indian Journal of Meteorology and Geophysics* 24(1), January.